PARTY FOOD

Sumptuous savoury snacks, cakes, biscuits, sweets, and ice cream!

CONTENTS

Guide to symbols

The recipes in this book are accompanied by symbols that alert you to important information.

 Tells you how many people the recipe serves, or how much is produced.

 Indicates how much time you will need to prepare and cook a dish. Next to this symbol you will also find out if additional time is required for such things as marinating, standing, proving, or cooling. You need to read the recipe to find out exactly how much extra time is needed.

 Alerts you to what has to be done before you can begin to cook the recipe, or to parts of the recipe that take a long time to complete.

 Denotes that special equipment is required. Where possible, alternatives are given.

 Accompanies freezing information.

Tzatziki

Serve this simple Greek dip with a selection of crudités.

INGREDIENTS

1 cucumber, peeled and coarsely grated
salt
350g (12oz) Greek-style yogurt
3 garlic cloves, crushed
2 tbsp chopped mint or dill
2 tbsp extra virgin olive oil
1 tbsp red wine vinegar

METHOD

1 Put the cucumber in a bowl, sprinkle with salt, and leave to stand for 30 minutes.
2 Rinse the cucumber well to remove the salt, then use your hands to squeeze out all the liquid.
3 Put the cucumber in a bowl, add the yogurt, and stir together. Add the garlic, herbs, olive oil, and vinegar and stir together. Cover with cling film and chill until required.

serves 4

prep 10 mins,
plus standing

Hummus

This chickpea and tahini dip is one of the most widely recognized of all Middle Eastern dishes.

INGREDIENTS

400g can chickpeas
3 tbsp tahini
juice of 3 lemons
3 garlic cloves, chopped
½ tsp salt
paprika, for sprinkling

METHOD

1 Drain and rinse the chickpeas, reserving 4–6 tablespoons of the liquid from the can. Place the chickpeas in a blender or food processor with 3 tablespoons of the reserved liquid.
2 Add the tahini, lemon juice, and garlic, then blend well for a few seconds until smooth and creamy. Add a little more of the liquid from the can, if required.
3 Season to taste with salt. Transfer the hummus to a small bowl, sprinkle with paprika, and serve at room temperature. Serve with flatbread and crudités.

serves 4

prep 10 mins

blender or
food processor

Taramasalata

Tarama is Turkish for the salted and dried roe of grey mullet traditionally used in this recipe. This version uses smoked cod's roe for a rich flavour.

INGREDIENTS
60g (2oz) fresh white breadcrumbs
250g (9oz) piece smoked cod's roe
juice of 1 lemon
75ml (2½fl oz) extra virgin olive oil
1 small onion, grated, patted dry
   with kitchen paper
paprika, for sprinkling

METHOD
1 Place the breadcrumbs in a small bowl and add 3 tablespoons of cold water. Leave to soak for 15 minutes.
2 Meanwhile, split the roe down the centre using a sharp knife and carefully peel away the skin. Place in a blender with the lemon juice and soaked breadcrumbs; blend well.
3 With the motor running, very slowly add the oil in a thin steady stream until the mixture resembles smooth mayonnaise.
4 Spoon into a small serving dish and mix in the onion. Cover and chill for 30 minutes, then serve sprinkled with paprika. This dip is good with olives, Greek or Turkish breads, and crunchy vegetable crudités.

serves 4–6

prep 15 mins,
plus soaking
and chilling

blender

Chicken liver pâté

The red wine adds lovely flavour and cuts through the richness of the liver.

INGREDIENTS

350g (12oz) chicken livers,
  thawed if frozen
115g (4oz) butter
¼ tsp dried thyme
150ml (5fl oz) red wine

10 chives, snipped
salt and freshly ground black pepper
sprigs of fresh thyme, to garnish

METHOD

1 Rinse the chicken livers and pat them dry with kitchen paper. Trim away any white sinew or greenish portions from the livers with small scissors, then cut each in half.
2 Melt half the butter in a large frying pan over a medium heat until it foams. Add the livers and cook, stirring often, for 4 minutes, or until browned.
3 Add the dried thyme, wine, and chives to the pan. Bring to the boil, then reduce the heat and cook, stirring occasionally for 4 minutes, or until the liquid is reduced and the livers are just cooked through when sliced open.
4 Remove the pan from the heat and leave to cool for 10 minutes. Add salt and pepper to taste, then tip the livers and sauce into a blender, and blend until smooth. Adjust the seasoning if necessary. Spoon the pâté into a serving bowl, pressing it down with the back of the spoon so it is firmly packed, then set aside.
5 Melt the remaining butter over a medium heat, then pour it over the top of the pâté. Chill, uncovered, for at least 2 hours. Serve garnished with sprigs of fresh thyme.

serves 4

prep 10 mins, plus
cooling and chilling
• cook 15 mins

blender

allow at least
2 hrs for chilling

freeze the livers
for up to 3 months
before using

Roast pumpkin, chilli, and ginger dip

This sweet, spicy dip is great with crudités or piled on toast, as shown here.

INGREDIENTS

1kg (2¼lb) pumpkin or butternut squash, peeled and cut into chunks

4 tbsp olive oil

4 garlic cloves, crushed whole with the back of a knife

1 tbsp grated or finely chopped fresh root ginger

salt and freshly ground black pepper

1 long red chilli, deseeded and thinly sliced

4 sprigs of flat-leaf parsley, leaves only (reserve some for garnish)

grated zest and juice of 1 lemon

150ml (5fl oz) Greek-style yogurt

drizzle of extra virgin olive oil (optional)

pinch of paprika

slices of grilled sourdough bread, to serve

grilled pancetta or prosciutto, to serve

METHOD

1 Preheat the oven to 200°C (400°F/Gas 6). Put the pumpkin on a baking tray, and toss with the olive oil, garlic, and ginger. Season with salt and black pepper. Roast for about 30 minutes until tender and golden. Set aside to cool.

2 Transfer the cooled pumpkin to a blender or food processor, and add the chilli, parsley (reserving a little to garnish), and lemon zest and juice. Blend to a chunky purée. Season with salt and black pepper.

3 Put the pumpkin purée and the yogurt in a bowl, and mix thoroughly. Season if needed, then spoon into a serving bowl. Top with a drizzle of extra virgin olive oil (if using). Garnish with the reserved parsley and a sprinkle of paprika, and serve on grilled sourdough bread, with grilled pancetta or prosciutto over the top.

serves 8

prep 20 mins, plus cooling • cook 30 mins

blender or food processor

Crostini with green olive tapenade

This easy-to-make dish is great as an appetizer or snack.

INGREDIENTS

2 tsp olive oil
1 garlic clove
100g (3½oz) pitted green olives
grated zest of ½ lemon
few basil leaves
freshly ground black pepper
12 slices of bread cut from a
   baguette, toasted
6 yellow cherry tomatoes or red
   cherry tomatoes, roasted, to
   garnish (optional)
12 flat-leaf parsley leaves, to
   garnish (optional)

METHOD

1 Place the oil, garlic, olives, lemon zest, and basil into a food processor or blender and
   process to a paste. Season with black pepper.
2 Divide the mixture between the 12 slices of toast and garnish each one w th half a
   roasted cherry tomato and a parsley leaf (if using).

makes 12

prep 10 mins

**food processor
or blender**

Anchovy and olive bruschetta

These salty canapés are ideal with pre-dinner drinks.

INGREDIENTS

12 slices Italian bread, such as
    ciabatta, about 2cm (¾in) thick
½ garlic clove
extra virgin olive oil
3–4 tbsp bottled tomato sauce
salt and freshly ground black pepper
115g (4oz) mozzarella cheese,
    drained and cut into 12 thin slices
1 tsp dried mixed herbs
6 black olives, pitted and sliced
60g jar or can anchovies in olive oil,
    drained and cut in half lengthways

METHOD

1 Preheat the grill on its highest setting and position the rack 10cm (4in) from the heat.
2 To make the bruschetta bases, toast the bread slices until golden on both sides.
   Rub one side with the cut side of the garlic clove. Brush the same side of each slice
   with a little olive oil.
3 Spread each bruschetta with about 2 teaspoons of tomato sauce and season with salt
   and pepper to taste. Put 1 slice of mozzarella on each, sprinkle with herbs and top with
   olive slices and 2 pieces of anchovy in a criss-cross pattern.
4 Grill the bruschetta for 2–3 minutes until the mozzarella has melted and is bubbling.
   Serve hot.

makes 12

**prep 10 mins
• cook 5 mins**

Stuffed vine leaves

Greek *dolmadakia* are vine leaves stuffed with a vegetarian mix of rice, herbs, and tomatoes.

INGREDIENTS

2 tbsp olive oil

2 onions, finely chopped

½ tsp ground allspice

200g (7oz) long-grain rice

600ml (1 pint) vegetable stock

3 tomatoes, skinned, deseeded, and chopped

1 tbsp chopped dill

1 tbsp chopped mint

salt and freshly ground black pepper

40 vine leaves

juice of 1 lemon

METHOD

1 Heat the oil in a frying pan, add the onions, and fry gently until softened but not browned. Increase the heat, add the allspice and rice, stir, and cook for 2 minutes.

2 Pour in the stock and leave to simmer for 10 minutes, or until the rice is tender and has absorbed the liquid. Remove from the heat, stir in the tomatoes, dill, and mint, and season to taste with salt and pepper.

3 Place a vine leaf shiny-side down and spoon a little of the rice mixture in the centre. Fold in the sides and roll into a parcel. Repeat.

4 Pack the stuffed vine leaves tightly in a large saucepan, squeeze over the lemon juice, and add enough cold water to just cover. Put a heatproof plate with a weight on top so they don't unravel, and simmer gently for 30 minutes, topping up the water if necessary. Carefully drain the vine leaves and serve warm or cold.

serves 6

prep 20 mins
• cook 50 mins

blanch fresh vine leaves for 5 mins; soak preserved vine leaves in hot water and then rinse several times to remove the brine

heatproof plate

Smoked salmon blinis

Blinis are melt-in-the-mouth bases for bite-sized party canapés.

INGREDIENTS
100g (3½oz) buckwheat flour
¼ tsp baking powder
¼ tsp salt
1 egg, separated
100ml (3½fl oz) milk
vegetable oil
120ml (4fl oz) crème fraîche
100g (3½oz) smoked salmon
1 small bunch of dill
freshly ground black pepper
1 lemon, cut into wedges, to serve

METHOD
1 Sift the flour, baking powder, and salt into a mixing bowl. Make a hollow in the centre and add the egg yolk and half the milk. Beat the egg and milk together with a wooden spoon, gradually drawing in the flour from the sides.
2 Add the remaining milk and continue beating the mixture until the batter is smooth and free from lumps. Whisk the egg white until it holds soft peaks, then gently fold it into the batter.
3 Brush a frying pan with a little oil and place over a medium heat. Add a few teaspoons of the batter (1 teaspoon of batter per blini), spaced well apart, and cook until bubbles appear, then turn over and cook for 2 minutes, or until golden. Remove from the pan, set aside, and cook the remaining blinis.
4 Leave the blinis to cool, then top each with a little crème fraîche, a piece of smoked salmon, a sprig of dill, and a sprinkling of freshly ground black pepper. Arrange on a serving plate with lemon wedges, for squeezing.

makes 20

prep 20 mins,
plus cooling
• cook 20 mins

Chicken satay

The authentic version is made with Indonesian soy sauce, *kecap manis*, but Chinese or Japanese soy can also be used.

INGREDIENTS

3 skinless boneless chicken breasts
½ tsp salt
2cm (¾in) piece of fresh root ginger,
  peeled and grated
2 garlic cloves, crushed
½ tsp ground cumin
2 tsp ground coriander
1 tsp lemongrass purée
4 tsp brown sugar
juice of ½ lime
2 tbsp kecap manis or soy sauce
vegetable oil
lime wedges, to garnish

For the satay sauce

250g (9oz) peanut butter
2 garlic cloves, crushed
30g (1oz) creamed coconut, coarsely
  chopped
1 tbsp dark soy sauce
1 tbsp dark brown sugar
1cm (½ in) piece of fresh root ginger,
  peeled and finely chopped
1 tbsp lemon juice
cayenne pepper
salt and freshly ground black pepper

METHOD

1 Cut chicken into thin strips. Place in a shallow, non-metallic dish and set aside. In a bowl, mix together the salt, ginger, garlic, cumin, coriander, lemongrass purée, sugar, lime juice, kecap manis or soy sauce, and 2 teaspoons of vegetable oil. Spoon over chicken, turning it until well coated. Cover and place in the refrigerator to marinate overnight.

2 To make the satay sauce, put the peanut butter with half the garlic in a pan and cook over a low heat for 2 minutes. Add 175ml (6fl oz) water, the creamed coconut, soy sauce, sugar, and ginger, and cook for 2 minutes, stirring until smooth. Add the lemon juice and remaining garlic and season to taste with cayenne pepper, salt, and pepper. Let the sauce cool, cover with cling film, and chill.

3 When ready to cook, thread chicken on to wooden skewers. Re-heat satay sauce over a low heat, stirring to prevent lumps. Brush chicken with oil and grill for 5 minutes, turning once, or until cooked through. Garnish with lime wedges and serve with the warm sauce.

serves 6

prep 20 mins,
plus marinating
• cook 5 mins

marinate overnight • soak wooden
skewers in cold water for at least 30
mins before using to prevent them
burning under the grill

wooden skewers

Devils on horseback

These spicy savouries are often served as pre-dinner canapés.

INGREDIENTS

1 tsp made English mustard
pinch of cayenne pepper,
   plus extra for dusting
3 tbsp mango chutney
salt and freshly ground black pepper
16 prunes, pitted
8 rashers of streaky bacon
4 slices of white bread
butter for spreading

METHOD

1 Preheat the oven to 220°C (425°F/Gas 7). Mix together the English mustard, cayenne, and mango chutney in a bowl, seasoning to taste with salt and pepper.

2 Make a small slit in each prune and fill with a little of the chutney mixture. Cut each bacon rasher in half across its width and wrap each strip around a prune, securing it with a cocktail stick.

3 Place the wrapped prunes on a greased baking tray and roast for 10–12 minutes, turning them over halfway through the cooking time. Cook until the bacon is crisp.

4 Place the bread under the grill or in a toaster and toast until golden. Remove the crusts and using the biscuit cutter, cut each slice into 4 small rounds. Butter the toast rounds and top each one with a bacon-wrapped prune. Dust with a little sprinkle of cayenne pepper and serve immediately.

makes 16

prep 15 mins
• cook 12 mins

cocktail sticks
• small biscuit
   cutter

Smoked salmon rolls

Easy to make, these can be served as a party appetizer with drinks, or as a first course with a salad garnish.

INGREDIENTS

350g (12oz) smoked salmon slices
1 cucumber
100g (3½oz) cream cheese
1 tsp chopped dill, plus extra
   sprigs to garnish
2 tbsp lemon mayonnaise
1 tsp creamed horseradish
lemon wedges, to serve

METHOD

1 Cut the smoked salmon into 16 strips measuring 12 x 4cm (5 x 1½in). Cut the cucumber into 16 batons measuring 4cm x 5mm (1½ x ¼in). Set both aside.
2 Put the cream cheese in a bowl and stir in the dill, mayonnaise, and horseradish until evenly combined.
3 Lay the smoked salmon strips on a board and spread with the cheese mixture, leaving 2.5cm (1in) clear at one short end. Lay a cucumber baton across each strip and roll up tightly from the short end where the cheese mixture comes to the edge.
4 Arrange the rolls on a serving platter, garnished with lemon wedges and sprigs of dill.

makes 16

prep 30 mins

Herbed fish goujons

Fish fingers for grown-ups.

INGREDIENTS

115g (4oz) fresh breadcrumbs
handful of flat-leaf parsley, chopped,
    plus extra leaves to garnish
½ tsp smoked paprika
salt and freshly ground black pepper
85g (3oz) plain flour
1 large egg

225g (8oz) white fish fillet, such as haddock,
    cod, or plaice, skinned and boned
sunflower oil, for frying
lemon wedges, to garnish
tartare sauce, to serve

METHOD

1 Place the breadcrumbs, parsley, and smoked paprika into a bowl, season to taste
   with salt and pepper, and mix thoroughly.
2 Place the flour into a bowl, whisk the egg with 1 tablespoon of water in another bowl,
   and put the breadcrumb mixture into a third.
3 Slice the fish into thin strips. Dust the strips with flour, then dip into the egg, then
   place in the breadcrumbs, and turn until they are completely coated. Place them on a
   plate and chill until needed.
4 Heat 2.5cm (1in) sunflower oil in a frying pan. The oil must be hot enough to sizzle
   when the fish is added. Fry the fish for 1 minute on each side, or until crisp, then
   drain on kitchen paper. Garnished with parsley and wedges of lemon, and serve
   with tartare sauce.

serves 4–6

prep 20 mins
• cook 10–15 mins

Falafel

Use dried chickpeas, soaked in advance, for the best flavour.

INGREDIENTS

225g (8oz) dried chickpeas,
  soaked overnight in cold water
1 tbsp tahini
1 garlic clove, crushed
1 tsp salt
1 tsp ground cumin
1 tsp turmeric

1 tsp ground coriander
½ tsp cayenne pepper
2 tbsp finely chopped flat-leaf parsley
juice of 1 small lemon
vegetable oil, for frying

METHOD

1 Drain the soaked chickpeas and place them in a food processor with the rest of the ingredients except the vegetable oil. Process until finely chopped but not puréed.

2 Transfer the mixture to a bowl and set it aside for at least 30 minutes (and up to 8 hours), covered in the refrigerator.

3 Wet your hands and shape the mixture into 12 balls. Press the tops down slightly to flatten.

4 Heat 5cm (2in) of oil in a deep pan or wok. Fry the balls in batches for 3–4 minutes, or until lightly golden. Drain on kitchen paper and serve immediately. Falafels are great in pitta breads with salad.

makes 12

prep 25 mins, plus soaking and chilling • cook 15 mins

soak the chickpeas overnight in cold water

food processor

Empanadas

These savoury Spanish pastries make very versatile nibbles.

INGREDIENTS

450g (1lb) plain flour, plus extra for dusting
salt and freshly ground black pepper
85g (3oz) butter, diced
2 eggs, beaten, plus extra to glaze
1 tbsp olive oil

1 onion, finely chopped
120g can tomatoes, drained
2 tsp tomato purée
140g can tuna, drained
2 tbsp finely chopped flat-leaf parsley

METHOD

1 To make the pastry, sift the flour into a large mixing bowl with ½ teaspoon salt. Add the butter and rub in with your fingertips until it resembles fine breadcrumbs. Add the beaten eggs with 4–6 tablespoons of water and combine to form a dough. Cover with cling film and chill for 30 minutes.

2 Meanwhile, heat the oil in a frying pan, add the onion, and fry over a medium heat, stirring often, for 5–8 minutes, or until translucent. Add the tomatoes, tomato purée, tuna, and parsley, and season to taste with salt and pepper. Reduce the heat and simmer for 10–12 minutes, stirring occasionally.

3 Preheat the oven to 190°C (375°F/Gas 5). Roll out the pastry to a thickness of 3mm (⅛in). Cut out 24 rounds with a pastry cutter. Put 1 teaspoon of the filling on each, then brush the edges with water, fold over, and pinch together.

4 Place the empanadas on an oiled baking tray and brush with egg. Bake for 25–30 minutes, or until golden brown. Serve warm.

makes 24

prep 45 mins, plus chilling
• cook 40–50 mins

9cm (3½in) round pastry cutter

Boreks

These cheese pastries from Turkey are traditionally made in cigar-shapes or triangles.

INGREDIENTS
175g (6oz) feta cheese, finely crumbled
pinch of ground nutmeg
1 tsp dried mint
freshly ground black pepper
8 sheets of filo pastry, 40 x 30cm
  (16 x 12in), thawed if frozen
60g (2oz) butter, melted
flour, for dusting

METHOD
1 Preheat the oven to 180°C (350°F/Gas 4). Place the feta cheese in a bowl, add the nutmeg and dried mint, then season to taste with black pepper.
2 Lay the filo sheets on top of each other and cut into 3 long strips, 10cm (4in) wide.
3 Taking one strip of pastry at a time, brush with butter and place 1 heaped teaspoon of the cheese mixture at one end. Roll up the pastry, like a cigar, folding the ends in about one-third of the way down to encase the filling completely, then continue to roll. Make sure the ends are tightly sealed.
4 Lightly dust the work surface with flour and keep the rolled pastries in a pile, covered with a damp cloth, while preparing the remainder.
5 Place the pastries in a single layer on a large greased baking tray. Brush with the remaining butter and bake for 10–12 minutes, or until crisp and golden. Best served hot or slightly warm.

makes 20

prep 25 mins
• cook 10–12 mins

Vegetable samosas

Serve these Indian pastries hot or cold.

INGREDIENTS

450g (1lb) potatoes
225g (8oz) cauliflower, chopped
   into small pieces
175g (6oz) peas, thawed if frozen
3 tbsp vegetable oil or ghee
2 shallots, sliced
2 tbsp curry paste or powder
2 tbsp chopped coriander leaves
1 tbsp lemon juice
salt and freshly ground black pepper

For the pastry

350g (12oz) plain flour, plus
   extra for dusting
½ tsp salt
6 tbsp vegetable oil or ghee,
   plus extra for frying

METHOD

1 To make the pastry, sift flour into a bowl with ½ teaspoon of salt. Stir in the oil or ghee and gradually add 120ml (4fl oz) warm water, mixing to make a dough. Knead on a floured surface until smooth. Wrap in cling film and leave to rest for at least 30 minutes.

2 To make the filling, cook the unpeeled potatoes in a saucepan of boiling water until tender. Drain and, when cool enough to handle, peel and chop into small pieces.

3 Blanch the cauliflower florets in a pan of boiling water for 2–3 minutes, or until just tender, then drain. If using fresh peas, blanch them with the cauliflower.

4 Heat the oil in a large frying pan and fry the shallots for 3–4 minutes, stirring frequently, until soft. Add the potatoes, cauliflower, peas, curry paste or powder, coriander, and lemon juice, season to taste, and cook over a low heat for 2–3 minutes, stirring occasionally. Set aside to cool.

5 Divide the dough into 8 equal pieces. Roll them out so each forms an 18cm (7in) round. Cut each round in half and shape into a cone, dampening the edges to seal. Spoon a little of the filling into each cone, dampen the top edge of the dough, and press down over the filling to enclose it. Repeat with the rest of the dough and filling.

6 Heat oil in the deep-fat fryer to 180°C (350°F) and fry the samosas in batches for 3–4 minutes, or until golden on both sides. Drain on kitchen paper and serve hot or cold.

serves 4

prep 45 mins, plus
resting and cooling
• cook 35–40 mins

deep-fat fryer or
large saucepan,
half-filled with oil

freeze, uncooked, for up
to 1 month; defrost, and
pat dry with kitchen paper
before frying

Mushroom vol-au-vents

French in origin, vol-au-vents, or "puffs of wind", are little puff pastry cases with savoury fillings.

INGREDIENTS
20 button mushrooms
4 tbsp olive oil
2 tbsp lemon thyme leaves, chopped
salt and freshly ground black pepper
2 tbsp tapenade
1 tbsp crème fraîche
375g (13oz) puff pastry
plain flour, for dusting
1 egg, lightly beaten

METHOD
1 Preheat the oven to 200°C (400°F/Gas 6). Put the mushrooms, oil, and lemon thyme leaves in a large bowl, season with salt and pepper, and mix together.
2 In another bowl stir together the tapenade and crème fraîche.
3 Roll out the pastry on a lightly floured surface. Stamp out 20 circles using the larger pastry cutter, then use the smaller cutter to make a shallow indent on each circle.
4 Transfer the pastry circles to a large baking tray and spoon a little of the tapenade mix on to the centre of each one, then sit a mushroom on top.
5 Brush the edges of the pastry circles with egg, then transfer them to the oven for 15 minutes, or until golden and puffed up.

makes 20

prep 20 mins
• cook 15 mins

6cm (2½in) and 4.5cm
(1¾in) pastry cutters

Goat's cheese croustades

Versatile, crisp croustade baskets can host a wide range of different fillings, such as this delicious combination of goat's cheese, mint, and roasted tomato.

INGREDIENTS

6 cherry tomatoes
olive oil, for roasting
salt and freshly ground black pepper
85g (3oz) creamy goat's cheese
6–12 mint leaves

For the croustade baskets

4 slices of white bread or
  wholemeal bread
1 tbsp melted butter or olive oil

METHOD

1 Preheat the oven to 180°C (350°F/Gas 4). Remove crusts from the bread, flatten the slices with a rolling pin, and brush with the butter or oil.
2 Using the pastry cutter, stamp out 3 pieces from each slice of bread. Push the bread, butter- or oil-side down, firmly into the bases of the muffin tin and bake for 12–14 minutes, or until golden and crisp. Remove from the tin and leave to cool.
3 Halve the cherry tomatoes. Drizzle with oil and season to taste with salt and pepper, then roast on a baking tray for 25 minutes. Remove from the oven and leave to cool.
4 Spoon 1 teaspoon of goat's cheese into each croustade basket. Top each with a tomato half, and garnish a few with mint leaves. Serve the croustades within 1 hour of filling.

makes 12

prep 10 mins, plus
cooling • cook 40 mins

5cm (2in) pastry cutter
• 12-hole mini-muffin tin

Chicken croustades

Tarragon and chicken is a popular combination.

INGREDIENTS

1 skinless boneless chicken breast,
  cooked
2 tbsp mayonnaise
1 tsp chopped tarragon, plus
  12 leaves, to garnish
1 tsp wholegrain mustard
1 tsp lemon juice
salt and freshly ground black pepper
12 croustade baskets (see Goat's
  cheese croustades, p40)

METHOD

1 Shred the chicken into small pieces and set aside.
2 In a bowl, mix together the mayonnaise, tarragon, mustard, and lemon juice, and season to taste with salt and pepper. Add the chicken and stir until well combined.
3 Divide the mixture between the croustade baskets and garnish each one with a tarragon leaf. Serve within 1 hour of filling, with lemon wedges.

makes 12

prep 15 mins

Sausage rolls

These bite-sized rolls are perfect for parties.

INGREDIENTS
400g (14oz) ready-made puff
  pastry, thawed if frozen
675g (1½lb) sausage meat
1 small onion, finely chopped
1 tbsp chopped thyme
1 tbsp grated lemon zest
1 tsp Dijon mustard
1 egg yolk
salt and freshly ground black pepper
1 egg, beaten, to glaze

METHOD
1 Preheat the oven to 200°C (400°F/Gas 6). Line a baking tray with greaseproof
  paper and chill.
2 Cut the puff pastry in half lengthways. Roll each piece out to form a 30 x 15cm
  (12 x 6in) rectangle, then chill, covered with cling film.
3 Meanwhile, combine the sausage meat with the onion, thyme, lemon zest, mustard,
  and egg yolk, and season with salt and pepper.
4 Lay the pastry on a floured surface. Form the sausage mixture into 2 thinly rolled tubes
  and place in the centre of each piece of pastry. Brush the inside of the pastry with the
  beaten egg, then roll the pastry over and press to seal. Cut each roll into 12 pieces.
5 Place the rolls on the chilled tray, make 2 snips in the top of each with scissors, then
  brush with beaten egg. Bake for 10–12 minutes, or until the pastry is golden and flaky.
  Serve warm, or transfer to a wire rack to cool completely before serving.

makes 24

prep 30 mins,
plus chilling
• cook 10–12 mins

freeze, uncooked,
for up to 3 months

Salted roasted almonds

Almendras Tostadas are served with drinks in Spain.

INGREDIENTS
500g (1lb 2oz) blanched
  whole almonds
2 tbsp sea salt
2 tsp paprika

METHOD
1 Preheat the oven to 220°C (425°F/Gas 7).
2 Spread the almonds out on a baking tray, and sprinkle with a little water. This will dry out, and the salt and spices will cling to the nuts. Sprinkle the almonds with the salt and the paprika, tossing to ensure that they are all well coated. Spread them out evenly again.
3 Roast the almonds for 15–25 minutes, depending on how brown you wish them to be, but take care that they do not burn.

serves 8

prep 5 mins
• cook 15–25 mins

London, New York, Melbourne, Munich, and Delhi

Editor Cécile Landau

Jacket Designer Mark Penfound

DTP Designer Kavita Varma

DK INDIA

Editorial Consultant Dipali Singh

Designer Neha Ahuja

DTP Designer Tarun Sharma

DTP Coordinator Sunil Sharma

Head of Publishing Aparna Sharma

First published in Great Britain in 2013.
Material in this publication was previously published
in *The Cooking Book* (2008) and *Cook Express* (2009)
by Dorling Kindersley Limited
80 Strand, London WC2R 0RL
Penguin Group (UK)

002-192715-Feb/13

A CIP catalogue record for this book is available
from the British Library.

ISBN 978-1-4093-2708-0

Printed and bound in China by Leo Paper Products Ltd.

Tracks of My Years

Ken
Bruce

Tracks of My Years

Sidgwick & Jackson

First published 2009 by Sidgwick & Jackson
an imprint of Pan Macmillan Ltd
Pan Macmillan, 20 New Wharf Road, London N1 9RR
Basingstoke and Oxford
Associated companies throughout the world
www.panmacmillan.com

ISBN 978-0-283-07069-3 HB
ISBN 978-0-283-07110-2 TPB

Typeset by Ellipsis Books Limited, Glasgow
Printed in the UK by CPI Mackays, Chatham ME5 8TD

For Kerith

Picture Acknowledgements

All photographs from the author's collection apart from:

Page 4: Peter Brookner/Rex Features
Page 5: top right, Mirrorpix, bottom © BBC
Page 7: top left, © BBC
Page 8: bottom, © Liz Hooper
Page 9: top, © BBC
Page 15: top © Owen Elias, bottom © BBC

Every effort has been made to contact copyright holders
of photographs reproduced in this book. If any have been
inadvertently overlooked, the publishers will be pleased
to make restitution at the earliest opportunity.

Contents

Acknowledgements

I would not have embarked on this book without the help and encouragement of Luigi Bonomi, Mark Wogan and Jo Gurnett. I would not have completed it without the expert guidance of my editor, Ingrid Connell, and the patience of my friends, colleagues and family.

Several colleagues helped to confirm my memories of individual episodes, although any errors that have inadvertently crept in are entirely mine. Iain Purdon and Robert Sproul-Cran were of particular help. My sister Isobel and brother Scott provided family photographs and details, as did my brother Alasdair, who sadly died in late 2008, much too young.

All of the above made what was an unusual venture for me much easier and they have my huge gratitude.

Finally, to all the announcers, producers, presenters and technicians who have made my career in radio so much fun, to the controllers of Radio 2 who have continued to employ me on the network, and to anyone who may have chanced upon one of my broadcasts over the last thirty-three years, my grateful thanks.

One

'The Wee Pest'

I was born before there were charts. Just writing this makes it feel like a time before memory, when the world was barely formed, when Moses had only recently descended the mountain with the bad news about adultery, and Jimmy Young had just started school.

But it wasn't so very long ago. The first singles chart in this country hit the public in November 1952, a simple marketing ploy by the *New Musical Express* in an effort to put one over on its rivals. The music press has been indulging in increasingly frantic battles ever since, usually involving the Music Police, that is, teenage scribblers, slagging off in a Year 5 manner any musician who is (a) over twenty-five, and (b) just, like, really boring, y'know.

Back in 1952, though, one Percy Dickins, such a rock 'n' roll name, phoned round twenty record shops, pooled the results and printed a Top 12 in the *NME*. Top of the Pops, though the phrase hadn't been invented yet, was Al Martino singing 'Here in My Heart'.

I was twenty-one months old when Al powered his way to number one, and had already managed to live through pneumonia, the chicken pox and being dropped in the bath, so it seems that the survival instincts which have so far enabled me to keep in employment at the BBC for thirty years were honed early.

To be born into a decade as flat and grey as the 1950s was a trial that succeeding generations do not fully appreciate. To 1960s children the world was beautiful and filled with love. Kids of the 1970s had fashionable clothes to wear and pop music aimed directly at them, and the 1980s generation had parents born in the 1950s who made damn sure their little lives were going to be a bit more exciting.

Britain was a nation exhausted in the 1950s. We'd won a war which had drained the country of men, money and resources. It had been a military and moral victory, but an economic disaster. In February 1951, rationing was still widespread. It had begun in 1940, at the height of the war when convoys were being destroyed and stocks of food, clothing and petrol were at risk. Somewhere in my loft, in a tin my mother kept until her death at the age of ninety-one, is my last sweet ration book. Yes, children, even the simple pleasures of sweets were denied you by the Big Bad Government.

So, when I made my entrance on 2 February 1951 at the Orchard Park Nursing Home, Giffnock, Glasgow, it was to a family which, like every other in the land, was having to hand over coupons to obtain all the things we now take for granted. Meat, eggs, cream, butter, cheese, margarine and cooking fats, clothes, furniture and petrol; all on the ration.

It must have been a bit of a jolt for my parents to have another mouth to feed; after all, my father was forty-eight and my mother forty-two, old for those days. I was their fourth child and a full six years younger than the last one. Isobel, the eldest, was already eleven, Scott a couple of years younger and Alasdair two years behind him.

To everyone's credit the word 'mistake' was never used in my hearing and I was only once aware of an old auntie saying, 'Is this the wee surprise one?' I was never for a moment made to feel a burden, and in fact my mother was probably over-caring of her little treasure, to the extent that I can remember having to tear myself away from her hugs when I considered myself to be too old for such babying. Mind you, I was twenty-three at the time.

Music was always playing around the house. With siblings eleven, eight and six years older, by the time I was five they were buying records and playing them on our parents' pre-war wind-up gramophone. I quickly mastered the art of propping up the heavy wooden lid, slapping the disc down on to the green baize mat and swinging the stylus over for the needle to make contact. Needless to say, my sister and brothers kept their precious records well away from the sticky-fingered Wee Bugger. So my early deejaying experience was limited to ancient recordings of Henry Hall and His Orchestra, and something called 'The Chum Song', which was made by Jack Hylton and His Band in 1930 to publicize a Chums Club run by a Scottish newspaper. Tragically, the record broke after many years of playing. Even more tragically, I still remember all the words.

I became adept at winding the handle just enough to ensure that the record would slow down halfway through; I could then add odd little turns to keep it wavering on-and-off key. You had to find some way of livening up the seven-hundredth play of the same song.

3

But let us not rush on; I realize I may have left you concerned at the mention of the dreaded pneumonia earlier. It's not a tale of great suspense, as it's fairly obvious the infant survived, but at the age of three months I did fall victim to the condition. I believe it was touch and go for a short while, the old guttering candle and such like, and the doctor coming out of the sickroom, removing his stethoscope and saying, 'Keep him warm – the next twenty-four hours will be the danger time,' or maybe I saw all that in a film somewhere. Anyway, the plucky little fellow pulled through; I'm not 100 per cent convinced that being stuck outside the house in my pram for most of each day in a freezing winter wasn't a contributory factor, but it was the habit of the time and I was back outside in the snow a couple of days later.

This episode may have made my mother a little more watchful of me as I grew up. I was always told I had a weak chest but never saw much sign of it, apart from a bit of a cough which developed at the age of fifteen. That may have had something to do with the twenty Embassy I was smoking each day though.

I say my mother was 'watchful'; my sister and brothers tended to say I was 'cosseted'. They were often to be heard, and indeed to this day can still be heard, saying, 'You were spoiled rotten,' and, 'We had to fight all the fights; you had it easy,' all of which is true, to an extent. I had a pretty carefree childhood; as long as I didn't do anything actually illegal, I was largely given a free rein by my parents, and my brothers used to put up with me following them when they went off on their bikes, with me pedalling gamely behind on my trike, shouting, 'Wait for me, pals!' They could have shot away from me easily but, mostly, they waited for the Wee Pest.

Issy being a girl, and nearly an adult by now, was a less present influence in my earliest years, although as adults, when age difference seems to diminish, we became much closer. The boys were in the main very good to me. Scott and I had similar features; Alasdair had a slightly different look, an altogether cheekier face. In later years, once I had learned the art of verbal retaliation, I would attribute this difference in looks to his being a 'throwback'. But they were good big brothers. Scott would carry me when I got tired and Atty, which was as close to a difficult name like Alasdair as I could get, once had a go at some bullies for me. I had been playing with a friend on a bit of open land near the railway line when some older boys came up and demanded sweets. Not exactly the stuff of Asbos, but we were a bit ruffled, and when I told my brother he set off to find them, offering them physical violence in some ripe language when he did

Scott, who had a finely formed wit from an early age, used to refer to me as Pesketh, and I was also known to them as the Wee Pest, the Wee Bugger, Buggerlugs, and the Wee Bastard. Not in front of Mum and Dad, of course; however, when they saw a billboard for the motor parts manufacturer Webasto, they at last found a name that they could call me at the table without getting shouted at.

And they found they could get me to do the swearing for them. At the time, the *Rover* comic ran a strip about the strongman Morgyn the Mighty. My brothers would stand me outside the kitchen window and tell me, 'You've to shout out the next word. Morgyn the Mighty; Shorgyn the ...?'

I would then excitedly yell out, 'Shitey!' They would run off laughing uproariously and my mother would pretend she hadn't heard.

Like most of us, I have few strong memories of my preschool years, just some images of the lamplighter, the 'leerie', coming round to fire up the gas mantles in the street lights outside our house. They went electric in the mid-1950s so I must have been three or four when that happened.

I think I was only two when I got lost on an outing to Tommy Strang's farm at Busby. I know now that with a largish family in tow, it's all too easy to assume somebody else is keeping an eye on the youngest and, sure enough, I wandered off unnoticed to look at the cows. I'm told there was quite a search for me, but I clearly remember feeling quite happy until I was found, whereupon I burst into tears, probably because everyone looked so upset and angry. Naturally, I put this down to my innate sympathy with other people's emotions. My family put it down to attention-seeking.

My brothers also clearly recalled, or said they did, an incident where I had strolled out on to the ice at the boating pond in Rouken Glen, one of Glasgow's finest parks, about a mile from our house. It froze over quite regularly in those days, less so now, and the perimeter was festooned with dire warnings about the dangers of walking on the ice. According to the boys, when they, in caring voices, tried to coax me back to dry land, I stood on the ice defiantly, successfully upping the stakes by stamping on it from time to time. The more they cajoled, the more I stamped. It took ages for them to persuade me back on to the bank.

I don't believe a word of it. First of all, I beg leave to

doubt that they used caring voices; I'm inclined to think that they called me every rude name under the sun and threatened me with all sorts of unpleasantness if I didn't comply. Secondly, the whole incident seems to bear too much similarity to an old *Tom and Jerry* plot to be believable. Thirdly, you'd have to believe that I was capable of being stubborn and contrary. Well, two out of three ain't bad.

My mother's family had roots in Caithness but were well planted in Edinburgh by the time she was born. My maternal grandfather, Robert Dunbar, was in the railway police, ending up as superintendent in Glasgow, and his children seemed to inherit the railway side of things. My mother, saddled with the unwieldy birth name of Williamina, was always known as Minnie. Before her marriage to my dad she worked for the railways in their Springburn offices; her sister, my Aunt Isobel, became a staff welfare officer; and their brother, my Uncle Bertie, took the management route and eventually reached the dizzy heights of the British Railways Board. I pass his old office at Marylebone every day on my way to work.

My father was part of a large family of nine brothers and sisters who lived in a large house in the Mount Vernon area of Glasgow. Grandpa Bruce was a businessman who was long gone by the time I came along. Born around 1860, his father had died when he was thirteen, so he'd gone out to work soon after as a commercial traveller, going all round the north of Scotland by train and carter's wagon. When he married he became a prolific and regular breeder. Peter, my dad, was one of the younger of the flock, born in 1903, and unsurprisingly I only knew his immediate siblings. Uncle Andy lived in Cheshire and had that strange hybrid accent that expat Scots develop, still obviously Scottish but with the heavy 'R' sound missing. And Uncle Tommy was a typical Glasgow man. By which I mean he drank. I once read a newspaper piece by the famous Glasgow journalist Jack House, in which he described a Saturday outing of Glasgow gentlemen in the 1950s.

This involved meeting at Glasgow St Enoch station at nine o'clock in the morning. In the large Gents' toilets by Platform 11, several trestle tables had been set up and beer was being dispensed. Crates were then loaded on to the train to Ardrossan, and mostly consumed by the time of arrival, whereupon the cast of characters embarked on a steamer bound for the Isle of Arran. A little fresh air may have been taken but most of the passage was spent in the bar, or 'looking at the engines' as the euphemism went, and on making land at Brodick all concerned trooped up the hill to the Douglas Hotel.

The return journey on the last boat and train of the day was not dissimilar. Lest you get the idea that these people were complete lushes, I must point out that ham sandwiches were provided at key points of the day.

This was the kind of company my uncle was completely at home with. As a young man, he'd got up to the usual scrapes; one night, after a particularly heavy session, he woke up knowing he was about to be sick so, with great presence of mind, rushed over to the bedroom windows, opened them and vomited out into the garden, returning to bed satisfied that he'd avoided a nasty mess in the room. Only in the morning did he discover that, rather than the windows, he'd actually opened the glass doors to the book-case.

Later in life his drinking became rather less amusing, and I was often bustled away when we had a chance encounter with him in town during the day. Uncle Tommy became a Terrible Warning of the Dangers of Drink.

Glasgow had a strangely ambivalent attitude towards alcohol. While the city boasted more alcoholics per head of the population than anywhere else in the country, it also claimed more teetotallers than any other city. There was an odd civil instrument known as the Veto Poll, where an elect-oral ward could vote as to whether or not to allow alcohol sales in the area. Unsurprisingly, the anti-booze brigade, a motley collection of prescriptive churches (even the Free Presbyterians, the famous 'Wee Frees', had a Glasgow outpost far from their West Highland stronghold) and obscure sects such as the Rechabites, were rather more motivated to go out and vote than the drinkers, who were ensconced in some four-ale bar or other, so large parts of the city were without pubs, off-licences or any outlet which could sell you even a can of Sweet Stout.

This led to some long treks before the rules were even-tually relaxed. At about half past eight in the evening, my dad would announce he was just going to put the car away for the night in the garage, a trip from the street at the front of the house to the little lane that ran along the back. This two-minute job would take upwards of an hour, as his route took him four miles out, past Newton Mearns to the Malletsheugh Inn, a farmers' pub where some years later I consumed my first underage half-pint of heavy. It was the nearest half-decent licensed premises. There was a pub in

Busby which would have been nearer, but it was not a place for the faint-hearted, or in fact anyone who wished to leave looking the same as they went in.

We were a solid middle-class family; for Glasgow, that is. Class divisions were much less clear in that city; it probably boiled down to whether or not you owned your own home. The size of that home didn't matter. I can never remember people being impressed by houses bigger than theirs. House envy had yet to be invented. If you had a council house, you were working class; if you had your own, you were middle class. There was no upper class. This was Glasgow.

Our life was comfortable and happy; we weren't rich, but we weren't poor. We always had plenty of food and clothes – although I never wore new clothes, except for school uniform. Everything else, apart from shoes, was hand-me-downs. My dad had a decent car, always a Standard Vanguard. He had three in succession, managing to roll the first on an icy road and putting him in dock with a broken leg. We kept the newspaper photograph of the stricken car for years, not as a terrible warning, more a badge of honour. We lived in a house that felt big enough to me in Giffnock on the outskirts of the city, a nice middle-class area but not as posh as Whitecraigs with its massive mansions, or Newton Mearns with its ranch-style bungalows. Ours was a large mid-terrace sandstone house with a small front garden, and a not much bigger back one which boasted a patch of grass, a few raspberry bushes and some rhubarb. Gardening was not my father's passion.

Luxuries didn't seem to come into our lives but nobody seemed interested in them; we weren't an acquisitive family and I think it's fair to say that all four of us have gone through life with much the same outlook. The one thing my father did spend on was education. My dad had put my three siblings through school, the fee-paying Hutchesons' Grammar, and even though my arrival when he was aged forty-eight must have caused him to blanch a bit, he coughed up for me to go as well. Whether his money was well spent is a moot point.

My dad was what I suppose we would now call a small businessman. He had a little newsagent's shop but his main occupation, the one he put down on forms, was manufacturer's agent. He dealt in shoes, and had an extremely untidy office at 75 Buchanan Street, Glasgow C1. As far as I understood it, he was the middleman between the shoe factories in England and the big department stores in Glasgow and elsewhere. The shoe companies would send him their latest lines, he would take samples to the shops and use his gruff charm to persuade the buyer to order 200 pairs. Or probably they just went to the pub together and put through the usual order. Two or three times a year he would head off on the sleeper to visit the factories or to attend the shoe fair held in either London or Harrogate, where business deals would be struck and many a whisky would be downed. He would then come back on the night train, where he always seemed to sit up talking all night and, in the course of this, meet the Stupidest Man in Scotland. One year this title was awarded to Matt McGinn, a fairly well-known Scottish working-class poet of the time, but whose oeuvre didn't seem to appeal to my dad. 'Poet? Call that working?' McGinn appeared to have been propounding communist theory and Soviet practice to all and sundry during the journey; just the kind of thing to have my father turning puce and very nearly spilling his whisky. He wasn't right-wing but he was an early adopter of the view that the Soviet model couldn't and wouldn't work. He had also never forgiven Stalin for dodginess during the war, and, in a spirit of fair-mindedness, thought the Americans were similarly untrustworthy from that period, owing to their lateness in arrival and desire to take any credit going.

There seemed to be thousands of businessmen like my dad in the city at the time, each of them with a small office in one of apparently hundreds of similar rabbit-warren-type buildings. The office of P. S. Bruce was on the second floor, reached by a lift in the adjoining lane operated by what Peter Cook would have called a unidexter. Harry was his name, a middle-aged man in a shabby suit who seemed deficient not only in legs but in the number and quality of his teeth too. He would hop off his chair and engage his passengers in what would have been merry banter if anybody could have understood his even-for-Glasgow impenetrable accent. The office was filled with shoeboxes, piled from floor to ceiling, and in the corner was a fabulous roll-top desk; my father would each morning ceremonially unlock it, roll up the front and then pick up all the bits of paper that had burst from it like a jack-in-the-box. The place was his solitary fastness. No one ever came in or out of the office, and the phone would only ring about once a day, and that probably while he was out.

His newsagent's shop was in Ingram Street, next to the fire station and across the road from what was then the *Daily Express* building. It therefore had a steady stream of cigarette-buying firemen, print workers, journalists and men and women from the nearby fruit market. He didn't work the shop himself, except on Saturday mornings when I would join him and attempt to eat sweets from every jar. His sister, my Aunt Jean, ran it during the week. She looked fearsome, with a round red face, a shock of white hair and a cigarette permanently balanced on her lower lip, the curling smoke from which had given her hair a nicotine-coloured streak. Underneath the forbidding exterior, though, she was kindly and, very occasionally, given to outbreaks of wheezing laughter at the comic rudenesses of the customers. She could give as well as receive in that department. On being asked by smokers at the counter for a match, she would say, 'Aye, your face and my backside.'

My Saturday trips were good fun, particularly getting to ring up the money on the cash register, which even my young eye could tell was a work of art, one of those magnificent gleaming affairs with silver scroll work. After closing the shop at one, I'd get in the car beside my dad to go home, he'd start up, drive a hundred yards, stop, switch off and get out. He then disappeared into a building called the Red Hoose, from which came shouts of merriment and smells of beer and whisky. I'd sit in the car with my comic and crisps for about forty minutes, then back would come Dad, now smelling just like the Red Hoose. It's an aroma I was to seek out again and again in later years.

My mum prepared three meals a day for all of us and seemed to spend all day washing, cooking, cleaning and then cooking some more, constantly on the move. I'm sure she must have sat down to eat with us but I can only remember her running round the table, putting dishes down in front of us or wiping our faces. She was a bright, cheery presence throughout our childhood and beyond, metamorphosing into everyone's adopted granny in the Highland village where she spent her last years and making tea and sandwiches for anyone who came near her door.

By the time I was starting school, in 1956, Britain was undergoing a military nervous breakdown at Suez, people were increasingly concerned that, only a decade after the war, they might all be blown to kingdom come by a nuclear explosion, and the nation was still as grey and dull as five years previously.

When I think of any event of the mid-1950s, I always see it in black and white; I assumed for a time that this was because all newsreel images of the period were in mono-chrome, but even when you see some of that washed-out colour film that exists of the decade, the predominant colour is still grey. Cars only came in black or, yes, grey; football crowds up to 100,000 strong were all men wearing flat caps and raincoats in grey and, occasionally, fawn; and, no doubt, with the tendency to pea-souper fogs in the days before the Clean Air Act, the sky was grey too.

To paraphrase the late Les Dawson, the 1950s gave a whole new meaning to the word 'drab'. No wonder we needed cheering up; and luckily, two new forms of music were opening up almost simultaneously to help in that task. In 1956, rock 'n' roll hit our shores, while at the same time our home-grown teenagers were discovering the joys of home-made music thanks to skiffle.

We weren't exposed to rock 'n' roll much; the BBC was a little reluctant to feature that type of record on its sedate programmes, and seemed to take a more approving attitude to skiffle. It was certainly the music my brothers and sister brought home – Lonnie Donegan with the 'Rock Island Line',

Johnny Duncan and the Blue Grass Boys singing 'Last Train to San Fernando' (what exactly did 'Beedy beedy bum bum' mean?) and Chas McDevitt and Nancy Whiskey on their 'Freight Train'.

Another of Lonnie's recordings led to Scott coming home from school severely chastised. His hit of 1958, 'Nobody Loves Like an Irishman', was quite popular in Scotland, despite the obvious inaccuracy of the title, and it contained a repeated inter-verse riff which had his band singing, 'Dum-dum-a-dimmy dum-a-dum.' Scott and his pals on the school bus thought they could improve on this lyrically, and wrote a perfect little replacement which went, 'Don't rub her belly, rub her bum.' Alas, someone unappreciative of this poetic genius overheard, reported them to the school, and sore hands all round ensued.

Giffnock Primary was the local school and I trotted off happily every day to Academy Road, to read Old Lob and Fred J. Schonell's spelling tests, with firstly Mrs Hamilton, a brisk lady in a green housecoat, and later Miss Graham, who seemed about 110 years old. She wore those voluminous black dresses that grannies seemed to specialize in, she had watery eyes which blinked non-stop and her steel-grey hair was hauled back into a bun from which protruded what I took to be pencils.

All of us had passed through Miss Graham's class at some point. My mother said she always knew when we'd fallen under her tutelage because we would come back from school blinking furiously, having picked up her peculiar facial tic.

Giffnock school was typical of the time: a traditional stone main building and a large playground into which had encroached 'new' buildings, in this case wooden-framed. At the back of the site, backing on to the railway line, were the outdoor toilets which, naturally, stank appallingly. In the playground, massive games of football would take place, thirty- or forty-a-side, or there would be British Bulldogs or Hopping Charlie. The toilets were brick-built, open-roofed and had a six-foot-high rear wall. The traditional sport at playtime would be to try to pee over this wall and hit the 10.34 train as it headed into town.

I'm not quite sure why, but every Friday, assembly day, I would wear a kilt to school, the sort of thing that would get you beaten up in the bogs now, but was considered unremarkable then. I was educated well, I think, and was certainly happy at school. It also played host to my introduction to the capriciousness of females, when a girl called Rhona allowed me to retrieve from her gym-knicker pocket a Callard & Bowser Creamline toffee. She then promptly peed the floor and told the teacher it was all my fault. I assumed an air of injured innocence; after all, it wasn't my bladder that had given in. Nevertheless, the kangaroo court decided that my fumblings for a warm toffee had been the major contributory factor and I was sent from the room.

As I stood outside, waiting for the 'janny' to arrive with his sand bucket, I experienced for the first, but by no means the last, time in my life that feeling where all the things you should have said, the crushing rejoinder, the vital piece of defensive oratory, come flooding into your mind two minutes too late. I couldn't go back in and shout, 'But she said I could!' The moment had passed. And it would mean sullying a woman's reputation. We Bruces have our Code.

And so, with some important parts of my education begun at least, the 1950s rolled towards a close with a man in space,

Col. Yuri Gagarin; a little bit of colour breaking into our lives (my dad's new car was a Standard Vanguard Mark 3 in, wait for it, coffee-and-cream!); and my realization that there were some quite good things on the radio.

We'd had a television since the beginning of Scottish transmissions, and my father dutifully tuned the beast into the Kirk O'Shotts transmitter to watch the Coronation. I don't remember any of this but apparently I was propped up in front of the box for large parts of my infancy, being particularly engaged, I'm told, by a bearded cook named Philip Harben. His daughter Pippa became a newsreader on the BBC World Service and was still there when I rolled up for an audition in the 1970s. Aside from Philip and the predictable *Watch with Mother*, I became addicted to the STV *One O'Clock Gang* programme when it began, and couldn't wait for each new episode of *Wagon Train* and *Rawhide*.

I was much less aware of the radio, but I did listen to Peter Brough and his ventriloquist's doll Archie Andrews in *Educating Archie* (what a brilliant bit of programme pitching that must have been), and Ted Ray and Kenneth Connor in *Ray's a Laugh*, as well as the frankly rather frightening Uncle Mac and his *Children's Favourites*. Those favourites seemed to be the same every other week, and consisted of a repeated diet of 'Sparky's Magic Piano', 'The Three Billy Goats Gruff', and 'The Ugly Duckling'. I can't help thinking these were 'producer's favourites', and chosen to represent what children *ought* to be asking for. There was always one piece of classical music which, if it was requested by a child at all, was obviously picked by some snotty little swot of the type vividly represented by Walter in the *Dennis the Menace* comic strips.

Although I was choosing to listen to these shows, I was obviously taking a lot more in, as I discovered many years later on hearing an old episode of *Take It from Here*, a series I was convinced I'd never listened to. I knew of the Glums of course, but thought my knowledge of them had come from spin-offs and other references. It was only when I heard the end of this old repeat and realized I was singing all the words to the closing signature tune and, not only that, knew every note of the playout music, that I appreciated that the radio had meant more to me than I thought.

It was to take on an even greater significance in the 1960s.

Listening to pop music really wasn't easy when I was young. You had to have the doggedness and ingenuity of a Hercule Poirot to seek it out, and when you found it, for instance on Radio Luxembourg, it tended to fade away into the ether after about twenty seconds. It amazes me that we ever heard any, let alone formed a view on which singers and bands we liked. We took what we were given, as in so many aspects of life.

The BBC had its Light Programme, the forerunner of today's Radio 2, but a very different animal. It was a mixture of speech and, as the name implies, 'light' music. Pop records were restricted to a few set outlets, such as *Pick of the Pops* on a Sunday, the programme that became indelibly associated with Alan 'Fluff' Freeman. It had started as a much more sober affair, the first presenter being Franklin Engelmann, a very accomplished broadcaster who became the friendly inquisitor of *Down Your Way*, but hardly the Voice of Youth.

David Jacobs was next man in ('Your DJ, D. J.'), and from here on it became the Appointment to Listen for any youngster with even a passing interest in music. There wasn't much else though. The fact that I used to tune in to *Desert Island Discs* because the guest very occasionally might choose a pop record may illustrate just how slim the pickings were.

Children's Favourites on a Saturday morning played a few. Very few. I repeat, I never believed real children made the requests on that programme; nobody I knew would ask for those billy goats, or, worse, Master Ernest Lough singing 'O for the Wings of a Dove'. Nevertheless, constant repetition of the same few records that the BBC approved of, week after week, has meant that each note and word of 'Nellie the Elephant' and 'The Teddy Bears' Picnic' is now stamped on my memory forever.

I blame this policy for the shaming fact that the first record I attempted to buy was not a rock 'n' roll classic by Elvis or Chuck Berry, not a Lonnie Donegan skiffle number, not even kiddypop like 'I am a Mole and I Live in a Hole'. No, my first foray to the little room above the newsagent's outside Giffnock station where the cardboard display boxes of records were racked was to ask for . . . Tommy Cooper singing 'Don't Jump off the Roof, Dad'. How very credible, even for a ten-year-old.

I was saved from myself by the simple fact that this tiny shop only stocked the narrowest range of discs and I was met with not just blank looks but slightly pitying ones too. When I eventually did manage to buy my first record, my taste hadn't developed much; it was 'I Remember You' by Frank Ifield. Still not exactly rock 'n' roll, but a step up from novelty songs.

I'm not embarrassed, though; like the children who allegedly requested Chopin sonatas, I've never believed the artsy types who tell the Sunday newspapers that they owned every Leadbelly recording before the age of ten. Any more than I believe the 'Day in the Life' features where they write 1,000 words before 6 a.m., eat a spartan breakfast of blueberries and sustainable wheatcakes, translate some Russian poetry in the yurt next to the organic garden and do a little cello practice before lunch.

I was busy being a proper child, pedalling around on my bike, annoying my siblings, getting muddy, doing the minimum possible at school, not washing enough and trying not to make adults angry. Just like the children of today, who do all of the above except, of course, the last named. Somewhere along the way in the last forty years or so positions have become completely reversed, in that children now seem immune to threats from adults, and it is now the grown-ups who live in fear of incurring the wrath of the young.

Life's boundaries were clearer then; if a football was booted into Mr Grumpy's garden, you wouldn't get it back, or if you did, it would be burst first. And if you moaned to your parents about it, they'd say, 'Well, what did you expect?'

My father was not a disciplinarian, but he didn't have to be. He was the line in the sand, the last threat. My mother would ask me to do something, I'd agree cheerfully and then not do it. She'd ask me again and I'd say, 'Why can't he do it?', naming whichever brother happened to be nearest. When after two or three more times of asking my father was brought into the equation, I'd know the game was up and submit meekly. I don't recall us ever having an argument.

He didn't have to shout or threaten. Once Dad had said, 'Do it,' I did it. The only time I ever remember him being remotely angry with me was when I inadvertently slammed his hand shut in the car door. Even then, all he said, with commendable restraint, was, 'Ow!' and, 'Open the bloody door then!' I wasn't hugely popular for the rest of that day but no further action was taken.

Two

'The Laziest Boy in the School'

Hutchesons' Boys' Grammar School was an ancient school in a new building. It had started in 1690, with twelve boys on the roll in the words of the school song, or, as we sang, 'Twelve boys on the dole.' For years it had been based in Crown Street, in the heart of the Gorbals, where the local roughnecks had taken great delight in taunting the posh kids in their uniforms and caps. A new concrete, glass and tile building at Crossmyloof had been raised in the 1950s and it was to this sparkling new school that I lugged my satchel in September 1960. I was nine years old, the age at which entry began, and had surprised myself by passing the entrance examination a few months earlier. My three siblings had all attended the same establishment, my sister naturally at the Girls' School, an entirely separate organization with whose fragrant pupils coarse boys were definitely not encouraged to fraternize. I don't recall feeling daunted by the move even though I had been told by all concerned that this would be a much posher school than Giffnock Primary. As I was to find out, money doesn't necessarily mean class.

It had a rector rather than headmaster, named, coincidentally, John M. Hutchison. He was a slight figure with prominent ears, earning him the nickname of Bunnylugs from the older boys, or, from the less polite, Buggerlugs. His manner was stern, dour and humourless, and each morning he would bring this cheering façade to the daily assembly.

On that first morning we stood in class lines, youngest at the very front, to hear our warm welcome to the school. There was none. Only an exhortation to work hard, and a barely veiled threat of what would happen if we didn't. I had found myself positioned next to a roundish lad who walked in with a bouncing gait and announced his name as Lang. Surnames only, you see. Posh or what!

We stood quietly, directly beneath the Rector's podium as he announced the names of this year's prefects, and then finally the school captain, one Arthur Slight. On hearing this name, Lang turned to me and said loudly, 'Arse or Shite.'

Under other circumstances, I'd have enjoyed the speed and vulgarity of this instant renaming, but the combination of surprise at such language in a grand school and the fact that John M. Hutchison, MA, was now staring hard in our direction caused any laughter to die in my throat.

In later life, with the experience gained from a lifetime of being caught next to people who were causing trouble, I would have turned round theatrically and looked behind me for the real culprit. At the age of nine, my diversionary tactics were not fully developed and the curse that was to follow me through my schooldays took over. I blushed, and by doing so confirmed my guilt to every teacher on the stage. Lang, naturally, had a look of great holiness on his face.

Blushing is the most maddening thing. The more you want it to stop the worse it becomes. Usually, the blush is over something you wouldn't normally feel embarrassed about.

Realizing this makes it worse again. Even today, I can still, about once a year, find a blush beginning to rise in my cheeks. Luckily, a long life of drinking and bad weather has given my face a fine red hue; the perfect camouflage.

My teacher for the next three years was Mr Terries, a tall man with slicked-back black hair atop a bean-shaped head. He was of the firm belief, as were all other primary teachers at our school, that bad spelling was something that could be cured by the application of the strap. Anyone getting less than fifteen out of twenty got a taste of the Lochgelly belt. Victoria Wood once said, 'They didn't have dyslexia in my day; you were just sat up the back with raffia.' So it was in our school, except that raffia-making was made slightly more difficult thanks to red and tingling hands.

Although not the most belted boy in the class, I had my fair share of being called out to the front, made to hold out my crossed palms, and then receiving a larruping. My spelling was good, so that wasn't the reason; it was usually talking, making a mess, or getting caught flicking neighbours with elastic bands. Six strokes of the belt was the maximum; Terries was a tall man but not athletic, so his beltings were not too bad. The kids with female teachers, against expectations, had it worse, only because the ladies felt that they hadn't sufficient strength to inflict the proper punishment so would send miscreants along to the gym teachers with a note which presumably read, 'Please thrash this boy to within an inch of his life.' Needless to say, being PE teachers, they were only too happy to oblige.

Whoever it was who first said that schooldays are the happiest days of your life was a Big Fat Liar. Any school student, as I believe they like to be called, who believes that this is as good as it gets should take heart. It gets a lot better. Childhood is, or ought to be, a glorious time, but the hours spent at school don't count as my happiest, or come anywhere near it.

I did the minimum necessary to get by, from the day I arrived to the day I left, and I still bask in the glory of being named as the Laziest Boy in the School by Fuzzy Cathcart, my geography teacher, during one of his frequent dissertations to the class on our character weaknesses. The title never rankled; it's always good to be outstanding at something.

I was lazy, but I know that the teaching could have energized me much more than it did, and I can only remember one teacher who really fired my interest: Arthur Meikle in English. I loved his classes and wanted to do well and I read and read all the books he suggested and many more. Other teachers failed to get me engaged, but Arthur taught me well, so that I was able to produce convincing book reviews of works I had never read. Perhaps not the testimonial that he would have wanted, but in later years this skill enabled me to conduct more than one lengthy radio interview with someone bundled into my studio without even their name to go on.

Ours was a rugby school, and at the age of eleven it became compulsory to play once a week. I was hopeless at the game, being too skinny to be of any use in the pack, but I was a fast runner, so I was placed at stand-off, from where I scored a few tries. It wasn't as impressive as it sounds as this was the duffers' team and nobody else could run at all, let alone at any speed. In the summer, cricket was the sport, and although my lack of prowess was just as marked here,

I liked the game and developed some accuracy as a bowler, counteracted somewhat by a deadly slowness that enabled any half-competent batsman to belt the ball for miles. Again, I was in the team for leftovers and no-hopers but I did get close to mixing with the better players by learning how to fill in the scorebook, so at least some usable skill came out of it, as well as a lifelong interest as a spectator.

I've spent many a happy day watching a Test Match, the intricacies of which are endlessly fascinating, and felt especially welcome at the Oval. Cricket crowds are good fun and rarely seem to show the ill effects of the large amount of drinking that goes on. One Friday of a final Test, I had a good seat in the stand next to my friend Graham Lambourne. It was a decent August day, dry but not over warm and I was wearing a lightweight pale-coloured suit. I ambled off to the bar to fetch a couple of pints, fell into conversation with a few hacks in the bar and then started off back to my seat bearing two of these bloody plastic glasses that regulations now insist on.

Reaching the outside, an over was in progress so I naturally waited for the end, nonchalantly leaning slightly back to rest my shoulder on a concrete stanchion. Unfortunately the post was a little further back than I had appreciated. When your sense of balance tells you something's up, all sorts of natural reflexes kick in. In my case both my hands gripped tightly. Had the glasses actually been glass this would not have been a problem. As they were plastic, they gave in to the pressure and the beer inside them shot upwards in two large jets and came down again all over my clothing.

I now had about half a pint in each glass and the best part of a full pint on my trousers. I couldn't put the glasses down to cover the damage so had to negotiate my way back to the seat looking like the victim of sudden spectacular incontinence. Not being the hottest of days, it took forever to dry, but even when it did, on the Tube home I smelt like the Chiswick Brewery. Despite this, I've still popped down to the Oval on occasion, but always in dark clothes.

Cricket in the summer followed rugby as the compulsory sport at the ages of eleven and twelve at our school; after that, you could choose another sport, or opt to spend the Wednesday afternoon given over to them in a classroom revising. Since I was not naturally gifted, I chose revision, but this soon palled and on the suggestion of another fifteen-year-old refusenik, Jeffrey Jacobs, we joined the school Curling Club. Jeffrey lived near me, a short, dark-haired lad whose beard growth was just about the heaviest in the school. He had five o'clock shadow all day and seemed to have started shaving at about the age of six. Like me, he was not athletically inclined, but felt that anything must be better than sitting in class for an hour or more doing algebra. So we signed up for curling, which was even less well known than it is now and about which we knew nothing other than it took place at the ice rink. As we discovered, it involves sliding heavy granite stones up the rink and knocking your opponents' stones out of the head, or target. Bowls on ice, really.

It turned out to be enjoyable, if a touch uncomfortable; we'd somehow failed to make the obvious connection between ice rinks and freezing temperatures and frequently watched our hands turning blue, but it passed the afternoon and we didn't break sweat too often. We stayed, played, and enjoyed it.

One of the good things about curling was that it revolved

around drink and no one seemed too bothered about sixteen-
or seventeen-year-old schoolboys smelling of beer when
they pitched up on the ice. Well, you need something to keep
out the cold. Every Wednesday and Saturday I turned up at
Crossmyloof ice rink and, though I say it myself, became
quite proficient at chucking great lumps of granite from one
end of the place to the other.

And so it was that, at seventeen years of age, I rose to
the only height I achieved in my school career: Captain of
Curling, for which I received my colours, or white piping
round the edges of the blazer, just like the rugger buggers,
but with about 10 per cent of the effort.

The pinnacle of my curling career was an appearance in
the Scottish Schools' Championships, for which I was
persuaded to appoint Jeffrey Jacobs as skip to our four, with
me playing third. In truth, I didn't need much persuasion,
as Jeffrey was a better tactician than I was and proved it by
steering us to a place in the final. I could have stood on my
dignity and insisted as captain that I should lead the team,
but this proved to be the moment when I discovered that
sometimes in life one has to accept that other people are
better suited to a job than oneself. It's an experience that
stood me in good stead in my later career.

Apart from this sport (!) my school life was undistin-
guished. I learned enough to scrape a pass in most exams
and ended up with enough Highers to have the choice of
going to university or entering a profession. The trouble was,
I had already decided what I wanted to do, and working in
radio wasn't what was expected of the alumni of Hutchesons'
Boys' Grammar School.

School had provided me with a few laughs and people

I got on well with, like Davy Hay, who once bet me he could jump across the frozen school pond. It was too wide to do it in one bound so the manoeuvre would require putting at least one foot on the ice without breaking it. His mistake was letting me go first. I crossed easily but I could feel the ice give slightly as I hit it. The inevitable happened: as his foot made contact with the ice, it parted completely and Davy went into the freezing water up to his armpits. He shot out and we both ran back to the classroom, not very speedily, he being hindered by the weight of about a ton of water in his uniform, and I being slowed by stomach-aching laughter.

My musical awakening happened not through school but in the unlikely surrounds of a Boys' Brigade trip. It was 1964 and we were off for two weeks in Austria, travelling by coach and train. The first leg was an overnight coach to London, and my first sight of the great metropolis was Cricklewood Broadway and the Finchley Road at half past five on a July Saturday morning. Not exactly the Elysian Fields.

For some reason, we had the entire day to pass in London, our train to Folkestone not leaving until about four in the afternoon. So, after going to look at Buckingham Palace and wandering round Victoria Station, we found a cinema nearby where the Beatles' film *A Hard Day's Night* had just opened.

I had never seen a film like it – it seemed set in real life, and there was none of the stagy stuff that all the movies I'd seen seemed to indulge in. The stars were four boys who were not much older than I was and they seemed to be reacting to events in much the same way I or my friends might. And above all, there was the music. I spent the rest of the holiday singing or humming the bits I could remember and trying desperately to recall parts of songs that hadn't stuck.

I went to see it again on the return leg through London, and then twice more in Glasgow. I bought the album and played it until I knew every word and note. It was my first overpowering musical experience.

Odd though it might seem now, the one everyone loved in the Beatles in those days was Ringo. The intervening years have made him the butt of many a joke, and I confess I've been as guilty as most. To a lot of people he's the one with the smallest footprint, but no less an authority than Trevor Horn once told me that Ringo was absolutely vital to the band's success, and was that most elusive of beasts: a drummer with an absolutely reliable tempo.

Ringo's appeal may have had something to do with the character traits played up in the film; he was certainly the one who seemed the most sympathetic and he was the one I warmed to. Watching him reignited my interest in drumming, for which I'd first shown a small, very small, aptitude in the Life Boys, the feeder organization for the Boys' Brigade, tapping along to our version of Perry Como's hit, 'Delaware'. I must tell you that my tempo was nothing like as consistent as Ringo's.

My brother Alasdair played bass guitar in a band and on the odd occasion when their drummer Hamish Whyte couldn't turn up to a rehearsal, I was allowed to use his kit and play for the band. A drum kit is a loud and slightly frightening thing to be in control of; to begin with I was tentative and hesitant, but very quickly I was too noisy and trying to take over. Typical drummer.

If the Beatles gave me my first musical wake-up call, I quickly went on to discover Motown. Again, not that you could hear much on the radio. But the Fab Four had done a few covers of Smokey Robinson songs, among others, and I became vaguely aware of this new sound emanating, I later discovered, from Detroit.

A local band called the System had cornered the market in dances around our area, and on Saturdays I would head off with my friends to Stamperland, where they regularly played. It was the basement floor of the tennis club, probably a store room during the week, but at the weekends the hub for those going to 'the jiggin'. Built into a slight hill, it had a low ceiling with water pipes running across it, from which, after about an hour of sweaty bodies bopping away, condensation would drip relentlessly. The girls would complain about their hair being ruined; the boys just sweated some more.

The System played Motown. I'd never heard the Four Tops singing 'I Can't Help Myself', but if it was better than what I was hearing, it must be brilliant. This was the beginning of my long love affair with the music of Detroit, although I knew nothing then about Berry Gordy and his stable of outstanding talents such as Smokey Robinson and Marvin Gaye, or the Funk Brothers, who laid down those pounding backgrounds for so many of the hits.

Again, the drumming made the difference. The Motown style, perfected by Benny Benjamin, wasn't simply the steady heavy rhythm heard on so many other pop songs; it provided that, but it also had a subtlety, inventiveness and lightness of touch more akin to jazz drumming. I knew good playing when I heard it but, alas, my own skills with the sticks were not in the same universe, let alone the same league.

Much as I loved music, I would never make a musician. But that strand of my life would tie in with my other growing interest: radio.

The Swinging Sixties never really reached Giffnock. The concept of free love may have been enthusiastically taken up on the King's Road but on the Kilmarnock Road it had yet to be embraced. As indeed had I and most of my friends. The young ladies of Glasgow's southern quarter seemed still rather Victorian in their views on sex; we lads were naturally keen supporters of the mantra 'Love the One You're With' but the girls tended to follow the rule 'What I Have, I Hold On To'.

Harold Macmillan had begun the decade by telling us we'd never had it so good. Through most of the 1960s, many of us never had it at all.

Similarly, the drug culture seemed to have become stuck somewhere on the way north. An aspirin dropped into a bottle of Coke was about as exotic as it got. Incidentally, did anyone ever feel any different after trying that? The aspirin was supposed to combine with the caffeine in the Coke to give you a massive high, but I can't say I ever felt anything. A brief effervescence followed by going flat and bitter. The Coke, that is.

Beer was the drug of choice for us. Put another way, we had no choice but beer. As soon as someone looked old enough, they were dispatched to the off-licence for two cans of Tennent's Sweet Stout, a disgusting concoction marketed as a drink for 'the ladeez' but drinkable by no one except desperate teenagers who couldn't yet stomach proper beer. Mercifully, it seems to have departed the market, probably since the arrival of alcopops, which teens can drink in large quantities without ever having to hold their noses. There's progress for you.

The 'someone' sent to the offie was usually me. For much of my life, I've looked older than my years. Naturally, I now look twenty years younger, but from about the age of fifteen I developed a five o'clock shadow and could grow side-burns, so could pass for eighteen, particularly with the old ladies who served in the shop, who probably mistook me for one of my brothers anyway.

Getting away with it in a pub was the next rite of pas-sage, and so, still fifteen, I went with an older friend to the Malletsheugh, which in those days was famous for not being too bothered about age restrictions, licensing hours and other tiresome details. It was also the pub my father used to drive to, but as he'd become more inclined to sit at home with his whisky I felt I was pretty safe. I consumed a half-pint of heavy, which tasted foul, and then I left quickly. Despite this unpleasant flavour I persevered and pretty soon had developed a taste for the stuff. Skiving off from the Boys' Brigade camp that summer, I managed to buy a pint of light in the Black Watch pub, Aberfeldy, for the least money I have ever spent on beer: 1s. 9d. About 8p today. Ah, my lost youth!

With the confidence of having passed the looking-eighteen test in a couple of pubs, I tried it out in others with equal success, so much so that one night my genuinely eighteen-year-old friends were thrown out of the Eglinton Arms, Eaglesham, while I, at sixteen, was allowed to stay; not only that, but I was told not to bring these kids with me again.

My stubble and sideburns may have worked on the publicans but they didn't seem to be impressing the female population of the area. I was awkward and easily embarrassed around girls. Attending a boys-only school from the age of nine hadn't helped; my friends went to the local Eastwood Secondary, an excellent school which I would probably have been happier attending, while saving my father a few bob into the bargain. They had a natural easy banter with the opposite sex, having grown up around them. I, on the other hand, treated each conversation with a teenage female as if it was a first date.

This improved when I started hanging around the local tennis club, which was only a matter of 100 yards from my back door. With my great sporting ability, the game was a bit of a non-starter, but I enjoyed the social side and slowly learned how to make the girls laugh without treating the encounter as if my life depended on it.

I could still freeze up, though; I stood shoulder to shoulder with a girl called Rosemary, quite a looker, as we both examined a poster for a dance. We were the only two people in the room, I fancied her something rotten, she was clearly interested in the dance and she might well have said yes if I'd just managed to find the right words, no, any words, to find out if she wanted to go with me. But I stayed completely mute; I just couldn't think of how to broach the subject and, after a few minutes of waiting for me to ask her out, she gave up and drifted away.

Perhaps this incident spurred me on; I did become a little better at chatting up the girls, although I don't think Leslie Phillips had much to worry about. A smooth-tongued Lothario I was not. And in any case, even he might have struggled, as most of the girls had firm views on how far they would go. The old adage about 'laughing them into bed' seemed wildly overstated. I could laugh them into the pub, or a café, or even a dance, but the laughter stopped abruptly at the garden gate. The boys tended to limp home.

One of the local girls, a policeman's daughter named Margaret, had a striking emerald green dress that she wore for special events, and one of our number reported to us that, thanks to a leg-crossing incident, he had discovered that not only was her external outfit bright green but she was colour-coordinated right down to her most intimate garments. The TV series *Green Acres* was popular at the time and only a slight adaptation of the theme tune was necessary to have us all singing every time she appeared, 'Green Knickers is the place for me!'

The fact that we could be interested in just a flash of a girl's pants says something about our lack of physical engagement with the opposite sex. Incidentally, the current trend for going commando was unknown, certainly amongst girls. One bloke I knew said he never wore underpants, but in his case I felt that it was more a sin of omission. As for the females, they would no more have gone commando than become one.

I had several well-established lads' boozing nights set up though, so the odd disappointing night out was easily forgotten in a sea of McEwan's Export or Younger's Special. The tennis club organized golfing weekends; I couldn't play but went anyway, to St Andrews or Cruden Bay, walked round the courses and drank in the bars at night.

And a group of us took a lads' tour of Scotland once. We must have been nineteen or twenty and there were four of us, Robin, Ronnie, Gordon and myself, in a rental car with no real aim in mind but to see a bit of our native heath and have a decent meal and a few drinks in each place we stopped, driving up the west coast and returning by the east. On our first night in Oban, our 'value' hotel overlooked the gasworks, so we set off to find a welcoming pub, which we did (not that its outlook was much more attractive), on a street set back from what passes for the main drag in the town.

This place must have been a contender for Smallest Bar in the World in the *Guinness Book of Records*. As you entered, the bar itself was along the left wall. There was room for a line of customers to stand at it and for a reasonably slim person to get past and no more. It was about eight feet wide at most. Past the bar there were about four tables and then you hit the back wall. Cosy is the word.

We took up position at the bar and it quickly became rather busy, although admittedly it wouldn't take more than about ten people to cause congestion there. I found myself next to a small elderly gentleman in a heavy coat with a tam-o'-shanter on his head. He had a wooden box at his feet which I paid no attention to until, after a couple of drinks, he bent down and produced from it a set of bagpipes.

I don't know if you've ever stood next to bagpipes being played in anger in a confined space. I don't advise it. As Wilfred Pickles once said, 'The bagpipes are best heard from a distance. We think England is about the right distance.' Certainly, standing next to a set of pipes in a tiny bar means you hear every nuance of the playing; the trouble is, you're unlikely to be able to hear anything else for the rest of the day.

Later in the week, we landed in Stornoway off the overnight ferry, drove round the island during the day and ended up back in the town at four o'clock, rather thirsty. We sat on the harbour wall opposite a closed and shuttered pub and waited for opening time at five o'clock. Promptly on the hour the shutters went up, the door unlocked and we charged in, the first customers of the evening. Except we weren't. Inside the bar was packed with red-faced drinkers, the tables stacked with full, half-full and empty glasses, and the overall impression was of a pub that hadn't stopped operation in the best part of a week. It seemed that licensing laws on Lewis were viewed as advisory rather than compulsory, a very nice utopian aim but hardly a realistic target. The Wee Frees didn't have quite the stranglehold on the community that we had thought.

On the eastern part of the journey we indulged in offshore fishing for what I trust will be the last time in my life – the North Sea is not the most relaxing place to be in a small boat – and we returned to Glasgow. After a few drinks in the local, I offered my mother's kitchen for toasted cheese all round. The trouble with cooking when ale has been taken is that you can be easily distracted. My friend Gordon Brown (no, not that one) spent a little too long talking after turning the gas on for the grill. When he eventually poked his head in and sparked up, there was a sudden hollow boom and he emerged with no eyebrows, gently singeing hair and a slightly sooty face. Needless to say, thanks to all the beer consumed, he was crying with laughter.

Aside from all the beer, it was obvious I would have to think at some point about a career. Truth to tell, I had already made my decision. It wasn't a terribly practical one, at least as far as the careers adviser at school was concerned. He hadn't even bothered to laugh when I muttered about liking radio and might there be any careers in that. He simply ignored my input and carried on talking about all the glittering professions I was not qualified for. 'You can't do law, as you haven't Latin; you wouldn't get into medicine, as your science isn't strong enough. No, I think all you could do is go to university where you might do an MA in French or English and get a job teaching, or with your maths, you might try accountancy.'

I enjoyed the way he was inadvertently denigrating his own profession by suggesting that I was such a poor candidate that I was only fit to teach, but at least he hadn't suggested going into the Church, so I suppose I should have been grateful.

Accountancy was the slightly more attractive option to me, as after six years of secondary education I'd had about enough of academia and wanted to get into some form of workplace. The bumf about studying to become a chartered accountant on a five-year apprenticeship within the profession was duly shoved over to me and I steeled myself for the task of sending off application letters to likely firms.

I had a bite from my very first, and was called to an interview in the St Vincent Street offices of a small company called Reid & Mair. I must have somehow convinced them that my heart skipped a beat over balance sheets and that tax notes were my constant bedtime reading, as I was offered an apprenticeship. I would do five years with the firm, working from nine to five in their office through the week, and then on Friday nights after work attend classes run by the Institute of Chartered Accountants of Scotland, at the end of which I would be able to append the letters CA after my name.

It hadn't been so very long since youngsters' families had had to pay the companies for the privilege of such an opportunity, so I suppose I was lucky that I was to be given the king's ransom of £350 in my first year, rising by £100 per year assuming I made progress in my exams. That turned out to be a pretty wild assumption.

Reid & Mair was, I suppose, a fairly typical accountant's office of the time; that is, it felt about a hundred years out of date. The atmosphere was solemn and quiet. The partners dwelt in private offices ranged around a largeish general office where about twenty apprentices, some nearly qualified, others, like me, just starting, toiled at long desks, going through the accounts of sweet shops, hairdressers and small manufacturing companies.

I was issued with a ticker and a bumper. The ticker was a pen-like article with, instead of a nib, a metal prong with a letter imprinted on the end. Mine had a W; I hesitated to guess why. The bumper was a rubber stamp with the firm's name and my initials on it. Armed with these tools of the trade, I was to check invoices and annotate entries on bank statements, by use of the ticker on the statements and the bumper on the invoices, and thus reconcile the accounts. It was every bit as exciting as it sounds.

My only respite came when the telephonist went on holiday and I was told to man the switchboard. I like to think I did this really well, using my best 'radio' voice, but

I remember overhearing one of the partners shouting, 'That stupid boy on the phones keeps putting calls straight through to me without saying who they're from!' So perhaps I wasn't quite as efficient as I thought.

My co-workers seemed pleasant but downtrodden, and there was very little fun to be had in the course of a day. At five o'clock each day there was a Gadarene rush for the exit, and we all came alive, as if we'd been released from some storybook sleeping spell.

By the time it got to Friday night, I felt as if I had done enough for one week and I was ready for some fun. We left the office at five o'clock; the classes didn't start until half past six, by which time I had usually been in the pub long enough to have got to the 'sod it' stage. 'There's always next week for the classes,' I heard myself saying with surprising regularity. So while my fellow trainees trooped off for their further education, I continued enjoying the revelry, and next week the pattern repeated itself. I did occasionally make it to the classes but they were just as dull as I had feared and there was little to encourage me to rush back.

This is not to denigrate those who have made accountancy their profession. Many of my best friends, etc., etc., and Lord knows where we should be without them on 5 April each year. It simply wasn't the work for me. It hadn't a hope of snaring me really, as I had decided some years before what I was going to do. I just didn't know how to achieve it.

Three

'I'd Like to Work in Radio'

I was about fifteen years of age when I decided I would like to work in radio. For a few years I found it quite difficult to answer when asked what had attracted me to the work, as I couldn't really identify any 'road to Damascus' moment. Naturally I had listened to the radio through my childhood and early teens, but not in any obsessive way and certainly not with any view to hearing myself on there one day.

The deciding factor for me was reading a book by Jack de Manio, the presenter of the *Today* programme during the 1960s. I had been sent to stay for a few weeks with my Aunt Isobel, not an arduous task as she was good fun, slightly bohemian, and in any case only lived about half a mile away. As I do when I spend more than five minutes in any house, I made a lunge for the bookcase. Other people's reading material is endlessly fascinating; there's always one book you would never dream of buying yourself but which turns out to be the best thing you've read all year.

So it was with de Manio. I heard him every morning over the cornflakes; not my choice, but child power was a force of the future. And when I read his book, it wasn't his current work that I found interesting, but his early years. He had been an announcer, one of those voices on the air that gave the time checks, linked the programmes, read the news and sometimes turned up on comedy shows, like *Round the Horne*'s famous Douglas Smith.

To read de Manio's book, the life of an announcer was fun and laughter all the day, with brief bursts of work punctuated by trips to the pub, the bookies or the shops. Those times when one was forced to remain in the studio were livened up by merry pranks and practical jokes. The book was clearly detailing the lighter side of broadcasting, but to this young reader it wouldn't matter if there were a serious side to the work; how could I not want to be part of such a lively environment?

He told how he had got David Jacobs the sack by making him laugh at an inappropriate moment, by holding a gramophone record above David's head like a halo while he was introducing a religious service. De Manio managed to turn this into a positive by arguing, not altogether convincingly, that in doing so he'd propelled David into his freelance career, and without this boost he would never have enjoyed all the success he was later to achieve.

He was equally cavalier about his own prospects. Booked to introduce a live string quartet recital from the Concert Hall of Broadcasting House, he made the opening announcement and then, noting that the first piece lasted more than twenty minutes, thought he might slope off to the pub for a sharpener. Duly refreshed, he trotted back towards the hall only to have the misfortune to bump into a senior executive on the stairs. 'Aren't you announcing the recital on the Third Programme?' was his enquiry.

'Yes, yes! Just popping down there now!' was Jack's breezy

reply, but it failed to satisfy his boss, who summoned him to his office that afternoon.

After a long dressing-down about unprofessionalism and flirting with disaster, he was asked to explain himself: 'Anything could have gone wrong. I mean, what would have happened if they'd broken a string?'

'Well, I'd be no help,' said de Manio. 'I don't carry any.'

This strange disparity between the formality of the sounds that came out of the radio and the schoolboyish behaviour of those making them intrigued me. Later I was to discover that the Reithian principles – inform, educate and entertain – had been upheld in the face of lax behaviour only with difficulty. According to legend, Lord Reith himself had been forced to deliberate on a thorny issue.

Some time in the late thirties, a producer had been caught *in flagrante* with a secretary in a studio in Broadcasting House. Worse, they had been engaged in the deed on top of the studio table when discovered. Reith's deputy reported the sorry tale to him. 'The man must be sacked! We cannot have such goings-on in this building,' was the Director-General's stern response. His assistant pointed out that the fellow involved was actually just about their very best producer, and was due to be running a major programme for the corporation very soon, which was pretty well bound to be a failure without his organizational skills. Reith pondered for a moment, then said, 'Very well, he can stay. But the woman must be dismissed.'

This time the executive said that the woman involved was the top secretary in the whole of Broadcasting House; she knew every system in the place and was vital to the smooth running of the BBC.

Reith fell silent for several seconds and then announced, 'In that case, get rid of the table!'

Pragmatism was always at the heart of the BBC.

The more I read about life in broadcasting, the more I wanted to be part of it. I began listening with a closer ear to find out what announcers did. The first thing I discovered was that they didn't talk like me.

While my accent wasn't exactly guttural, it was certainly not Oxbridge and, as far as I could tell, all announcers spoke like a minor member of the Royal Family. However, the announcers on the Scottish Home Service had accents that were a little closer to mine and I began to follow their activities by poring over the *Radio Times* and listening to a great deal of the output, from early morning to closedown.

Ah, closedown. A concept that means little to today's radio listeners, who demand and get twenty-four-hour service from all their stations, even if it means their combining with another to keep the sound flowing. To the BBC of previous decades, all right-thinking people should be in bed by midnight and those who weren't were probably not deserving of quality radio programmes.

I listened intently and, with the help of a feature in the *Radio Times* one week, discovered who the Scottish announcers were and what they did. Could I do it too? I cut some bits out of the newspaper and used my brother's tape recorder to record a news bulletin. Playback revealed a thin squeaky voice with a nasal Glasgow tinge. It seemed I wasn't going to walk into a job on radio just yet. Being only fifteen, it may have been a long shot anyway. So I resolved to get myself ready for the chance when it came.

I learned how to pitch my voice for the microphone and

practised gap-filling by picking up the *Radio Times* and ad-libbing trails for a couple of minutes. I made sure I could talk to time and make sense. Strange that such niceties don't always seem to bother me now.

I grew in confidence and once I reached the age of eighteen was ready to offer myself up to BBC Scotland, who would, no doubt, clasp me to their collective bosom as one of their own. I wrote to the presentation organizer, whose name had been very helpfully printed in the magazine article, and was delighted to be asked up for an audition.

In my Sunday suit I arrived at Queen Margaret Drive, Glasgow, and was greeted by Pamela Patterson, the senior announcer. She was one scary lady. Tall, thin, and with a severe appearance, she guided me into the continuity studio, where the links between programmes were made, and where I was astonished to discover there was a square of paper pinned to the wall on which was printed the name of the station. How could they not know it? I knew it as well as my own name. What I didn't realize then was that the simplest things, like the station name or on occasion even one's own, can easily vanish from the brain at a critical point; also, the corporation had been struggling with the identity of the Scottish Home Service since the names-to-numbers changes of the national networks in 1967, leading to the clumsy construction in use by 1969: 'This is BBC Scotland Radio 4.' Nobody could be expected to remember that.

I recorded a brief news bulletin and a bit of trail reading and, before I knew it, was back out on the street again, desperately trying to file in my memory everything I'd seen, done or touched. This was a moment I didn't want to fade from my mind. A few weeks later, a letter arrived from the

BBC thanking me for coming to see them, and while there weren't any vacancies at present, they'd keep my name on file. I was young enough not to know that this meant, 'Don't ring us,' so went around buoyed up for some months, confident that the 'file' would be regularly consulted by the top brass, all saying to each other what a shame it was that no vacancy had turned up to allow the boy Bruce his much-deserved opportunity.

It was only when I heard a new announcer on the air that I realized that I'd been body-swerved and they were managing rather well without me. Miss Patterson had advised me in a kindly fashion as I left the building to go out and get some experience; Forces Radio was, she said, a good way in.

I fired off a letter to the British Forces Broadcasting Service and received a reply saying to make an appointment to come in if I was ever passing. In the way that a school leaver from Giffnock, Glasgow, was often in the vicinity of Dean Starley Street, London W1.

Naturally, I made it my business to be passing. I made the appointment, took a day off and used my savings to buy a return air ticket to Heathrow. A worthwhile investment; after all, I'd make the money back as soon as I got the job.

I spent the journey weighing up the options of working for BFBS; Gibraltar would be nice, or Malta, perhaps Cyprus, yes, any of them would be fine. It wasn't the BBC, of course, but after a couple of years with the forces, I'd walk into a job there, wouldn't I?

After a flight on a Vanguard with disturbingly wobbly wings, I made my way into Central London and mooched around the Westminster area until the appointed hour, whereupon I was warmly greeted by a very nice man who smelt strongly of gin and tonic. It was half past two, after all. He listened to what was even to my own ears a vague explanation of why I wanted to get into radio (I couldn't very well say, 'To get plastered on gin and tonic at lunchtime, like you'), and sent me to a studio for an audition.

There, a slightly offhand engineer with an Australian accent recorded my squeakings and I returned to my friend with the Gordon's aroma for the verdict. It is to my eternal shame that I cannot remember this man's name, because he did me the great service of being honest with me.

I can understand why some people criticize Simon Cowell for his apparent cruelty on shows like *Britain's Got Talent*; he can seem too blunt in his dismissal of certain acts. But believe me, it is much worse to allow someone with no ability to continue to waste their lives in the delusion that it will all happen for them someday. There are ways of delivering the news, sure, but give me an honest appraisal any day.

This gentleman, in an entirely kindly fashion, pointed out a couple of pronunciation errors and stylistic points and in summing up said that I showed some promise but I probably wasn't right for them just at present. It was a bit of a blow, but a much-needed blast of reality, and I thanked him for his time. Just as I was leaving, though, he said, 'Whatever happens, don't give up the idea of broadcasting.'

I was pretty downhearted at the dashing of my hopes of immediate employment but as I left the building I paused for a smoke and met the rather dour Aussie engineer again. 'Have you done this sort of thing before?' he asked.

'No, not really,' I replied, to which he said, 'Well, you're better than most of the people who come in here for try-outs.'

I headed for a pub, filled up with beer and set off for the airport and home, thinking, 'Nice try, but better settle into real life again.' And so it was back to accountancy by day and beer nights at the Orchard Park (once the nursing home where I was born, now a pub). But those two slightly encouraging remarks had lodged in my mind and every so often would re-emerge to niggle at me. Was it worth one more try?

Accountancy was not going well; I'm sure the profession itself was thriving and profits were being made with senior partners living lives straight out of *The Arabian Nights*, but for me, the outlook was gloomy. My aversion to attending the after-work classes was having the inevitable result and I scored poorly in the exams. Nevertheless, I progressed into my second year with the massive incentive of a salary of £450 per annum. Bloody hell, I might have to start paying tax!

If I had, I wouldn't have known how to work it out, such was my detachment from the work I was supposed to be enjoying. To no one's surprise, my second year exams were a disaster. At a meeting with one of the partners, it was decided that Reid & Mair could probably manage to struggle on without my talents and I left the room in need of a job. Oddly, for a man facing the Labour Exchange, I was elated. I decided not to tell my parents, with whom I was still lodging, until I had fixed myself up with something else. That way, I could do the good news/bad news trick and soften off any explosions or wailing. Finding other work was not difficult. This was the beginning of the 1970s; unemployment was low, the economy had not yet hit the skids, and there was an optimism left over from the 1960s still in the air.

Some student friends had part-time work washing cars for a hire firm, so I pottered along there and got myself taken on by the manager, David Ness, a tall, sandy-haired, energetic man with a brisk line in conversation. He was to be called Mr Ness at all times, except behind his back where he was only referred to as Eliot. In the accountants' office, every partner had had to be called 'Sir'; when I responded, 'Yes, Sir,' to Eliot, he thought I was taking the proverbial so I was soon cured of that. I had stopped shaving on leaving the accountancy profession – oh yes, ever the rebel – and his first words to me were, 'Are you growing a beard? Not very tidy, is it?'

He had, I learned, a hatred of beards and didn't want any facial hair cluttering up his office. But he appeared prepared grudgingly to allow the below-stairs greycoats to look a little less smart and signed me up, mainly because they were short-staffed.

The work called for me to fill up and wash cars and vans as they were returned, and show punters over the controls as they went out. Most of the other workers were part-timers, students making up the grant, HGV drivers, firemen and even policemen earning a few bob on the side. They were a good bunch, characters all, and I felt quite at home. The banter was typically Glasgow: hard, cruel even, but softened off with a laugh.

One particularly work-shy individual, who had hardly ever been known to wield a brush in anger, came up to the others one day, outraged at the state his hands had got into doing some small task. 'Look at these!' he moaned, holding out two grimy palms. 'Oh,' said a concerned voice, 'did you fall?'

The job certainly improved my driving skills. I got my obligatory damage in early, scraping a van off the pillars of the underground car park, after which the unofficial rule-book said you relaxed and turned into a good driver. I was being paid at an hourly rate and working long hours and soon found that I was earning roughly twice as much as before with much less time to spend it. And I was having fun.

This life of stress-free work and money in my pocket couldn't last and, sure enough, it didn't. Responsibility came calling in two forms: I was taken out of the garage and put into a suit in a desk job in the office, and I got a regular girl-friend.

I had known Fiona for a little while; she was a local girl, fair-haired, good fun and very attractive, but she was going out with someone else. I gazed on from afar, but when she suddenly became unhitched I asked her out, having by this time realized that simply standing saying nothing did not usually lead to meaningful encounters with the oppo-site sex. To my surprise she said yes, and we became an item.

Work involved answering the telephone and processing the customers who came into reception. Basically it was selling car hire. Except we were rather reluctant salesmen. The attitude we were encouraged to adopt, perhaps not surprisingly in Glasgow, was that everyone who walked in was out to steal our car. Only when we were sure that the person would bring our car back did we start to employ conventional selling tactics.

Our standard interrogation would probably have had Gestapo officers wincing and saying, 'Oh, go easy.' We had to quiz every punter about age, occupation, driving experience, where they lived, what they wanted the car for and where they'd be going in it, before even hinting that we might have one available. Only satisfactory answers to the above led to the change in treatment from suspect to prospect. Unsatisfactory answers meant further detailed questions about date of birth, place of work, and type of work; the list of banned occupations was as long as your arm and I sometimes marvelled that we agreed to rent a car to anyone. Journalists, actors, musicians were complete non-starters. Travelling show people were similarly dismissed out of hand. Builders were slightly more respectable but still on the suspect list; 'They'll be carrying bricks in the boot.' Hardly any occupation seemed automatically OK. The moderator of the General Assembly of the Church of Scotland might just have been approved, but only if he promised not to drive further than 50 miles in a week and covered the car on his own insurance policy. In our office, everyone was guilty until proved innocent.

This attitude spread to home visits. Once a car was overdue, that is an hour later than the due time, the phone calls began, and if the address given was a 'bad' area, off we went to check and, if necessary, retrieve. Our assistant manager Bruce Forbes took me out on one such trip, to Easterhouse, one of the 'baddest' addresses. 'Put your raincoat on,' he said as we set off, 'and don't say exactly who we are.'

The object was to give the impression, without ever saying so, that we were the police and thereby encourage whoever we spoke with to tell a little more of the truth than they might to a couple of car-hire men. It seemed to work overall as we had a much lower rate of disappearing cars than our competitors.

'He's roon' the pub,' offered the woman who answered the door in Easterhouse when we asked to speak to her man. 'Don't tell him I telt ye or he'll knock the shite oot o' me.' Bruce said he wasn't sure we could keep her name out of it, but he'd do his best for her.

'Just follow me and keep your eyes open,' I was told as we marched into one of Glasgow's rougher pubs. 'John McEwan!' boomed Bruce, followed by, 'We've come to get the car keys off you.' This is the day I die, I thought, as every face in the bar turned towards us, but amazingly, after a few seconds of silence, the McEwan man said, 'Oh, aye, right, here yese are. Sorry, boys.'

'There's the matter of the day's extra hire charge,' said Bruce; '£15 will cover it.' And McEwan meekly paid up A receipt was quickly written, but not quickly enough for my comfort, and we left the bar. I drove the hire car back to the office, where further advice was given. 'The trick is to look like the cops when you're dealing with one person, or two maximum, but if there's a crowd of them, crack on you're bailiffs,' I was told. They'd gang up against the police, but bailiffs were just part of everyday life and their arrival on any scene was regarded as a natural hazard.

Mostly our cars came back. From time to time, though, one escaped, and until such time as it turned up, parked on some estate in the north of England, or abandoned at the

My christening photo.

July 1953, at Hunter's Quay.
My brother Alasdair, me, aged two,
and brother Scott.

Apparently hailing a taxi
aged two and a half, on holiday
in Hunter's Quay, Argyll.

Being paraded around Dunoon in what passed for a pushchair in the fifties by Scott.

Scott looking after the wee . . . in Dunoon.

Scott in trendy shades me, Mum in her summer frock, and Alasdair in baggy shorts on the seafront in Dunoon.

Myself and Alasdair blissfully unaware of the soaking we are about to receive at the seaside in 1955.

Scott, me, and Alasdair on holiday in Wester Ross in 1955.

The family house
in Broomley Drive,
Griffnock.

School photo
as I arrive at
Hutchesons' Boys'
Grammar School
in 1960 aged
nine.

Mid-sixties
colour shot of
me, Alasdair and
our dog Bruno.

A school photo
aged seventeen
in 1968.

Scott and I, the
gawky teenager,
modelling
matching cardies.

The adult Bruce,
modelling a beard,
1981.

Taking over the Breakfast Show in 1984.

In the Glasgow studios
in 1984.

With Ray Moore (centre).
Left to right: me,
Derek Jameson and Simon Dee.

The Radio 2 Presenters' Christmas Dinner, 1986.
Left to right: David Jacobs, John Dunn, Frances Line, Jimmy Young, me,
David Hamilton, Derek Jameson, David Treadway, Bryant Marriott.

On the ferry
with Campbell
and Douglas,
1986

My Dad and Mum
moving into
their house in
Carrbridge,
Inverness-shire,
'The Steading'.

The Radio 2
Railshow at
Scarborough 1987,
with producer
Carolyn Smyth.

ferry terminal at Dover, whoever had dealt with the hirer would have to traipse up to police headquarters to go through the mugshot book. The first time I had to do this, I came across the faces of two of our part-time workers within ten minutes.

Should I tell the boss? I decided not to, but kept an eye on them when they went near the till.

One of our staff did turn out to be a crook. His name was Bill, although his driving licence gave his first name as Idris. He explained the difference quite reasonably: 'Would you walk around Glasgow with a name like that?' There was another disparity, which for some reason didn't set our alarm bells ringing, although it was the kind of inconsistency that would have had us sending a prospective hirer packing.

This was still the time of the little red driving licences. What most people didn't know was that the inside page with your name and address on it had a number at the top from which certain facts could be ascertained. DL6A was the normal one but, for example, a DL2 indicated someone who had been driving before the introduction of tests, which began in 1934. Therefore, by the early 1970s, only someone aged over fifty-five ought to have one of these. If a twenty-five-year-old punter offered up one, we refused to hire them a car, said we'd keep the licence and post it back to them. We then gave it to the police.

Bill was thirty, so clearly shouldn't have had such a licence, but he spun a plausible story about how he'd been sending it back and forth to the authorities for mistakes to be rectified and they never got it right. Our normal suspicions were overlooked and we took him on trial. He proved to be an exemplary worker: good fun, efficient, bright and trustworthy.

Until the day when the polis arrived and carted him off. Fraud, apparently.

It taught me a couple of things. Firstly, if the facts are all pointing in one direction, it's probably the right one, despite plausible explanations. Secondly, good people do bad things. Bill was a nice guy; we checked everything he'd ever laid his hands on but couldn't find any trace of him having done us over. He'd had access to expensive cars and had even taken the cash bag overnight, but nothing was ever taken. His problem was that he just couldn't stop himself from gulling people.

He'd been involved in a host of frauds and misrepresentations. David Ness went to court as a character witness but Bill got the clink. I had a few trips to court myself, mostly to give evidence against those Glaswegians who believed in the socialist utopia of shared property. Specifically, our cars.

Once though, the case was against one of our own staff. Wee Harry was well named, rising only to about four foot nine. He had an untipped cigarette seemingly permanently glued to the corner of his bottom lip, the smoke from which had been curling upwards for so long that his left eye was always half-closed and there was a nicotine-yellow streak in his otherwise white hair.

The company was quite generous about use of its cars. Staff could use them overnight if any were available and also for holidays, again provided they were not needed for hire. There were two times in the year when all the cars we had, and even some we didn't have, were booked out: Christmas, and the Glasgow Fair fortnight. We always overbooked, as the airlines do, on the basis that a fair proportion of prospects wouldn't turn up, and always got away with it; old Eliot was a past master at judging how far to push it but Fair Friday night was the tightest of all. There was never a car left in the garage at night and even the manager went home in a van.

One year Wee Harry had booked his holidays for the Fair. He'd asked about getting a car but had been told only if one was free, which was very unlikely. Harry appeared to take matters into his own hands and put a Morris Marina aside early in the day with a 'Booked' note on it, then at six in the evening sailed off in it. By eight o'clock the whole staff was searching high and low for it, when someone recalled seeing the wee barra driving away in it. Eliot went ballistic; a customer had to be fobbed off until the morning, phone calls were made, someone was dispatched to Harry's house to find it, but he was long gone.

Two weeks later he returned to a still-seething David Ness and Harry was told he'd be getting a bill for two weeks' car hire at the full rate. He said he wouldn't pay it and handed in his notice, which was immediately accepted.

And so, some months later, we all found ourselves at the Sheriff Court, Harry having refused to pay his bill, convinced he had moral authority on his side. Presiding was Sheriff J. Irvine Smith, something of a local wit, who I noticed early on in proceedings was beginning to enjoy the comic possibilities of this case. Harry himself had a theatrical style despite his lack of inches and was smartly dressed in a blue suit. He'd even detached the fag end from his lower lip for the occasion. I'd been told just to give my brief and strictly formal evidence and get back to the office but I was enjoying the event too, so hung around to hear Harry's defence. After an impassioned speech about his rights, the heartlessness of the company and the chance of taking his poor benighted wife on a measly two weeks' holiday in a nice car which wouldn't be missed out of a fleet of 200, he delivered his closing clincher of a line: 'As God is my judge, Yer Onner, I'm innocent.'

This gave J. Irvine Smith the opportunity he may have been waiting his entire career for and which he wasn't going to let slip. The good Sheriff replied, 'He isn't, I am, and you're not.'

This got a great laugh from the whole court, with the exception of Harry, whose air of injured innocence deepened. He found himself having to pay up with costs. I saw him afterwards outside the court when the cigarette had resumed its rightful position on the lower left lip and commiserated with him. 'Tell Eliot I can come back to work again now,' he said. I chose not to, to spare the Ness blood pressure.

Weekend working was part of the deal and the only consolation was that Sunday was usually quiet, and it was split into two parts, closing at lunchtime and then opening for a couple of hours in the evening. After a hard morning's fiddling with paper clips, we naturally felt like a drink. Scotland's licensing laws were still of the wartime 'don't let them near the munitions drunk' type, so pubs were officially closed on a Sunday.

Hotels were allowed to open to serve 'bona fide travellers', a category we fell into, having come all the way from Mitchell Street. They could only open their bars from 12.30 p.m. until 2.30 p.m. It was usually well after one o'clock by the time we piled into the Blythswood Hotel on Argyle Street, by which time the bar was three-deep in waiting customers. Worryingly, as this was the nearest drinking establishment to Central Station, about 90 per cent of the thirsty punters appeared to be train drivers. I always tried to avoid rail travel on Sundays.

The old trick of multiple ordering was used, especially at last orders, when at least two pints each would be ordered and swilled down before the ten-minute drinking-up time window had elapsed. At this point the traditional Glasgow barman's cry went up: 'Get it down ye, get ootside and get it up ye!'

The evening 'ten o'clock swill' led to some pretty drunken scenes, though I suspect not any worse than the two in the morning falling out of bars that seems to be the norm nowadays. However, when the licensing laws were relaxed a few years later, there was a marked improvement; drinks were consumed in a relaxed fashion and people actually, shock horror, left before closing time.

On Sunday nights, we occasionally blagged our way into the Merchant Navy Club, which was quieter than the hotels and rather cheaper. Only one of us had ever served in the Mercantile Marine, Highland Angus, and he was given the task of talking us in, which he did in exactly the same way every week by saying we were off the *Rangitoto*. I suggested he might like to change the name of our alleged vessel now and again but he insisted on using this one, as he'd actually been a crew member on it and therefore wouldn't forget.

Quite why the doorman never noticed that the same New Zealand-based ship was docking in Glasgow every Sunday night and only the same four sailors ever came off it, I don't know, but it was a relatively civilized place to pass a couple of hours and gave me the chance to discover that I had a taste for dark rum.

Working at the car-hire company was enjoyable, even if

it didn't leave a vast amount of opportunity for socializing. But there had been plenty of time for Fiona and I to realize that we wanted to marry; I popped the question, in no doubt an entirely unromantic manner, and we set a date in 1976. Life was looking very settled.

But now and again, the old idea of broadcasting did rise to the surface, and I began to realize that I would have to give it one more shot or I would be haunted by 'what ifs' for the rest of my days.

One evening, with a few beers on board, I called up the BBC and asked to speak to the duty announcer. To my surprise I was put through. Later, I realized that sitting alone in a continuity studio for six hours or more could reduce my normal critical faculties to such an extent that I'd even accept calls from double-glazing salesmen, just to lighten my evening. In fact, I'm not sure I didn't begin to call them.

Whatever his reason for doing so, Bob Christie took my call and was kind enough to discuss career possibilities and to suggest I get some experience at hospital radio. He gave me the number of a man called Eric Simpson. Eric ran the Hospital Broadcasting Service for Glasgow and the West of Scotland, HBS Glasgow for short, which served a varying number of hospitals (many of them long-stay geriatric facilities) from studios in the city centre, and quite soon I was sitting in his office in Argyle Street.

Eric ran a tight ship. He was a good-looking, fair-haired man who, by day, ran one of the city's more prestigious libraries, but did not conform to the stereotype of that profession, being anything but meek. Standards expected of his broadcasters were as high as any I came across in later years, and if someone wasn't performing, they were taken off. It was also not acceptable just to swan in, do a show and float off again. The unsexy stuff, filing, manning phones and ward visiting, had all to be done too.

I was shown around and asked to do a little trial, a couple of records and a few links, as Eric assessed my worth. Afterwards, I met a boy in school uniform who was obviously a trusted operator around the place and who already had the voice of a man twice his age; one Charles Nove, who is still very much a part of my everyday experience thirty years later.

It was decided I passed muster and I was given two hours on a Sunday night to play with in a programme called *Open Line*, in which listeners would phone in their requests and these would be passed to the studio for me to read out and play their chosen record. Many of these had a desperate predictability about them, with Jim Reeves showing up rather too frequently for my liking, but I learned the lesson early that being on the radio didn't mean only playing your own favourite music. The customer, while not always right, wasn't always wrong either.

Eric had some useful warnings: don't say, 'This'll get your feet tapping,' as not all your listeners would have the full complement of pedal extremities; don't talk about going home soon, as some may not; and above all, watch out for false names. Eric himself immediately sent through one which I fell for and announced, a request for 'I Don't Know How to Love Him' for a Les Behan.

He also had two golden rules of music presentation: if you've nothing much to say, don't say anything much; and if you want to talk over an introduction, either talk right up to the vocal or don't even start. Good advice in both cases;

ever since, I've tried, but failed, to keep to the first, and never had a hope of following the second, implying as it did some element of pre-thought.

To say I loved the work is to come nowhere near the feeling of complete satisfaction with a hefty tinge of elation, the sense of being in my natural element, the absolute rightness that I felt every time I stepped into a radio studio. It held no fear for me; I knew that whatever happened in there, I'd cope and enjoy doing so. I had come home.

There were many talented people there: Paul Coia and Ross King were near-contemporaries, and there was a vision mixer from STV, John Frame, who wrote very funny scripts for features and comedy shows. Hospital radio struck me then, and still does, as a way of getting people involved in charitable works who might not otherwise. Many people, myself particularly, were there for their own reasons, doing something they really wanted to do and enjoyed but, almost as a by-product, doing some good in the community.

I harboured some doubts about the effectiveness of what we were doing, thinking it seemed too much fun to be really helping, until I met a patient who told me that, yes, they had access to television and the major radio stations but, he said, 'You have no idea just how important it is when you're stuck in hospital to hear your name mentioned and to know that someone is there just for you.'

And the advent of hospital television has not ousted radio any more than it has in the outside world, because of the special bond between broadcaster and listener that is so much more personal, so much more intimate than the experience of TV viewing can ever be.

Whatever good it was doing others, it was certainly what

I wanted. The ducks were all in a row now; at the age of twenty-five I had a decent job, not spectacularly paid but solid; my hobby was something I'd dreamed of doing and had achieved; and I was about to get married.

Fiona and I found a flat in the Pollokshields area of the city. Like all first-time buyers we had begun by looking at small houses, then large flats in the best areas, then small flats in the good areas and then finally lowered our sights to what we could actually afford. At least, unlike today's first-timers, we could actually afford a house of our own.

Pollokshields was a strange mix of great wealth and some poverty, with Shields Road as the dividing line. West of that lived some of the city's most moneyed families in huge mansions. East lay tenements of varying degrees of dilapidation.

Our flat was, yes, east of the Great Divide but it was in good nick, in appearance at least, in a grey sandstone tenement block in Melville Street, and it was huge. It had three bedrooms, a dining kitchen, bathroom and a vast living room with an ornate ceiling rose and a walk-in alcove bar on the back wall. All this for £7,700.

It also had running water. Down the walls. We discovered this after a couple of weeks, following a night of heavy rain. Considering we were on the first floor and there were two other flats above ours, the amount of water coming into our bedroom was quite impressive. It had begun with a small but repetitive drip, drip, during the night. The flow increased until a bucket had to be employed. And increased again until the bucket was having to be emptied and towels put down on the floor.

As you may know, it can rain a little in Glasgow. I use

the word 'little' in the same way the late Willie Whitelaw did; arriving at a reception and asked what he was having to drink, he would invariably say, 'I'd like a little whisky please.' And to avoid any misunderstanding, he would add, 'And when I say a little whisky, I mean a large whisky.'

The measures down our walls were roughly the same. After one particularly heavy downpour, the water was not only running down the windows and walls but had somehow found its way into the ceiling space and was pouring out of the ceiling rose on to the bedroom floor. We both had to go out that day, so I placed the tall swing bin from the kitchen under it to make sure we weren't flooded. I came back at lunchtime to find that bin full to the brim and overflowing.

It was utterly depressing and I often found myself waking in the night with a cold fear gripping me, imagining I'd heard a drip. In the peculiar way of Scottish property ownership at the time, the house was ours but ground rent or feu duty had to be paid to the feu master, who was responsible for the upkeep of the building, delegated to a firm of factors. Just getting through to the factors on the phone could take a week, after which they would promise to send out somebody to fix the roof. No one ever came. 'Too wet for them to work,' would be the catch-22 explanation after a further week of phone calls.

It took a year before scaffolding went up and the drips stopped. The only thing that stopped me feeling completely sorry for myself was the thought of what it must have been like for our upstairs neighbours. More than thirty years later, though, the sound of a drip in the night can still snap me awake.

Overall, life was good, although money became a bit

tighter as Fiona had given up her job as a lab assistant to retrain as a teacher. On a Saturday we would go round the Fine Fare supermarket in Victoria Road with a five-pound note to cover our entire weekly shop, which felt like tough times for us, but we were only too aware that there were plenty of folk worse off than we were.

I was now assistant manager of the Glasgow branch of the hire company, with a whole £100 rise to go with it, and there were hints that a new branch was opening in Hamilton and I might be in line for the post of manager there. Progress, then. And because I was getting my fix of radio at HBS, I had put all thoughts of a full-time job in radio on the back burner. In fact, I think I had turned the gas off.

There were only about nine announcers at BBC Scotland, so vacancies did not arise very often and when they did, they would not be advertised, as the corporation didn't want to wade through five thousand applications from pig farmers and hairdressers whose mothers had always said they 'talked nice'. Their attitude was that if anyone was interested in such work, they would already have made themselves known.

Iain Purdon was one of the select band and he paid the odd visit to our studios; he was ex-hospital radio himself and only a couple of years older than me, and we always got on well. Still do, to this day. I enjoyed the gossip he brought with him but gave little thought, if any, to the possibility of any jobs coming up. Until, one day, he casually mentioned that one of his colleagues had handed in his notice.

All the dormant ambition within me was instantly rekindled. Here it was, the one last chance to see if I could break through the door of the BBC. The chances were that they would have somebody in mind for the post, but if I didn't have a go I would spend the rest of my life regretting it. So I put together a short tape of my reading a few items of news along with a few bits of a recent programme and popped it in the post.

I had a terrible habit of working out how soon I could expect a reply. A day to get there, a day to lie on his desk, a day to listen and two more to write and post a reply, so it would definitely arrive the day after that. Of course, it didn't, but after about another week it did arrive, and I was invited up to meet the presentation organizer, Cecil Hawthorne.

Memory plays some strange tricks, and while I remember my previous auditions and interviews in some detail, I can scarcely recall anything about this encounter. One exchange only is lodged there; Cecil asked me if I felt I could do the job better than the existing announcers. I was savvy enough not to say yes, mainly because I didn't believe that I could. I did think I could learn to do the job as well, so was able to answer truthfully without sounding horribly complacent.

Of the voice test and other parts of the conversation, I can remember nothing. I went home not terribly confident and returned to work, wondering how long the letter of rejection or, just maybe, acceptance would take to arrive. If I was the man for the job, they would surely get back quickly. Weeks dragged by; my confidence ebbed. Finally, when I could stand it no longer, I called Cecil Hawthorne and asked if he could tell me anything about how my interview had gone.

He sounded slightly surprised to hear from me. This was not the response I wanted. 'You haven't had a letter from us?' Profuse apologies followed, and through them all any possible future in the corporation seemed to diminish. 'Yes,'

Cecil continued, 'I understood our Personnel department were writing to you. We're offering you a three-month contract from June.'

I only just stopped myself from handing in my notice that afternoon. I got through the rest of the working day without blurting it out, although one of my colleagues did wonder why I was so bloody cheery for a change, and got home to tell Fiona. It was an easy decision for me, less so for her, as she was still an impoverished student, we had a hefty, for us, mortgage and I would be giving up a steady job for a measly thirteen-week contract, after which, well, nobody knew.

It was no contest, really, and so I prepared to become a BBC announcer.

Four

'Pop, Prattle and Parish-Pump Piffle'

On my first morning I was ushered into the office of the head of personnel or, to give him his dreadful BBC acronym, S.Pers.AOS. There is a rumour that there was once an engineering information officer whose title was EIEIO, but I am not convinced.

S.Pers's first question puzzled me. 'Where do you see your career going in the BBC?' Who cared? I was in the door, and doing a job I had wanted to do for years. What else could I possibly want to achieve? Only a few months later I would have an answer to that, and only a few weeks would pass before I began the traditional activity of all corporation staff: complaining about the management. I had definitely settled in.

The BBC's Scottish Headquarters was in Queen Margaret Drive, Glasgow, a handsome building, designed by Alexander 'Greek' Thomson, and formerly home to a trio of bachelor brothers called Bell, thereafter becoming a girls' college. The BBC had moved in and, as it always did, added bits on and changed things around so that internally it was like a rabbit warren.

My fellow announcers were welcoming and friendly,

encouraging and helpful. Giving advice without patronizing is not easy, but they managed it, and I was honestly thrilled to be working alongside some of the famous voices I had known for years. Many of them were gay, not the easiest lifestyle to lead in Glasgow in the 1970s. Most people of my parents' generation had never knowingly met a homosexual, and many straight men appeared to live in fear of being propositioned by gays, an attitude which hilariously implied they were irresistibly attractive.

Even within the business, I was told, 'There are two types of people in the BBC: engineers and queers.' I found I got on well with both; I even met some who *were* both, and, needless to say, I was never propositioned.

The senior announcer was Pamela Patterson, the same lady who had scared me at my first tryout some eight years earlier. If she recalled that day, she gave no hint of it and I didn't wish to remind her. She was still pretty forbidding, but I soon discovered she was a kindly and considerate boss who took great care to look after her 'boys'; mostly by presiding over long drinking sessions in the BBC Club. The Club had, for reasons of the licensing laws of the time, to be housed in separate premises, which turned out to be an agreeable townhouse a few hundred yards away on the other side of the River Kelvin, which ran behind Broadcasting House.

Pam's rules were clear: gin at lunchtime, whisky in the evening. Delivering a gin, large of course, to her table after five o'clock would result in her staring at the glass with an incredulous, 'What's *this*?'

There was a heavy drinking culture there at the time, which I fell into for a spell. Beer drinking had been my forte, but limited time between news bulletins meant I soon began to follow Pam's rules. Lunchtimes were a particular challenge when I was working the middle shift, which began at noon.

The early announcer toddled off to the Club with Pam, taking my drink order with him, invariably a large gin and tonic. At one o'clock I could leave the studio as we opted in to *The World at One* from London. The walk from the continuity studio over to the Club took six to seven minutes. The first drink was downed and lunch ordered. A second large G&T would accompany the meal and then there was just time for a small gin before heading back to read the two o'clock summary. Five measures, quarter-gill ones at that, in forty minutes. A gill was a quarter of a pint so work that lot out yourself.

After a seven-minute walk back and a couple of minutes to look at the stories, the news was duly read. Not too badly, considering. My main hazard was the handback to the programme into which this bulletin fell. The final words were always, 'Now back to *Woman's Hour* and Sue MacGregor.' No matter how well I had navigated my way through the difficult pronunciations in the news, I could never quite cope with this lady's name, possibly all that gin sloshing about in my stomach being a contributory factor. Every time, what came out sounded more like 'Soomacerror'. Luckily, she being in London and me in Scotland, she never heard the mangling her fine old surname received at my hands.

The Bravehearts amongst us might hightail it back to the Club for another quick one before closing time at half past two, but I tended to stay put, have a thoughtful smoke and long for the day someone with an easier name would take up the reins of this fine programme.

The next most senior to Pam in the department, and therefore the most experienced on air, was Harry Gray, a figure
I had heard on radio and indeed seen on TV since my youth.
He was a heavy-set man and had always seemed a bit threat-
ening, a bit of a hard man in the Glasgow parlance, so to
find he was one of the sweetest men you could hope to meet
was a pleasant surprise. He spoke in a Scottish flavoured
Received Pronunciation, well, most of the time, but when
the gin had slipped down he lapsed more into his native
Selkirk, with language to match.

His partner was an actor by the name of Charles Baptiste,
who was what would now be termed mixed-race; a tall,
distinguished and commanding figure. Their sexual procliv-
ities and his racial background had led the macho wits in
the newsroom to dub them the Govan Fairy and the African
Queen, but it was done with affection as they were much
liked. They were not in the least camp, and in fact I once
heard Harry refer to some very flamboyant and loud people
in a bar as 'bloody poofs'. Such attention-seeking behaviour
was not his idea of a gay lifestyle.

Charles had done some broadcasting and had a deep,
resonant voice but his radio career had been cut short because
of heart trouble. Not that he was unfit; simply that the early
version of the pacemaker with which he'd been fitted made
so much noise it could be heard on microphone, ticking
away like a grandfather clock. He, too, could lapse into
thick Scottish when the mood took him, and he was the only
man I have ever heard employing the phrase, declaimed in
theatrical cadences in the Club bar, 'He can go and get stuffed
with the broad end of a ragman's trumpet.'

My announcer colleagues were all individuals, a polite

way of saying slightly eccentric, a trait inherited from the previous generation. The former senior announcer, Alastair Macintyre, was the chief of the clan which bore his name, and drove a Bentley to and from his home in Edinburgh, pausing at a distinctly dodgy pub on the Maryhill Road for a post-shift drink with some of his 'chums', by all accounts the kind of nice chaps you see committing murders in *Taggart*.

Alastair had been an actor at one time; you can catch one of his performances in the film *The Arsenal Stadium Mystery*, which still crops up on TV from time to time, and in which he played the team physio, with a broad Scottish accent very different from his own normal patrician drawl.

He had the distinction of being the only person ever to use the F-word on BBC Scotland in the 1960s. Prior to the nine o'clock news one morning, he had been trailing ahead to a lunchtime music show called, unhappily, *Folk 'n' Pop*. This was a title asking to be misread and, sure enough, he obliged in spectacular style: 'And then at 12.30, Alastair Clark will be here with *Fuck 'n' Pope*.'

This story was relayed to me by the Rev. Murdoch McPherson, a Church of Scotland minister turned sports producer, who had been sitting in his car at traffic lights when it happened. After a brief moment of wide-eyed silence, he had burst into helpless laughter, and looked around to see everybody else in the queue similarly doubled up.

Another old hero of the Scottish Home Service was Ivor Phillips, who lived in some style in a castle in Fife. He was a former dance-band drummer with a musician's robust sense of humour. He used to take great pleasure in telling colleagues in the canteen that he'd just been appointed to a new job, 'SADG'. When he was asked what that stood for he would reply, 'Sexual adviser to the Director-General.' Pressed for an explanation, he would say, 'Well, I took some of my programme ideas up to the DG the other day, and after he'd looked them over for a minute, he said, "Phillips, when I want your f***ing advice, I'll ask for it."'

This was the tradition I found myself proudly joining, and I relished every day I spent at work, although perhaps not the early rises. Leaving the car-hire company had meant leaving my car behind, so, after a few weeks of bus and train travel, and BBC taxis for the late nights and early mornings, I bought an old Hillman Avenger from a relative of Fiona's. I had found the uncertainty of standing looking out of the window at half past five in the morning wondering if a cab was going to arrive too stressful, so it was a relief to have my own transport sitting outside.

Unfortunately, the Avenger had an intermittent electrical fault which meant that, from time to time, turning the ignition key gave only a clunk and total silence. This proved even more stressful than waiting for taxis, but on the one occasion when I slept in for the early turn, it started first time, making me only ten minutes late rather than about two days.

The work was hugely enjoyable; even today, I think of those first years as an announcer as being my happiest, possibly because it was all new and fresh, but also because there was such variety to the work. Whenever anyone would ask me why I wouldn't prefer being a disc jockey somewhere instead, I would reply, 'What, and play the same records day after day, making tired old jokes?' Before you point out the obvious similarities between that statement and what I've been doing on Radio 2 for twenty-odd years, the records aren't the same every day. Well, not all. But the jokes are tired.

As far as I was concerned in 1977, variety was the spice of life. In the space of a week, I could be reading news, making continuity announcements, introducing a symphony concert for Radio 3, reading the football results and the shipping forecast. It was all terrific experience and taught me the importance of tailoring your performance to your surroundings.

The announcers were well thought of, being a kind of 'emergency services' of broadcasting. If anything went wrong, we were there to cover the moment; if a presenter didn't turn up or fell ill, we could step in and do a professional job. Mostly, though, we were newsreading and in the continuity studio. Some shifts were better than others. I dreaded Sunday shifts, in the first instance as they were longer, but also because the programming was dull, there was no news to read and there was no one around to share your pain. Listening to a Gaelic religious service on a wet Sunday afternoon, with its mournful, interminable tuneless psalms, must rank as one of the least pleasurable ways to earn a living ever recorded. Doing it for reasons of faith is one of the greatest of sacrificial acts.

On Sunday mornings, the announcer was almost literally the only person in the whole of the headquarters of BBC Scotland. There was a security man on the front desk, but no one in the newsroom, the corporation having taken an executive decision that nothing happened between Hadrian's Wall and Shetland at weekends, so we had to phone up the Glasgow Weather Centre and take down the weather forecast at dictation speed before we could broadcast it. There was no one in maintenance either, as I discovered one morning in deep winter when the heating packed up and I sat in the studio all morning in coat and gloves.

Weekday mornings were much more fun, as you had a real sense of being the voice of the nation, bringing people the latest news over their breakfasts. Our sustaining service at that time, providing the bulk of programming, was Radio 4, but we opted out to do many of our own programmes and almost all of our own news bulletins. We even blanketed the London continuity announcements, that is, opted out and did our own version, going back in for the start of the programme. This required the utmost cooperation from our London colleagues and the frequent phone calls between us to check times and details led to my striking up many lasting friendships with the likes of John Marsh, Peter Donaldson and Eugene Fraser.

It required a certain slickness from us, too, as we had to make our announcements while keeping half an ear on what the Radio 4 announcer was saying in our headphones and then fading up the programme once they'd finished. This led to many missed first words and syllables, with a particular favourite being the daily ''Ternoon theatre'. One of our number, David Findlay, had such problems with missing the beginning of the Greenwich time signal that he was known as Five-Pip Findlay.

The *Today* programme did not get an airing in Scotland; instead, we had our own programme, *Good Morning Scotland*, presented by a variety of Scottish stars of the time, including Magnus Magnusson and Mary Marquis, who had been a major figure in TV and radio for several years. Mary was the only person I knew who made up for the radio. She would invariably arrive at the last minute before going on air, or even frequently after we had started, always looking impeccable. What seemed perfect to me was obviously not enough for her as, after the first twenty minutes on air, she would unplug her headphones and leave the studio during the seven o'clock news for the Ladies', where she would restyle her hair around the headset.

She may have been careful about her appearance but was not in the least 'grand', and was very good fun in the studio. Amongst the research staff on the programme at the time was a fresh-faced young graduate called Kirsty Wark. No idea what happened to her.

It was a happy programme to work on but one exception sticks in the memory. There had been some romantic intrigue amongst the team, and a presenter and producer who had been living together split up. The female producer had moved in with a male producer on the show, and the presenter involved had to carry on working with both of them. He had taken the whole business hard, and some late nights with the bottle had been the result; a bad mix with early starts.

One morning he turned up for the programme completely ratted, and, what's more, the duty producer was his ex-lover. His state was so obvious that she had to come in and take him off the air to sober up. I had to be in the studio to read the news and was an unwilling witness to the whole scene; suggestions he might like to step out were met with a terse, 'No.' An offer of a cup of black coffee got the response, 'Why?' and there followed a very brittle conversation with rather more detail about their relationship and the alleged flaws of the 'new man' than I was keen to hear. Eventually he was persuaded to leave, on the understanding that it was just for a few moments, and he was filled up with caffeine and allowed to return to presenting duty, with the heavy inter- views having been quietly reassigned. I had buried my face in a newspaper and only just stopped myself from singing, 'La, la, la,' to blot out the intimate details, but it was just about the most excruciating time I endured in a studio.

I enjoyed the company of the news staff, but found they tended to have split personalities. In the Club, they were witty, kind and relaxed. At work, they bustled about with pencils in their mouths, often scowling and with little patience. A cultural thing, no doubt, many of them coming from newspaper offices, but I found the falsely created excite- ment and the compulsory 'serious news' face, even when the only story in town was a missing cat, more than a touch ridiculous.

I also found it bewildering and a little irritating that, of a newsroom staff of about thirty people, only one was assigned to the hourly radio bulletins. Everyone else was in some way involved in preparing the nightly television programme, *Reporting Scotland*. It was the first time, but not the last, that I would experience how television claimed the lion's share of resources, attention and kudos.

Radio was a Good Thing, of course, and absolutely vital to the corporation, and so on, but it was not seen as sexy and, frankly, not many people wanted to work in it compared with the apparent glamour of TV. Public perception seemed much the same, and I was frequently asked when I would be promoted to appear on television. I usually gave a with- ering reply, as my harsh view at the time was that success on television was predicated almost entirely on looks and had little to do with ability. A fair proportion of small-screen stars would be quickly found out if they ever came to radio. My views have, of course, modified since then. But not too much.

While journalists were not my complete soulmates, I soon found that professional musicians were. There were two full-time orchestras at BBC Scotland at that time, the Scottish Symphony, which continues to thrive today, and the Scottish Radio Orchestra, so the Club bar was always full of players. Their attitude to work matched mine and I especially warmed to the SRO, whose repertoire ranged round big band, swing and jazz. Not for them the scowls and moods of news; they did their jobs professionally, accurately and in many cases with great flair, but spent a great deal of their time laughing, telling tasteless jokes and taking the piss out of their colleagues.

They had nicknames for everyone; Pam Patterson, my immediate boss, was great friends with a viola player, Esme Haynes, and their long gin sessions in the Club led to them being christened the Bevvy Sisters. The wonderfully accomplished and amply proportioned piano player Peggy O'Keeffe was renamed Leggy O'Beef, and the conductor Iain Sutherland was called Zorro, as a result of his flamboyant baton technique.

The SRO, and in particular their brass and woodwind players, were big drinkers, many of them being ex-jazzers, and it was alleged that afternoon sessions were hardly worth recording as a result. Certainly, they could get into some states. I was having a quiet drink in the Club bar one lunchtime when Dave McLelland, the lead trumpet of the band, walked in. Ordering his drink, he asked if his instrument was behind the bar. It was; he'd left it the previous night on becoming a little over-tired. 'Good job you didn't have a session this morning,' I offered. 'Oh, we did, I've just come from it. I just sat in my seat and kept my head down. Nobody noticed.'

When the Club had to close for refurbishment, the musicians went into panic, until someone made an arrangement with the owner of a small hotel just outside the gates of Broadcasting House. A key to his bar was given to the band, and they could use it for all their breaks. No staff would be there but the thirsty players could serve themselves and an honesty box would be placed on the counter. The manager was heard to say that even if they only put in half of what they drank he would make a profit on sheer volume.

By late August my initial three-month contract was drawing to a close and I had heard nothing. I was unsure whether to speak up, thereby reminding them that I should be got rid of, or keep quiet and hope that no news was good news. I opted for the latter, and when the rota came out for the first week in September and my name was on it, I relaxed a bit. Once the date had arrived, I decided it was safe to enquire about my continued employment. I had been surplus to requirements as far as staff numbers went and had merely saved them hiring in holiday relief over the summer, so an extension of the contract was by no means certain. The announcer who had handed in his notice had withdrawn it, so there was no real post for me.

However it was done, a new contract was forthcoming. I heard later that although strictly speaking I should have been allowed to drift away, the BBC were planning an expansion of the service within the next year or so, and they would rather I stayed than went off to some other station. The term was extended to a year and, even better, the money went up. Fiona and I could now think about moving house to get away from the running-water problem, and even buying a reliable car. They both turned up in short order, the house being the top half of a converted villa, on the 'right' side of Shields Road, and the car being a Honda Civic with one careful owner, a priest from Ardrossan. How priests could afford new cars I never knew, and judging by the state of the gearbox, he must have been driving back and forth to the Vatican every other week and then clocking the odometer. Either that or he was a dealer who had changed his first name by deed poll to Father.

I was now a fully fledged BBC announcer, and revelled in the work and the slight recognition that came with it. Listeners don't tend to take in newsreaders' names and it can take some time for a new presence to be registered. But, very occasionally, on being introduced to someone they would say they'd heard me on the radio, and occasionally guests visiting the studios would react to the name. When Archbishop Thomas Winning came in to record a programme of his choice of music, I was slated to make the opening announcement. When we were introduced, he looked me up and down and said, 'Oh. I had you down as a wee fat man. I see I wasn't right; but I wasn't completely wrong either.'

One of the most experienced broadcasters there was Howard Lockhart. He had been in the BBC since before the war, had produced Sir Harry Lauder and had presented *Housewives' Choice*. For many years his main outlet had been a weekly greetings programme, which was gentle, home-spun and innocent. So much so that he had caused some consternation when mentioning a couple who had written to say that they were about to enjoy two weeks' break. Howard's line was, 'I hope you'll have a lovely time, whether you're going away or having it off at home.' No amount of explanation could make him see what was wrong with it.

Perhaps innocence went with the age. His contemporary, Kathleen Garscadden, who ran the Scottish *Children's Hour*, had caused a near-walkout by insisting that an actor had to read, live on the radio, a story called 'The Sucking Foal'. Again, she could not understand his refusal.

I would have been even more vehement than that poor actor; I seemed to have a problem with spoonerisms. In one of my early bulletins, instead of saying, 'Apart from,' I started to say, 'A fart . . .', and then stopped myself. This wouldn't have been so bad if I hadn't been talking about 'strong winds across Scotland'. In a story about the Middle East, I got as far as, 'Best,' before correcting myself and saying, 'West Bank.'

Plenty of other broadcasters have suffered from this; sometimes the problem is exacerbated by correcting too early, as in the case of the Royal Horse Artillery, where the offender drew attention to the mistake by stopping after saying, 'And there, the great spectacle of the Royal Arse.' On the other hand, if you start to go wrong with the Chief Constable of Kent, the sooner you stop, the better.

Errors apart, I was having a great time and even managed to liven up dull Sunday shifts by popping down to the control room to see the Big Valve. This sounds like some initiation trick played on new recruits, but was exactly what it said on the tin. Just like a valve in the back of granny's radio, but about a hundred times the size. Legend had it that if you stood close up and shouted right into it, your voice could be faintly heard on the output. Well-refreshed members of staff could often be heard trying it out after closing time.

It was around this time that I was offered my first programme. For most broadcasters this would be the pivotal point of their career, the opportunity to break free of the relative anonymity of the announcing role, get their name in the *Radio Times* and launch oneself on a public who didn't know what they were missing. Not me. I was flattered, naturally, but surprised as it wasn't at all the kind of offer I had anticipated. It was to present and conduct interviews for a current affairs programme, the subject for that week being some story of a split in the Church of Scotland. I couldn't think why I had been chosen as I had no experience of this kind of reporting; nor did I know anything very much about the Church.

My first reaction was to decline the offer. I didn't think it was right for me. Luckily, Amanda Ashton, the producer, had another try and persuaded me that I ought to give it a whirl. My natural diffidence was partly to blame for my hesitation, but also, more cynically, I didn't want to be seen as a 'religious' broadcaster. Much as I liked Thora Hird, I didn't want to be her.

The work turned out to be much more enjoyable than I had feared, and I learnt a lot about interviewing and editing. How to ask questions in a way that couldn't be answered with a yes or no but gave you a reply in a proper sentence that could stand alone in the finished piece. How to cut out parts of an answer while not changing or misrepresenting the interviewee's point of view. It was invaluable, and I was grateful for the chance.

As part of the preparation, I had to go along to the headquarters of the Church of Scotland in Edinburgh and interview a senior cleric. A senior producer, Robin Malcolm, had been sent along with me to act as my minder. During our pre-interview chat with this distinguished minister, he said he'd been interviewed by someone else from the BBC recently, and was struggling to remember his name. We tossed in a few likely ones, none of which rang any bells, and then, to help us, he said, 'He was an awfully Catholic-looking chap.' I nearly choked on my coffee. In sectarian-aware Scotland this was a shockingly direct description to hear, especially from a man of the cloth. It was effective though, as Robin and I both immediately knew who he was talking about, although we hummed and hawed a bit longer before coming up with the name to make us look a little more sensitive than he was.

When my first year came to a close, I was put on the staff, something I had been keen to happen, for no other reason than it validated my existence. It was nice to be in a pension scheme, I suppose, but few twenty-seven-year-olds worry about what might happen to them forty years down the line, and I was no exception. As is the way with ambition, almost as soon as I had achieved this minor goal, another one rose on the horizon.

Much as I enjoyed the work and the company at BBC Scotland, I had my eye on London. I felt I wouldn't really have cracked it unless I was good enough to work there. So when a job came up at the World Service, I filled in my form, sent it off and in due course was given a date for my 'board'. The BBC never did interviews; it had appointments boards, confirming its status as a branch of the civil service rather than a creative organization. I had even had to sign the Official Secrets Act when I became an announcer; simply telling you this means that I can probably be prosecuted or, more likely, dragged up a back alley off Great Portland Street and garrotted with a bit of piano wire.

The board went nicely; there were three inquisitors, a very quiet person from the Appointments department, an extremely tall gentleman who was high up in Editorial, and a hearty lady with a deep booming voice who wore a tweed suit and sat with her legs apart.

Nice it may have been, but soon enough a letter arrived saying that I had not been appointed to the post. About three years later, when I was enquiring about something else, I discovered that they had in fact offered me an attachment for a few months, which is what the BBC did when they had given the job to someone else but wanted you to have a shot at it. Somehow this information had got lost; according to my informant it could have been deliberate, to avoid messing up Scotland's plans, but, knowing the way things work, I am pretty convinced it was down to cock-up.

I also applied for an announcer's job at Radio 4. Once again, someone else was appointed and I was offered an attachment, but this time they managed to remember to tell me about it. It made no difference; Scotland couldn't release me for some time, and events took a turn which changed the direction of my career.

That was a little way in the future, though. In 1978, the prospect of Radio Scotland becoming an all-day home-grown station was imminent. No longer would we be opting in and out of Radio 4; we'd be running our own programmes from six in the morning to midnight, and the announcers would be an important part of the output. A number of new voices were recruited and I found that I had responsibility for looking after them on some shifts. I had only been doing the job for eighteen months but the logic appeared to be that I was the closest in age to them and the learning process might still be fresh in my mind. A young lady by the name of Sheena McDonald was amongst them. I got on best, though, with a bloke by the name of Ian Aldred, who was my own age but had less hair than me – I always liked to meet people in that situation – besides which, he had a dark and some-times revoltingly vulgar sense of humour. I can't think why we got on.

The BBC was going through one of its periodic spasms of relocation. With the relaunch of the station it was decided, not before time, to beef up the radio side of the newsroom, with many more dedicated staff compiling the bulletins and reporting specifically for radio. A brilliant idea, but marred by the decision to relocate the operation to Edinburgh. The thought behind this was that devolution was in the air and a Scottish Assembly would be set up in the capital within a short time, and we would be right there, ready for it A Scottish Government did happen, but not for another twenty years, by which time the corporation had moved its radio news operation back to Glasgow. Planning, eh?

The other difficulty was that all the new announcers would be sent there to read the news. This meant that all the highly experienced newsreaders the public had heard for years would be confined to continuity, and inexperienced staff would be thrown in at the deep end. It took only a few weeks before a rethink was necessary, and there then followed a long period in which Glasgow-based voices would be sent through to Edinburgh and vice versa. It did improve the sound of the station, and also did no harm to the operating profit of British Rail as we all plied our way back and forth.

On one journey east I met James Cox, one of our most accomplished news and current affairs presenters, on the platform at Glasgow Queen St. We were having an enjoyable conversation when the train came in, at which point I realized that he had a first-class ticket while I had a second. News division obviously had better budgets than Presentation. Rather than break up the discussion, I simply followed Jim into the plusher seats and prepared to pay the difference.

After about twenty minutes, our chat subsided, having run through all the available gossip, and we fell to reading our newspapers. Shortly after, the inspector appeared; Jim showed him his ticket and resumed reading and I smiled and explained my position. 'I only have a second-class ticket but I met my friend here who was travelling in first and decided to join him.' At which point James Cox looked up from his newspaper just long enough to say loudly, 'I've never seen this man before in my life.'

The ticket inspector shook his head gently with a 'why can't they just own up' look on his face while I laughed weakly and said, 'He's joking, of course,' and all the while Cox kept his face buried in his newspaper.

The 'new' Radio Scotland was a mixed-format station. The main news programme at breakfast remained, followed by a consumer-based show presented by Jimmy Mack and then a pop show with Tom Ferrie. The press immediately took against it, calling the music shows 'pop and prattle' and the news programmes 'parish-pump piffle'. Scottish journalists have long had a weakness for alliteration. The announcers were given the *Night Beat* show to present and I was one of the team allocated to that.

I was also asked to be the presenter of the Saturday edition of *Good Morning Scotland*, the idea being that this would be a lighter version of the weekday show, with more features, a little music and more local news. In short, it would combine all the bêtes noires of the newspapers: pop, prattle and parish-pump piffle in one programme.

I had been a little nervous about taking it on, as there would be several interviews in each show about the major news stories of the day, and my background was not in formal journalism. It was a time when much play was being made of the necessity of having done 'hard news' before you could really understand a story. Since a fair number of the news staff had come from local papers where the hardest thing they had to cover was a garden fete, or taking the names at a funeral, I couldn't see how this gave them greater insight into an industrial dispute or war zone. So I just asked questions that a member of the public who read the papers might ask, or, put another way, the questions I myself wanted to know the answers to. The main thing I learned was to have your questions written down. It didn't matter if you didn't use those exact ones in the event, but always have them there with you. Of course, the very fact of taking this precaution ensured that it was never needed.

Presenting this show meant I was regularly given the Friday late newsreading shift to be followed by the Saturday morning show, which meant an overnight in Edinburgh. Ian Aldred very kindly offered me the use of the sofa in his flat for those nights, not that I spent long on it as we would hit the town after my last read of the evening at ten o'clock. Before it in fact, as there was a long wait from the previous bulletin at seven o'clock, so it was only natural to wander round to the Abbotsford or the Beau Brummell, the two handiest pubs.

Naturally I would limit my intake, but sometimes a slight misjudgement meant that the ten o'clock became a mine-field. It was a ten-minute read, so you couldn't just take a deep breath, run at it and hope for the best. Mostly I got it right, but there was at least one occasion when I had to close one eye in order to focus on the script.

After the Abbotsford closed, we would move to the late-night club known as the Calton Studios, which stayed open until two in the morning, and then I would hit the sofa for a few brief hours before getting up to host the morning show. Luckily, this arrangement only lasted about eighteen months, otherwise I might not have lived to become the healthy specimen you see in the photographs.

Edinburgh was, I quickly discovered, a very different city from Glasgow. It had an Establishment for a start, or at least people who thought they were: lawyers, academics, moneymen, authors and poets who held court in bars like the Abbotsford and seemed very pleased with themselves. Glasgow felt like a much more equal society where you could meet all of the above but mixed in amongst the rest of the population.

And Glasgow was friendlier and more direct; as a well-known journalist recounted, when some Glasgow ladies accosted him in an Edinburgh street, saying, 'You're that Jack McLean, aren't you?', he said, 'You're not from here, are you?' When asked how he had known that, he replied, 'You're speaking to me, for a start. Second off, you didn't ask me who I was, you *told* me.'

I did enjoy my days working in Edinburgh, though, with news staff who were good at their job and committed to radio. One of the news subs, Hamish Leal, had a habit of using spurious names in scripts when the actual reporter whose voice was to be used had not been confirmed. Nora Shagnasty was one of his favourites. Unfortunately this name sometimes made it into final versions, and only a panicked glance to the top of the page where the real reporter's surname would be noted meant that Nora was prevented from becoming nationally famous.

Hamish had a proprietorial air over his bulletins and would shuffle the order and remove words and sentences during the transmission to deliver a well-balanced summary. A special newsreading booth had been built in the Edinburgh building, fashioned out of an old toilet. They do spoil us. It still had the frosted glass on the windows and gave on to a central well which was a roosting place for a large proportion of the city's pigeons. It was therefore necessary to close the windows before broadcasting, otherwise the news was accompanied by loud cooing noises. One day, having dutifully shut out the chorus, Hamish and I sat down side by side for the three o'clock.

With a couple of minutes to go, he had given me the various stories to glance over and check for foreign names or other stumbling blocks. As you know, almost all news is bad. People sometimes complain about this, saying they'd like to hear more positive stories, so news editors will put in a lighter story at the end, an 'And Finally' to cheer us all up for fifteen seconds after nearly five minutes of unrelenting gloom. The tailpiece for this bulletin was to be a story about an escaped goat in Brora.

Just before transmission time, Hamish took all the pieces of script back for further editing, leaving me with only the lead story. We got on air and I sailed through to the end of the lead and paused, waiting to be handed the next one. Nothing happened. Hamish had become engrossed in his work and was busily chewing his pencil.

To jog him into action, I gave his right arm a gentle nudge with my left hand. I say gentle, but it is possible I hit him a little harder than I intended or perhaps I simply caught him awkwardly under the forearm; in any event the result was his right hand shot upwards and the news stories contained therein were launched into the air. They fluttered down to earth with Hamish flailing about trying to catch them. He managed to retrieve one story from the floor and handed it to me. There had now been several seconds of, well, not silence, as the listeners would have heard a degree of rustling only previously experienced on stocktaking day in a brown-paper factory.

However, off I went with the second lead; except it wasn't. It was the story about the goat which had escaped in Brora. And halfway into that was when the giggles set in. Hamish's great shoulders were heaving and my voice was slipping into falsetto. Four minutes may not sound a long time but when laughter is rising in your throat and tears are filling your eyes, with all the most serious news stories still to be read, it can seem like eternity. A wheezing, shaking 14-stone subeditor by your side is of no help.

Oddly, no listeners appeared to notice anything wrong with this broadcast, but Hamish was subject to a number of barbs from colleagues about his news priorities.

This was a time before staff cutbacks, and there seemed

to be plenty of people around to do the necessary work. Almost too many; there was a TV producer who was habitually to be found in the Club bar every lunchtime, puffing on a pipe and completing the *Times* crossword over a couple of pints. Some older staff could just remember the last time he had a programme on screen but no one could quite recall what it had been about. Still, at least he turned up.

Legend had it that there was a producer in the Light Entertainment department in London who would call his secretary from home on a Monday afternoon at five o'clock and ask if anyone had come looking or called for him that day. If the answer was in the negative, he would say, 'Right. In that case, I was in all day and I'm having a bisque tomorrow.' The bisque was not, as the name suggests, a nourishing soup, but was a kind of sanctioned 'duvet day'. All staff were allowed two bisques per year, which gave you a day off for no good reason, just because you felt like it. Needless to say, this producer phoned up again on Tuesday afternoon, asked the same question and pushed the bisque on to the third day if his absence had not been noticed. Even if it had, his secretary was primed to say he'd just popped out to buy some cigarettes and he'd ring them, which he did, by phone from home. It's said that by using this device he had reduced his appearances in the office to about once a month and, naturally, scarcely any programmes with his name attached ever reached the airwaves.

Laziness on that scale was rare though, and most producers used the free time they had to indulge in what is amusingly called nowadays 'blue-sky thinking'. Many insisted the best programme ideas they ever had came from relaxed conversations with colleagues in the canteen or the pub rather than slaving away at the desk. It's an argument I have a certain sympathy with. Now, in the twenty-first century, the pendulum has probably swung too far the other way and most of the production staff I know are inundated with work, especially the numerous compliance forms they have to fill in, to the extent that they are constantly running fast to stand still.

In those more leisurely times, every producer devoted a good few hours every week to studying the latest BBC jobs in the house newspaper, *Ariel*. My friend Ian McLaren Thomson spotted a misprint one week where a job was advertised as attracting a 15 per cent shift allowance. On the page the letter 'f' had been omitted from the word 'shift'.

His letter, pointing out that he had been producing programmes that had been described as such for years without any extra payment, was not printed.

I mentioned earlier the 'emergency services' attitude of announcers and the 'show must go on' mentality that prevailed amongst us. This was never better demonstrated than on the night of a leaving party, where almost all of us were enjoying several drinks, but one brave soul was on lemonade, having the late bulletin to read. After he had left the pub to return to the studio, some bright spark thought it would be amusing to ring the bar and pretend to be calling from the BBC to say that the newsreader hadn't turned up and could anyone take over. No sooner had the request gone up than about half a dozen of us rushed for our coats and headed for the door, despite being in hardly a fit state to walk, let alone broadcast. One of our number was so keen he had to be chased up the street and restrained before he barged into the studio, demanding in slurred tones to be allowed to read the news.

It was a happy time, and despite the foregoing tales, we were serious about our work and kept our revelry under control. We prided ourselves on knowing how much we could take; sounding even slightly slurred on air would be regarded as simply unprofessional.

My work pattern settled into a nice mix of newsreading, the Saturday morning show and an evening or two on *Night Beat*, a late-evening music and interview show. Charles Nove, the schoolboy from hospital radio, had now joined BBC Scotland. He was a few weeks short of his eighteenth birthday when he started, and under the rules for employment of minors was not allowed to work after ten o'clock at night unless accompanied by a responsible adult. Unfortunately all he had was us. Soon, though, he was free to work until midnight and became one of the regular presenters of *Night Beat* with Iain Purdon and myself.

One night when I was on the programme, a new announcer by the name of Robert Sproul-Cran was on the evening shift. I had been in earlier to make sure he was happy and returned later to find him looking slightly troubled. At a certain point in the course of the evening, he had a call on the 'hotline' from Edinburgh, from the Head of Radio Scotland himself. This was the beginning of what would become known as the 'Queen is dead' incident.

Robert recounted the sequence of events to me. The hotline had buzzed and there had been HRS and his deputy, who, without any of the usual pleasantries, said, 'The Queen is dead. What are you going to do?' Robert was no fool, and immediately thought he was being set some kind of trap, although he had no clear idea of what it might be. He asked, 'Are you genuinely telling me the Queen has died?' To which he received the reply, 'I am telling you the Queen is dead. Now you tell me what you are going to do about it.' At this point, judging by the tone and sound of the questioning, he decided that it was a form of test, although the language used was quite unequivocal. He was being told that the monarch had passed away. As he said to me later, 'I could have put the phone down then and there and gone into full Royal Death scenario.' When I heard the story, that's exactly what I thought. A clear message from the management of the station to an inexperienced member of staff, telling him the Queen was dead.

Robert said he had continued the conversation for a little while, running through the options he might employ in this situation, but likened his approach to humouring a bore in the pub. Needless to say, he had not taken the station off the air and begun playing funereal music. As far as I was concerned, he had done exactly the right thing; the likelihood was our esteemed bosses would not remember the conversation in the morning, but to protect himself Robert ought to write a full report in his log.

It must have made interesting reading, certainly to the upper echelons of the corporation, because within hours, the ordure had hit the air-conditioning. Our presentation organizer took a dim view of the pressure this young announcer had been put under and the way in which it had been done, and he was far from alone. Enquiries were begun, reports were written and within days a story appeared in the *Glasgow Herald*. After that, the jig was up and resignations were required. Head of Radio Scotland went, as did his deputy.

I don't doubt that the whole thing could have been easily swept under the carpet and explained away if the higher reaches of the BBC had had utter confidence in this particular management, but it seemed that someone somewhere wanted these heads to roll, and roll they did. If this incident hadn't happened, another way would have been found. But as a lesson in watching what you say on the telephone, it is what you might call a sobering one.

It gave the corporation the chance to relaunch the station, to counter the pop-and-prattle criticisms of the press, and soon meetings were being held, huddles gone into and anxious faces waited for puffs of smoke to come out of the third floor. As a staff announcer, I was less anxious than some; much as I enjoyed presenting programmes, I would be happy enough to go back to standard duties if that was the way they wanted it.

Somewhat to my surprise, I was called in by Ian Mac-Fadyen, one of the steering committee 'rescuing' the station. Ian had just retired as the senior TV Light Entertainment producer in Scotland, responsible for almost everything tartan on telly, in particular the New Year shows, for which he had become known as the Ayatollah Hogmanay.

He was a fairly gruff sort of bloke and not given to huge outpourings of praise, and, sure enough, I wasn't subjected to any. He simply offered me an afternoon show three times a week, to be produced by Ben Lyons, one of the most experienced producers in the building. It would go under my name, the first time there had actually been a *Ken Bruce Show*, but I would still be a staff man and would work shifts on the other days. I agreed, and was out of the door in under ten minutes, possibly even five. No fuss, no tears, no manly hugs, just a muttered, 'Right, then,' and the deal was done.

Ben devised a show of music and features, which ran for an hour on Mondays, Wednesdays and Fridays and started to gather a small but regular audience. The music we played was chosen by Ben but, like all good producers, he made sure it was to the taste of his presenter. When I wasn't doing the show, I was stuck into Schools continuity, introducing all those programmes we used to sleep through when played into our classrooms. You know the sort of thing: 'Listen to the music and pretend to be a tree. And rest.' There was a geography programme called *Exploring Scotland*, which I managed to introduce once as 'Exploding Scotland'.

I got to know Ian MacFadyen rather better in the course of that year, as he came back to produce my show as a freelance relief once the dust had settled, and I found that beneath his gruff demeanour there lurked a good man with a nice sense of humour. He had funds of stories of Scottish show business, having been at the heart of it for many years; using the name of Neil Grant he had provided the music for many of Andy Stewart's hits, including 'Donald Where's Yer Troosers'.

We particularly bonded one day when he had booked a pre-recorded interview with Alex Hay, the golf commentator, just before the Open. Alex was very good value and gave us a great interview, until the end, when I asked the stock question about any embarrassing moments. This is the story he told.

He and Peter Alliss had been commentating on a women's match and at one point there had been a lull in play while one competitor took a long time lining up her putt. So much so that they had begun discussing the state of the course. At this point they had both made the classic mistake of not looking at the monitor but gazing out of the window right under which the lady player was busily examining the run of the green in the classic manner, bending down with her nose near the ground. From the window, all was fine. On their unwatched TV screen, the picture was from the rear and looking directly at this woman's backside.

Peter Alliss chose this moment to say, 'You know, this has always been one of the nicest little holes on the circuit.' And Alex then compounded it by adding, 'But not as tight as it used to be.'

It was some time before I could speak. On the other side of the glass MacFadyen had turned bright purple and appeared to be suffering a choking fit. I thanked Alex Hay profusely, even as I knew that we could never broadcast this, the best story we were ever likely to get on the programme. Radio Scotland was not quite ready for it.

As well as these shows, I was continuing to work with the Scottish Radio Orchestra. My few attempts at symphony concerts had been no better than passable, because I found the formality required at these events, and the very strict rules laid down by Radio 3, slightly daunting. I much preferred the more relaxed freedom of the lighter material. And I loved the way that these wildly differing musicians, from conservatoire-trained violinists to jazz-pub veterans, could come together and play as a unit. They all shared the ability to pick up a sheet of music they'd never seen before and play it with flair and style.

I had been booked to present the SRO Road Show in 1978; previously my friend James Alexander Gordon had been brought up from London each week to do it, but presumably the BBC was going through one of its regular bouts of cost-cutting and so the local boy was given the job. The first show I had done went quite well; my script made the band laugh (always a sign that you've pushed taste boundaries a little too far) and at the end the producer said he'd like me to do the whole series.

Three weeks later I found that he had booked someone else to do at least two shows in that same series. This was my first experience of 'forked-tongue syndrome', in which an executive will tell you what you want to hear rather than what is the actual case. The syndrome is, I can tell you, still thriving.

What made it even more educational was that when I returned to the show after the other presenter had done his brace of programmes, the same producer told me exactly the same thing, he'd like me to do the whole series, without a flicker of déjà vu crossing his face. Naturally, I made no reference to the previous conversation, and simply said something like, 'Well, how kind,' and thanked him politely.

That was something else I had learned. I have, from time to time, been offered work by someone who has either previously rejected or overlooked me. There is a very strong temptation to say something like, 'So, you've come crawling back, have you?' or, 'Took your time but you saw sense in the end.' While that may offer a warm glow of satisfaction, even without the addition of a thumb on the nose and a 'Na, na, na-na-na,' the feeling only lasts about ten seconds. After that you either have to work with the guy or face being replaced again, so it's better simply to accept the offer with good grace and keep the triumphalism for when you get home.

The SRO Road Show did what the title said; the orchestra went round Scotland, or at least the central belt, and played an hour of music to the local populace in Airdrie, Falkirk, Stirling and anywhere else that had a stage big enough for sixty musicians and a couple of guest singers. We had musicians of the calibre of the harmonica player Larry Adler and singers like Dennis Lotis, Tony Monopoly and Rosemary Squires. Brian Fahey was the orchestra's musical director and most of the arrangements played were his. No bad thing, as he was one of the best orchestrators in the country.

One concert had Sheila Buxton as the guest. She was famed in radio circles as having been the resident vocalist on *Make Way with Music*, in which Roger Moffat introduced the Northern Dance Orchestra in irreverent style. They were renowned for being high spirited and the story went that Moffat and Buxton, along with some of the band, were drinking illegally after hours in some Manchester dive when there was a police raid. Moffat whispered to Buxton, 'Don't give your real name,' and, sure enough, when the coppers came round with the notebooks asking for names, he glanced at the bar taps for inspiration and replied, 'Roger Worthington.' Upon which the officer with the book said, in measured tones, 'Thank you very much, sir. And now, Miss Buxton, what name are you going under tonight – Guinness?'

Sheila's concert with us in Airdrie was marked by her arrival. She had come up from the south by train, and on being deposited at Glasgow Central had hailed a cab to take her to Airdrie. The cabbie must have thought it was Christmas, as a 20-mile trip was about 18 miles longer than his normal fare. She had obviously felt a little thirsty on the train, because when she arrived at the Sir John Wilson Town Hall she was tired but ebullient. She had a run through her songs, after which it was decided that one of our programme staff might feed her a few coffees and wash her hair. It was only at this point that the cabbie came into the hall, asking who was going to pay the fare which had been steadily ticking up outside for the last hour.

The washing and caffeine seemed to have the desired effect and Sheila did a barnstorming performance, at one point with her arms draped round Brian Fahey's neck as she sang, with feeling, 'My man, I love him so.' After we had finished and the hospitality wine bottle was opened, Sheila raised her glass and said, 'First today!' and couldn't understand why everyone present fell about laughing.

On the occasion when Larry Adler was guest, I had put into the script a little gag about the SRO's pianist Allan Cameron, to the effect that when he was born the doctor took one look at his fingers and predicted he would be either a gifted pianist or a pickpocket. 'So,' I mugged away, 'watch your wallets tonight!' It got a bit of a laugh, and I added a bit about being surrounded by tea leaves here tonight and moved on. When I got off stage I noticed that Mr Adler was looking a touch stony-faced. I was well used to my jokes being received like that so thought no more of it until I mentioned his look to one of the band, who said, 'For God's sake! Didn't you know? Larry Adler was arrested for shoplifting last week!'

I was thunderstruck and began frantically to think of ways to grovel and put things right. I prepared a little speech of contrition and apology and was pacing up and down and about to go up to him after the show when I was stopped by my 'friend', who admitted he'd made up the whole story on the spur of the moment just to see me squirm. Well, I had squirmed. Marmite and piccalilli together could not have made me squirm more.

A couple of years later, once the heat had died down, I had to interview Mr Adler for my show. He could be somewhat spiky; and this abrasiveness was not helped by his being in a London studio while I was in Glasgow, a situation that encouraged a sense of distance. The first rule of interviewing is never to ask a question to which you do not know the answer. Like most rules, you can often get good results by breaking it, but I had done my homework and studied his press clippings, or 'cuts' as the Americans call them, and asked my first question, to which I of course knew the answer: 'Is it true that you were once . . .' I had hardly got any further when he barked out, 'Well, it's all in the cuts, I suggest you read them.'

Now, I am an even-tempered man by nature and don't get riled very easily but this immediately made my blood pump. I had spent an hour wading through yellowing newspapers and jotting down the minutiae of his life and here he was treating me like some lazy oik who had just turned up without knowing who he was interviewing. I rose to the fight.

'I have read the cuts, but our listeners haven't, so I'm asking you to fill in a little about your background, but if you'd rather not we can talk about something else.' Oh God, I thought. I have to speak to this man for twenty minutes and I've started arguing with him already. The interview limped on for a short while until I decided to remind him of the concert where he had been so warmly received by our Glasgow audience.

I started sweating a little because I recalled my tea leaf remark and thought he might too, and it was some time before I remembered that the entire story had been invented. The memory of the concert must have been an agreeable one, as he thawed audibly and became almost pleasant. By the end of the interview, I won't say we were Bezzie Mates but diplomatic relations had definitely been restored.

One of the other oddities I worked on at this time was a new comedy show for the radio station. Phil Whittaker, a studio manager turned producer, had commissioned the well-known Scottish writer Cliff Hanley to come up with an idea. Cliff's plan was to base the series on a fictional radio station, with music links and news items to provide the lead-ins to the sketches. For the music, Phil hired Bernard Sumner, a fine pianist who had been the BBC's staff accompanist in Scotland, but despite that prim-sounding background was outrageous in both behaviour and humour. Two experienced actors were signed up, Paul Young and Mary Riggans, these days running her shop in *Balamory* as Suzie Sweet, and as the newsreader I completed the cast.

We spent a day doing a pilot, and I thought it was all rather good. Cliff had written a witty script, Paul and Mary could do any voice required, I did my bits, and Bernard wrote and delivered a lot of music in the form of an original theme, parody songs, cues and jingles. Of the performers, I was definitely the cheapest, the letters SNF, or Staff No Fee, appearing after my name; Mary and Paul were well regarded so would be being paid more than Equity minimum; Cliff had done more than one draft so presumably had put in a bill to reflect that; and as for Bernard's input, well, that kind of stuff doesn't come cheap, even at BBC rates.

The net result was one very expensive show. The bosses liked the pilot but as soon as they saw the amount spent blew a fuse. I was told half the annual development budget for the station had gone on this one show. The plug was pulled, no more episodes were made and I don't think the pilot was ever transmitted.

Radio Scotland was still going through Dr Jekyll-like spasms of transformation by the end of 1980. While I was happy in my work, with a mix of announcing and programmes, I still had no firm idea about what I wanted to do into the future. Radio 4 was a possibility, given my promise of an attachment, and I was keen to get into the London swim. On the other hand, I enjoyed the lighter end of presentation, and people around me in the BBC couldn't understand why I wanted to try something other than what I appeared to be doing best.

In the end, a decision was forced on me. At the end of the year, I was offered a full-time daily show on Radio Scotland, to run mid-morning through to lunchtime, a blend of music and interviews. In order to take this on, I would have to leave the staff and become freelance. I would lose the security, but I would be given a year's contract, more money and I would be free to take on other work outside the BBC. It was not a hard decision to make. I was about to join the ranks of the self-employed.

Five

'Like a Younger Sean Connery'

As I was a freelance broadcaster, the letters SNF would no longer appear after my name on the programme budgets. No more Staff No Fee, now I was an OC, Outside Contributor. This did not always mean I was paid a fortune, but it did mean I was paid for every appearance. The corollary of this was that non-appearance meant non-payment. No sick pay, no holiday pay either, but the assumption was that vast freelance fees would more than make up for those lost days. I didn't take any holiday for more than six months, but, despite being very healthy, I had to go off sick sooner than I thought.

My first day as a freelance was 25 December 1980. I did not work. I actually started on the new show the following Monday, and was due to work through the week and on the Friday night act as presenter for the radio New Year celebrations, a nice earner. By the Thursday night, I had developed a diarrhoea bug. There were only three ailments that could prevent me broadcasting: losing the voice, which even with heavy colds never seemed to happen to me; vomiting, which was a thankfully rare occurrence; and the trots, ditto. Not so rare that it didn't strike me down within a week of self-employment. The annoying element is that with modern treatments the dodgy tummy is controllable, but back then I did not dare move too far from efficient plumbing. I had to phone in sick for the Friday show, but resolved to be in to do the Hogmanay show.

I managed it, but in a weakened state, and it was certainly the most sober New Year I had seen in for some time. In my innocence, I thought that the BBC might just pay me for the missed show, it being my first week and Christmas time to boot. No; they docked my weekly cheque by one programme fee. Just as well I had shown up for the special, or my loss on the week would have been even greater.

Here were some other good lessons. I had left the corporation and it was not responsible for me. I shouldn't expect sympathy or special treatment. And the best lesson of all was – don't get ill.

Much as I tried to avoid them, I did succumb to a variety of illnesses, mostly inflicted by my family. I had missed a show for the birth of my first son, Campbell, but that had been as a staff member. When Douglas was born, just three months into my new status, I managed to attend the birth, buy the flowers and wet the baby's head, all without dropping any bookings.

Later in the 1980s, I would be plagued with a series of youthful ailments, some of which were fairly uncomfortable but none of which generated much sympathy, their comedy value to my friends and colleagues being too attractive. The mumps caused me to take a week off, so were the worst in terms of missed work, but least unpleasant in terms of effects. No, they didn't swell up, before you ask. Everybody did ask at the time, with many a ribald comment along the lines of,

'Bet you wish something else had!' accompanied by much nudging.

I had caught mumps from a work colleague who had generously come into the office for two weeks complaining about swollen glands. Chicken pox I had caught from the children. Naturally, they sailed through the illness with only a few spots and regular applications of calamine lotion. For me, in my thirties, it was a miserable experience. The spots hurt rather than itched, I looked like a victim of the Black Death, and sleep was nigh-on impossible. When I did venture out, I wore an old hat pulled down over my face but still managed to frighten the unwary.

When glandular fever afflicted me, it tired me out, but it was difficult to judge whether I was any more dozy than usual. I was over the worst of it by the time it was diagnosed in any case. Tonsillitis had been the medical profession's opinion for some weeks and I had been given antibiotics which caused raging diarrhoea, none of which I had needed to endure. As is often the case, the cure was worse than the disease.

After these three childhood complaints in short order, I began to wonder if nappy rash or colic would strike me next; but happily, my immune system seemed to remember what it was supposed to do and, from 1984, I never had to take a day off work for illness until 2008, when I fell victim to a dodgy ready meal one evening when catering for myself.

After my missed day in the first week of the new show, both I and the format settled down. We followed the *Jimmy Mack Show*, an engaging consumer-based show that had built up a good audience, and Jimmy himself was popular with the listeners. Our brief was to deliver shorter punchier speech pieces, larded with quite a bit of music. We were also to give space to a new soap opera within our slot, to be called *Kilbreck*.

This was a quite separate production from us, delivered by the Drama department in Edinburgh, and it was to be partly funded by the Health Education Council. It was intended to be a strong drama set in a fictitious new town and, here was the rub, health messages were to be included somehow, either as storylines or as conversations between characters. The former *Archers* editor Bill Smethurst was brought in, with his experience of blending agricultural topics into the action on that serial, to help the team achieve the same seamless mix of fact and fiction. What fell naturally into place in Ambridge did not seem so easy in Kilbreck.

Shaping the plots wasn't too difficult, as some old bloke or other could always be found to be suffering from an incurable whatever as a result of a misspent youth, but the 'natural' dialogue seemed to be more awkward to capture. The writers, who had their own ideas about what any character might say, found themselves having to shoehorn into their scripts conversations about brushing your teeth for a minimum of twenty seconds or the importance of washing your hands after touching raw fish. Even with the abilities of the most skilful writers, these little homilies stood out like a sore thumb (this infection being simply avoided by washing your hands after touching raw fish).

I also felt for the actors, who included the aforementioned Paul Young, who gave it their all but couldn't bring much life to lines like, 'Isn't it awful the amount of sexually transmitted infections going around these days?' Naturally, my reaction to it was to take the rise, ever so gently.

I gave a rousing cheer, though, when Paul's character,

having been made redundant, was given the magnificent line, 'Twenty years I've been here, and ye're just treated like so much shite!' His delivery was, I thought, heartfelt.

I suppose we did resent the inclusion of *Kilbreck* within our timeslot. Why, I wanted to know of the bosses, did I have to stay in the studio for an extra fifteen minutes just to say goodbye? As tends to happen, BBC management, confronted by a complaining presenter, resort to unconvincing flattery. You'll be helping us out, they say. You're so popular/trusted/able, depending on circumstances. We would have asked X but we thought you'd do it so much better. As I say, totally unconvincing. But, strangely, it always works.

The main body of the programme was taken up with one heavy news story, one light one, a feature or two, and any showbiz faces who happened to be in the area. We had a strong team of producers and researchers, and some good interviews and interesting guests started to pass through the studio. Mostly I stayed in there, but occasionally I went off with my portable tape recorder and stuck a feature together.

These recorders, manufactured by Uher, were portable only in the sense that a holiday suitcase is. They were heavy and unwieldy but highly efficient and simple to operate. The only trap was the pause button. Everybody who ever went out with a Uher has come back at least once with a totally silent tape, thanks to forgetting to lift that little device.

These machines were treated like gold bars in the corporation. There were never quite enough to go round, and anybody who damaged one, no matter how inadvertently, was more or less cut from polite society. Their value was drummed into staff from their first day. I know of a trainee reporter who was rushing back to Broadcasting House in London with an interview when he was hit by a taxi. His instinctive behaviour was not to protect himself, but to hold the Uher out of harm's way. Having crashed to the ground, bruising several ribs but saving the machine, he staggered to his feet and carried on towards BH with a wave of apology to the taxi driver. If it proves nothing else, it's certainly a tribute to the effectiveness of BBC training. Techniques learned during the war, no doubt.

One of the missions I took my Uher on was the appearance in Glasgow of the Harlem Globetrotters basketball team, whose effortless combination of ball skills and comedy was, I was assured, a great item in the making. I soon realized that it was a great item – for TV. Almost all of their appeal was visual. After half an hour all I had on my tape were echoing shouts and cheers and the squeak of trainers on wood. I managed to fill it out with interviews with the players and some fans, and luckily discovered that the MC on the tour was the radio sports commentator Norman de Mesquita, so I immediately enlisted him to convey some of the spectacle rather better than I could. I got a fairly decent report out of it but once again learned to investigate the prospect thoroughly before leaving the office.

Back in the studio, there was a regular flow of the interesting, the quirky, the downright odd and the famous. Sometimes all at the same time.

I have no idea why Telly Savalas was in Glasgow, but we got him and he came in, eyeing me suspiciously from the start. I used to wonder why these stars agreed to be interviewed at all, as some clearly didn't want to talk, had little idea of where they were or, in some cases, who they were, and gave a very good impression of someone who would rather drink a nourishing glass of strychnine than answer a single question. My sympathy for them increased a bit when it dawned on me that the interviews had very probably been arranged without asking them by a PR who was desperate to get publicity for the project, and the star concerned had in all probability done six interviews already that day and been asked the same questions every time.

I made it my business to look for different angles for my interviews and studied their press files closely, looking for the offbeat parts of their lives. This worked in the case of Mr Savalas, as after our wary start he warmed up nicely, talking quite openly about some unhappy aspects of his youth which I had come across in the cuttings.

Not everything went so well. Jimmy Logan, the Scottish actor and impresario, came from a showbiz family. His sister was the jazz singer Annie Ross and his mother and father had been music hall artistes, Jack Short and May Dalziel. One day the announcement came through that Jack Short had died. He was a fair old age and had been ill for some time, but it was the passing of an era of entertainment, so we put in a request to see if Jimmy would come in and talk about his father.

He agreed, and the next day he came into the studio in an understandably subdued state. While the news was on I offered my sympathies for his loss and said we'd play a bit of music and then talk about his father. So wrapped up was I in my conversation with him that I failed to appreciate that the track I had lined up to play was a Joe Jackson recording of an old swing number going by the title of 'Jack, You're Dead'.

At times like these the only course of action is to plough on, avoid mentioning the title or drawing any kind of attention to the gaffe, and hope nobody notices. We had no complaints, so it seemed we had got away with it. But there was a look in Jimmy Logan's eye that told me we hadn't.

One of the peripheral bits of banter around the show at this time was my imagined similarity to Sean Connery. It grew up because of my one-word impression of his voice: 'Yesh,' and I made great play of being just as rugged and handsome but with the advantage of looking younger. The usual old rubbish, in other words. When the chance to meet Connery cropped up, the production team leapt to it.

He was promoting a film called *Five Days One Summer*, directed by the great Fred Zinnemann of *High Noon* fame, in what would turn out to be his final film. Some of the shooting had taken place at the shipyards in Port Glasgow and a press call was arranged down there where the stars and director could be interviewed.

We duly trundled off to the yard office and milled around with the stars and crew, along with a selection of Scottish newspaper journalists. We got an interesting interview with Fred Zinnemann and a good one with Connery himself. No press call was complete in those days without a healthy amount of free booze being supplied to the thirsty hacks, and this proved to be the case here. It turned into quite a jolly do, but someone present had obviously sampled a fair bit and thought it would be really hilarious to tell Mr Connery of my on-air comparisons.

Radio is unlike the written word in that you operate in a strange half-reality, cocooned from the outside world; you say something but it's gone immediately. It's easy to believe that any remark is not being taken seriously or, quite frequently, even heard at all. The prospect of Sean Connery ever knowing that I was using his name in this way on air had never occurred to me. It was so unlikely as to be impossible. Well, of course, he hadn't; until this moment.

He sauntered up to me with a faint grin on his face and said, 'I hear you think you look like me.' I muttered awkwardly, 'Oh well, sometimes on one of my good days . . .' To which he responded, 'And one of my bad ones.'

He walked away, seemingly amused, but nowhere near as amused as my colleagues.

One of the other stars I met at this time, under less personally trying circumstances, was Ella Fitzgerald. She was in her late sixties by then, an age when many singers have given up or are only doing guest spots on other people's shows, but here she was on a major international tour. The Scottish stop was to be at the Playhouse in Edinburgh, accompanied by a specially formed orchestra directed by Brian Fahey and recorded for Radio 2.

I was asked to present it, the sort of invitation that doesn't need to be made twice. The chance to appear on stage with a legend? Oh, now, let me think . . .

I arrived early at the theatre so I could hear the whole rehearsal. Very often on jobs like this, on the evening itself, I have to stay backstage or in the wings and don't get the full effect of the performance, so I like to catch the experience from the stalls earlier. The first half of the show was to be the orchestra playing half a dozen pieces, and the great Ella would join them for the second half, in which she would sing all her classic songs.

I parked myself in a seat in the stalls and settled down

to enjoy the moment. After the band's numbers, Brian went offstage to fetch the star and introduce her formally to the musicians. When he reappeared he was linking arms with a frail-looking elderly black woman whose eyesight was evidently not wonderful as she wore bottle-end specs and required guiding to centre stage. Oh dear, I thought. But perhaps when she begins to sing . . .

Alas, when the orchestra struck up, Ella, perched on a high chair, simply hummed and mumbled along, with only about half a dozen notes given anything like full volume. I sank deeper into my seat in the stalls and wondered how the production team would be able to make anything of this. Each of her songs was approached in the same way, more or less walking through with only a brief glimpse or two of the great Ella voice.

After the rehearsal, I went down to her dressing room to introduce myself and found this terribly sweet old lady, as I was now thinking of her, surrounded by dozens of Perrier bottles. Just the little 330ml bottles, not the litre ones, but loads of them, right round the table and along the shelf on the wall. She squinted at me through her pebble glasses and very charmingly signed my programme, as I checked how she wanted to be brought on and so forth.

Ah well, at least I would have the autograph of a great entertainer even if I had not seen the best of her.

At the evening performance, after the interval, I went back on stage and made the announcement to introduce Miss Ella Fitzgerald. On she came, once again on the arm of Brian Fahey and still with her thick specs on. She parked herself at the microphone, Brian gave the downbeat, the orchestra began, and from that instant, the years slipped away. Ella sang tremendously, with power, volume, style, timing, phrasing, wit and feeling. It was as if she had transformed into a forty-years-younger self over a four-bar intro. I stood in the wings, straining to catch every note of every song.

It was one of the most impressive live performances I have ever seen, and I felt truly privileged to experience it. The Edinburgh audience, which has occasionally been thought to be cold, needed no extra warmth that night. They loved her and showed it.

Afterwards, I went to her dressing room again and there once more was the elderly lady I had seen in the afternoon. To my enthusiastically complimentary gush, she simply said, 'Well, I think we could have done it better in places but thank you so much for saying that,' making me, just an oik from Scottish radio, feel as if my view on her performance mattered to her.

I am no hero-worshipper and normally find it extremely easy to treat the great and the good as perfectly normal people. I don't kowtow or turn to jelly in the presence of the famous. But Ella Fitzgerald was the exception; for the first, and possibly the last, time in my life, I was star-struck.

We were to return to Edinburgh throughout the early 1980s each summer for the Festival, or more exactly, the Fringe. Coverage of this on Radio Scotland had previously been the preserve of the Arts department but we managed to persuade the management that a more popular approach would work. Radio 2 were setting up a sort of mini-club in the Caledonian Hotel and we offered to pool resources and use the same facilities for my show in the morning and Brian Matthew's *Round Midnight* programme in the evening.

We had left booking rooms too late, so our accommodation was in Musselburgh, which seemed almost as far to the east of Edinburgh as our homes in Glasgow were to the west. We were hardly ever there, though, as we spent all day and evening going to shows and inviting the participants to come on the radio in the morning and give a taster of their performances. Such is the struggle for attention and audiences on the Fringe, acts were falling over themselves to appear and give their box office a boost.

So that we were properly 'badged', the BBC broke into its publicity piggy-bank and provided branded sweatshirts for the team. On our first day in Edinburgh, as I emerged from a pub at lunchtime, my sweatshirt was bombed by a seagull which had evidently been suffering severe digestive problems. My distress and immediate demand that someone should give up their shirt for me to wear caused nothing but helpless mirth from all my colleagues. So much for the dictum, 'Protect the Turn'.

The acts we booked were of varying types and, indeed, abilities. Student revues, major stars, buskers, classical musicians – the only thing they had in common was a desire to sell tickets in an overcrowded market. Peter Ustinov was followed on to the interview seats by an American brass ensemble, a stand-up comedian and an itinerant guitar player who completed every number with the words, 'Thank you, music lovers.' Each in their own way interesting, the latter for the complete lack of self-awareness he showed with that remark.

In succeeding years we would expand the offering by including a resident singer, Art Sutter, who would later step into my presenting shoes when I left Scotland, but at that time provided the musical breaks in what would otherwise have become a rather speech-heavy show. His trio were part of our team but also did some work for *Round Midnight*.

I discovered that Radio 2 had a different attitude towards the musicians, as they were not granted the same rights to a drink after the show at night as they were by us. When we came off the air at lunchtime, everyone repaired to the green room the BBC had booked in the hotel, where drinks would be dispensed and everyone thanked. When the lads worked at night, they were somewhat surprised to be refused a drink by the producer, who said, 'Sorry, it's for programme staff only.'

The green room was shared, but there were separate drinks cabinets for each production. Luckily, the band had the key for our cupboard so refreshed themselves from that. The following night, Radio 2 lost their key, and when the same producer asked if he might borrow a bottle from our cupboard, the sax player Frank Pantrini took great pleasure in replying, 'Sorry, it's for musicians only.'

The constant rush of performers on and off the stage at the Caledonian was lightened by the presence of this band, who could always be relied upon to liven the day with a remark about the acts or some piece of horseplay. They were positioned right next to the raised dais where I and my guests sat at one end of the room, so while visible to the audience, they were not in direct line of sight, especially if all eyes were on the interviewee. During one dullish interview, the drummer Murray Smith thought he would pass the time by showing the others his party trick: an ability to put a drumstick up each nostril and leave them hanging there unsupported. Admittedly, it's not a skill that many would find useful, but it amused his colleagues. My cue to the band came sooner than he expected, partly because the interview was indeed very boring but also because I had noticed what Murray was doing and wanted to throw a little confusion his way. I gave the quickest of wind-ups: 'Well, thank you for a fascinating (!) chat but now it's over to Art Sutter and His Trio.' The boys leapt to their instruments, Art's hands darted to the piano, Brian Payne hoisted his double bass to the upright, and Frank planted the sax in his mouth.

Murray whipped the sticks out of his nose and started to play without missing a beat. The speed of the sticks' removal, though, had obviously disturbed some part of his nasal passages as his nose began to bleed, quite heavily, on to his snare drum. The sight of Murray trying to continue playing while mopping blood spots from his snare, with the blood still dropping on to it noisily, is something I have treasured for years. Sympathy for his predicament was not widespread; many said the blood drips were keeping better time than he was.

Drummers can often be the butt of musicians' jokes. During an orchestra session which was going slightly awry, the drummer threw down his sticks in frustration and shouted, 'There are three different tempos going on in this orchestra!' only to get the instant reply, 'Aye, your bass drum, your hi-hat, and your snare.'

The Edinburgh Festival programmes were always great fun, if rather tiring. After the first week's programmes I would go home and sleep for almost the entire weekend. One of our engineers had got home, nodded off in his child's Wendy house while playing with the kids and had been found there, still snoring, the next morning.

We were to return for several years, to a list of performers of dizzying variety. In one programme we had the conductor Klaus Tennstedt, on the next Oscar Peterson, rubbing shoulders with undergraduates from the Cambridge Footlights and flute players from Peru. Comedy acts as different as Victoria Wood, Jeremy Hardy, Angus Deayton and Hale and Pace all trooped through, as did the Hull Truck company and the National Youth Music Theatre, in which one of the outstanding talents was Toby Jones, whose career I have kept an eye on over the years, up to Dobby in the *Harry Potter* films and an Olivier award. His father, the wonderful actor Freddie Jones, came to watch proudly.

I had harboured thoughts about working on the national networks for some time, but there was a settled stable of accomplished broadcasters there already and I couldn't see much space for me. However, Radio 2 began asking some regional broadcasters to sit in on holiday relief. In fact, the first I knew of it was when I saw the name of Jimmy Mack, my Radio Scotland colleague, in the *Radio Times* as host of the *Early Show*. Fond as I was of Jimmy, I thought, 'Bugger that. If he's getting a go, then I am too.' So I sent off a letter to David Hatch, the Controller of Radio 2, asking to come and see him. I had a week's leave coming up so made plans to motor to London. A date was agreed and I duly presented myself on the fourth floor of Broadcasting House.

David Hatch was a bustling dynamo of a man, open, direct and to the point. His conversational style was friendly but combative. To his immediate enquiry, 'Well, now, why do you want to see me?', I replied that I knew he was trying out new people and I just wanted to let him know I existed. False modesty and understatement were not something to be tried with David.

'Of course I know you exist, it's my job to know about people like you. The question is, why should I employ you?' I was all for plain speaking so I gave an account of myself, ending with the phrase, 'So I thought you ought to give me a try before you made any final decisions.'

'I'll bear what you say in mind. Thanks anyway for coming in.'

Well, there we are, I thought, he doesn't like me, but at least I had given it a try. I set off for home convinced that I had got on his wrong side and my chances of getting a toe in the water at Radio 2 had slipped away. Not for the first time, my reading of situations proved so accurate that a call came very soon after, inviting me to sit in for Ray Moore on his next holiday.

It was September 1982. I had no leave booked, and anyway didn't want to seem to be too eager to ditch my Scottish responsibilities, so I arranged that after each morning's Radio 2 show I would do my Radio Scotland show 'up the line' from a London studio. In fact, on the Friday of that week, I had also been asked to present an edition of *Friday Night is Music Night* from Largs in Ayrshire, making it my first three-programme day. The things you do when you're young.

Radio 2 seemed very trusting. I had spoken to the producer, Dennis O'Keeffe, on the phone beforehand, and he told me just to turn up at Continuity C, where I would find the programme box and a technical operator, and he would see me after the show. This was absolutely standard practice at the time. Most daily record shows had no producer present; the presenter was left to get on with it. A box of records, a bunch of letters, a microphone and a bloke talking. That was all there was to it.

The programme slot ran from five o'clock until half past seven in the morning and for the first two hours was broadcast on Radio 1 as well as Radio 2. Apart from a recorded edition of Pause for Thought round about quarter past six, and various news bulletins, there was no other formal content, no guests, no features. As an exercise in making something out of nothing, it was wonderful training.

I drove down on the Sunday, with time in the evening to pop in to have a quick look at the studio to make sure I knew where everything was before checking in to the hotel immediately across the road from Broadcasting House, where the BBC had arranged a room. It was not the most salubrious of rooms but at least the bed was sleepable in, for the few hours I would get. On retiring for the night I asked the night porter, a tall, sinister man with a completely shaved head, in the days before such sights were commonplace, to call me at half past three. His response was incredulity mixed with outrage. 'I haven't got time to be knocking your door in the middle of the night! I've got things to do.' I retreated quickly, wrongfooted by his unexpected unwillingness to undertake what I imagined to be an integral part of his job, and also slightly fearful of just what these 'things' he had to do might be.

So, under my own steam, I rose at half past three and tottered over to BH for my first Radio 2 programme. Ray Moore had told me to get in early, as sorting the cards and letters took quite a while, but more importantly, it took the best part of an hour for the coffee to start working.

Luck plays a central role in anyone's career. Talent, ability and aptitude all have their place but without luck they are largely meaningless. The roadsides are littered with talented people who never got the breaks, never managed to be in the right place at the right time. This turned out to be my lucky day.

The programme went well enough; Ray had, typically, invited his listeners to write in to welcome me, and they had, in sufficient numbers. In the days before faxes, texts and emails, a few dozen cards were all you would get, and very grateful I was for them. The duty newsreader that morning was my old Radio 4 friend John Marsh, who was similarly trying his hand out on Radio 2, so I had familiar faces around.

Having got to the final half-hour, with two hours behind me I was comfortable and coasting towards a tidy finish at half past seven, when the news came in that Terry Wogan had slept in and was going to be late. Wonderful, I thought, just the chance to give me a few jokes at Terry's expense and a bit of banter when he arrived, presumably after about ten minutes. After twenty minutes, there was still no sign of Terry.

I had run out of records in my box, so his programme box was brought in and on I ploughed, past the eight o'clock news and into another half-hour. It was half past eight before he made it to the microphone, and I had been on air for three and a half hours. God knows what I talked about in those last sixty minutes but I had kept going, which in those circumstances seemed to be enough.

It certainly seemed to please the hierarchy, as I had visitations later from various representatives of management, all patting me on the head. This was not what I was used to. Terry was a big star and what he did made news, so the press took an interest, and the following day I found my name and face splashed across the newspapers. As an introduction to national broadcasting, it was pretty good. As the stroke of luck every career needs, it couldn't be bettered.

In a single bound, as the old comics liked to say, I had become a known quantity. Good though that was, it would only carry me so far. In the 2000s, a single burst of publicity is usually enough to ensure media work for two years; in the 1980s, the initial publicity had to be backed up by some proof of competence. I enjoyed my week in London, and went to lunches, shows and, yes, just pubs throughout my days, in sufficient amounts for David Hatch to hint in his gentlest manner that I ought to make sure I got enough sleep.

I have never needed more than one 'quiet word'. Much as I enjoy my socializing, no matter how late the night, I have always kept a careful eye on my next work engagement and would be deeply ashamed to get caught out in a tired and emotional state on air.

There was once a fairly boozy Christmas Eve in Broadcasting House where the drinks flowed in the Control Room well into the night. The Radio 4 duty newsreader, who had done the late shift to be followed by the early Christmas morning shift, as was the custom, indulged a little too freely and read the first news of the day in a 'relaxed' state, though by all accounts he didn't sound too bad at all.

Nevertheless, when our man realized that he had read the Christmas morning news in a slightly inebriated condition, he was so crestfallen at his lapse that he immediately wrote out his resignation and left it on his boss's desk. When management finally returned after the holiday, since no complaints had been received, his letter was simply torn up and the whole incident consigned to the dustbin.

I like to think I would have had the courage to do something similar, although I would probably have been a little more pragmatic and waited to hear if any complaints had come in before I offered my head on a plate. In my case they might have been keener to take it.

So I slackened off on the roistering and completed my stint, having established some credentials at least on the national airwaves. The Friday night concert was the climax of this intense week, and my recollections of it are unclear, as by this stage I was becoming a little weary; after the *Early Show*, I had done the Radio Scotland programme and then dragged myself off to Heathrow for a flight to Glasgow, where I picked up my car at the airport and drove to Largs. Having got up at 3.30 a.m., I would finish my working day 400 miles away and 18 hours later. I do recall that it was the only concert I have ever done where there were three separate orchestral pianists. Only one piano, but three people to play it.

Allan Cameron, the pianist booked first, was a beautiful player but a fragile character. He was happiest in a studio, and when he had to confront an audience and play as part of a large orchestra he had a tendency to become extremely nervous. To counteract this, he would have a drink or two, or possibly more, and his playing would deteriorate accordingly. While he would cope with the normal demands of the odd orchestral piece without having recourse to the 'nerve tonic', solo work would have him bellying up to the bar, so for the jazzier and more exposed piano parts that the programme included the producers hired the gifted Peggy O'Keeffe.

All well there, but when it was discovered that one of the orchestral arrangements contained an interpolation of part of Grieg's Piano Concerto, Peggy politely but firmly said she couldn't and wouldn't attempt it, so the call went out to Bernard Sumner, who turned up for that one piece alone.

To see this procession of pianists playing musical chairs on the piano stool must have had the audience wondering just how the BBC chose to spend their licence fees.

With my busy week finished, I was able to resume being a family man once again, but I was energized by my reception at Radio 2 and further ambitions had been fired in me. I couldn't see it happening at the time, but work was beginning to take the upper hand in the constant balancing act of life, and I was setting myself up for a fall.

I now had a successful daily programme on radio in Scotland plus regular other programmes and concerts, further requests to come and deputize at Radio 2 were in the offing and I was even being offered the odd television appearance. To this day, I've maintained a healthy distance from the box. I always regarded myself as a radio broadcaster first and foremost. Television work, like writing, was a pleasant change, a treat, but not something I wished to pursue specially. That said, I was happy to do the odd turn if it appealed to me.

I became something of a regular on *The Best of Brass*, as the guest supporter or presenter of the Scottish band that made it into the show, usually the Whitburn Burgh Band. Their conductor, Major Peter Parkes, told me about another brass band programme they had been on, presented by the singer Bill McCue. 'I couldn't believe the jokes he was telling the audience,' he said, 'women and children included! I wouldn't have told them to my soldiers!' I knew Bill, and I could believe it.

One such, delivered off air to the kiddies, went like this. A man walks into a café and looks at the menu. 'I'll have some of your pissoles,' he announces. The waitress frowns, takes the menu and studies it, then says, 'Oh, that's a misprint. It shouldn't be a P there, it should say R.'

'All right then,' says the man, 'I'll have R soles.' Like I say, family fun.

Another television excursion found me freezing my intimate parts off on the esplanade of Edinburgh Castle beside Keith Chegwin one wintry Saturday morning on the *Multi-Coloured Swap Shop*. I was swathed in thermal underwear but could still hardly speak for teeth chattering. It was my first meeting with Keith, who was, and remains, as mad as a box of frogs. In a very nice way, though.

I did a *Children in Need* show for Scotland alongside Mary Marquis, whose composed and cool exterior on screen covered up a highly witty and amusing woman. We were teamed up again later for the radio coverage of the Queen's visit to Glasgow.

Radio bosses don't like their carefully constructed schedules messed around with and in this case, to minimize disruption, one programme was cancelled and we were allotted its space, between the midday news summary and the main news programme at half past twelve. This looked good, as Her Majesty was due to alight from her limousine in George Square at midday, process around the square glad-handing the locals and mount the steps to the City Chambers in time for lunch at half past.

Mary and I were parked at an office window overlooking the square and provided with notes on the statues and history of the buildings in case the need to fill should arise. Otherwise, we were simply to describe the royal progress, so we worked out between us how we would split the commentary and sat back.

The first sign things were not going to go swimmingly was the arrival of a large black car in George Square at ten minutes to twelve. At first we thought it was some flunkeys or minor royals, but no, out stepped Her Maj. and she set off on her peregrinations a full thirteen minutes before we were due on air. We shouted back up to Broadcasting House, but to no avail; the schedule would run as laid down and we would still have to wait for the news summary to finish before we could get going.

By the time we received the cue, the Queen was a tiny figure in lavender on the far side of the square, and within five minutes of our getting underway she had disappeared up the steps and into the Chambers for, no doubt, a refreshing pre-prandial drink. This left us with approximately twenty-one minutes of airtime and no activity to describe. The crowds melted away, leaving behind a street-cleaning van and a few billowing newspapers. Mary and I soldiered on, recounting the exact route Her Majesty had taken round the square and desperately trying to remember what sort of people she had talked to, with a considerable amount of time taken to describe in great detail just what she had been wearing.

As the clock ticked achingly slowly towards half past twelve, our airy banter had descended into back alleys like,

'I don't know if you know the background to the statue over on the far side of the square, Ken, but . . .' and, 'Well, Mary, this information kiosk down in front of us is a little older than it looks . . .'.

I knew when I heard myself referring to the stops where the night buses left from that we had run this particular well dry, so I handed back to the studio two minutes early, and sod the consequences. I was due to rush back to the studio to start my own programme at 1.40 p.m. but I made sure I stopped off at a pub on Great Western Road for a quick sinew-stiffener.

The call to do a little more Radio 2 work came in early 1983, and I found myself sitting in again for Ray Moore, for a whole month this time, which was a real chance to connect with the audience. I thought, in my youthful foolishness, that an extended period of early rises would make them more bearable. The reverse was true; the 3.30 a.m. alarm is less and less welcome with each passing day. I would go out for meals in the evening and nod off during the main course. I went to theatre shows and had to be woken up at the interval. Ray had become a good friend, and this friendship was to blossom in the years to come as we found we took much the same views on work and life. He confirmed to me that early starts never got any easier; doing it day after day simply made it less of a shock to the system.

I sat in for John Dunn on his drivetime show, too. This was closer to the format of my Radio Scotland show, with interviews throughout. I wanted to show that I could do this sort of work but I was quietly discovering that my preference was for the 'box of records and you're on your own' type of programme. At first glance, these seem more difficult, as there are no signposts or crutches to help you on your way, but as far as I'm concerned the reverse is true. The lack of things that must be mentioned or done at certain times gives an enormous freedom. I also always felt that a guest coming into the studio broke the bond between listener and broadcaster. It changed the nature of the communication: in a sense, I stopped talking to the listener and started talking to this other person in the studio.

It's why I've never really gone for the co-host idea; the danger is that you talk to each other and the listener becomes simply an eavesdropper. Some people make it work brilliantly, Jonathan Ross for example, but for me radio is best when it's one person in a studio talking to one person listening. I was coming to the conclusion that this was the style of programme I wanted to do.

Meanwhile, the daily show back in the Glasgow studio underwent a change in 1983 with a switch to an afternoon slot. Well, all afternoon in fact. I was to pick up after *The World at One* at 1.40 p.m. and carry on until 5 p.m. This was a considerable upping of airtime from the hour and three-quarters I had been doing, and made it by some margin the longest show on the network.

One element that did not survive was the soap, *Kilbreck*. Its Health Education funding ran out and that was that. I was not to get away without some outside influence though; once a month I would have to give up an hour to *Scottish Question Time* live from the House of Commons, and every

afternoon I would have to incorporate a pre-school children's programme by the name of *Nickety-Nackety*. Scheduling
on Radio Scotland was often a matter of necessity rather
than choice.

Nickety-Nackety was the Scottish answer to *Listen with
Mother*. I am greatly in favour of radio programmes aimed
at the under-fives. I am somewhat less in favour of them
when they are wedged into my show. The host of this delight
was the experienced actor Harriet Buchan, later to become
the wheelchair-bound wife of Taggart, and her sidekick was
a scarecrow by the name of Tumshie the Tattie-Bogle, played
with more care than the part deserved by Jack Shedden.
They gave it their all, but however well crafted it was for
toddlers, it stuck out even more than *Kilbreck*; not so much
a sore thumb, more the whole arm up to the elbow.

Scottish Question Time was one of those things that BBC
Scotland had to do. Charter Output is the internal term for
an activity that no commercial organization in its right mind
would undertake, but which falls neatly under the banner
of public service. As far as I could see, the only people being
serviced were the politicians, who could prove to their
constituents that they were both present and awake in the
House at least once a month. An hour of this vital debate
meant I was effectively doing two separate shows on those
days, except that I couldn't wander off to the canteen in
between times in case the line to Westminster went down
and I had to pick up.

On normal days, the throughput of items was fairly heavy.
There was to be an interview roughly every twenty minutes,
with the exception of one half-hour slot given over to a star
guest, and of course the toddlers' time. Needless to say, we

had been given no increase in budget or staffing to achieve this increased output; do what you've been doing, but do more of it, was the message. Our production and research team worked wonders in coming up with fresh ideas and guests, but we naturally became more reliant on new books or surveys in magazines than we would have liked.

I would be doing seven or eight general interviews each day, from briefs supplied by the team, plus the star guest whose piece I personally researched from the cuttings supplied by the library. I worked out that I was conducting more interviews than any other presenter on the station, including the morning news guys. I pointed this out after the first year in my contract negotiations, without of course making any impact on the fee.

BBC Scotland's Contracts staff had a long tradition of charmingly but firmly refusing to part with any cash. A pained expression would pass across their faces and it would be explained that, while they would love to pay more, so many other parts of the corporation would be deprived of funds, staff would be laid off, their children would starve, their houses would be repossessed and so forth, that it would be quite impossible. I didn't really see how giving me an extra fiver a day would have all these devastating effects, but they were immovable.

If you have ever fretted about the BBC being profligate with licence payers' money, I can only say that a meeting with any of these staff would have left you thinking the money was as safe as if it were in the deepest vault in Threadneedle Street. Not a pound left their grasp without a spirited fight being put up for its retention. Had they been in the vicinity of the Scotland–England railway line in 1963,

Ronnie Biggs and his mates would have left with only a half-crown postal order.

The actor Jameson Clark, who as well as appearing in every British film from 1945 onwards which required a Highland policeman turned out 'little pieces for the wireless', once told me that he had been booked by a BBC radio producer in London to narrate a series, with a very healthy fee being mentioned. He did the work, but when the contract came through it was for less than half the amount agreed.

Jimmy Clark rang the producer, who couldn't understand why the full fee hadn't gone through, and he promised to check. He traced the detail through the Contracts department in London, all right there, and then got to the Scottish end, where, sure enough, he found that the fee had been halved. On enquiring why this might be he received the stunning answer, 'We can't have people in Scotland getting used to this kind of money.'

A couple of attractive ways of supplementing my income came my way; I was now able to freelance as a voice-over artist, so I had joined Equity, the actors' union. Membership was a prerequisite for voicing television commercials in those days, but, wouldn't you know, it was years before any of that work was offered. However, I found a niche doing trade films and the like, and BBC Scotland hired me back to do the odd television continuity shift.

This was the most technically complex work I had ever done, or would ever do. On joining the Presentation department I had trained in it, but much preferred radio so had hardly had the opportunity to use the skills, which involved vision mixing, sound mixing, cueing videotape, slide loading, clock fixing, caption typing and, oh yes, speaking on the telly, all at the same time.

Our job was to opt out of the BBC1 network after each programme, put up our own symbol, the spinning globe, and say, 'BBC1 Scotland,' instead of the generic ident, thus fooling the Scottish public into thinking that everything from *Basil Brush* to *The Nine O'Clock News* was specially tailored to a Celtic audience.

It goes without saying that the viewing public cared more about whether the programmes were worth watching than whether a Scottish voice had introduced them, and the same went for home-grown output. They wanted locally produced programmes but they had to be as good as the national alternative. Naturally, any time a local programme went out, a national one had to be sacrificed. Listings magazines were less detailed then, so viewers would not necessarily know what it was they were being deprived of for the privilege of seeing Calum Kennedy singing Gaelic songs, unless something went wrong in presentation.

One announcer neglected to put his desk in circuit, meaning the scheduled episode of a show called *Castles in the Air*, which featured nice singers delivering Scottish songs to the backdrop of some of the country's stately homes, failed to go out on air. It was a reasonably popular show, so this alone would have generated several complaints. When the Scottish viewers were treated instead to an edition of *Steptoe and Son*, they realized what they had been missing and the phones started buzzing. Worse still, after five minutes, the announcer realized what he had done and threw the transmission key, abruptly losing Harry H. Corbett and Wilfrid Brambell and immediately gaining Peter Morrison singing 'Ae Fond Kiss' perched on a parapet atop Glamis Castle. That was when the phones went into meltdown.

No wonder any shift I undertook in television continuity was accompanied by flop sweats at every junction. The question I was most asked about the experience concerned the globe. How big was it? About the size of a tennis ball was the answer. It was plastic, lit from within, and had a concave mirror behind it. It was also black and white; the colours were synthesized on to it and could be changed. I passed many a bored hour by trying it out in magenta or lime green, almost forgetting to return it to the required blue and gold on one occasion.

The operation of the desk was complex and was not helped by its occasional failure. Once, about to introduce the Sunday morning religious service, one colleague found that none of the controls reacted to his commands. Understandably frustrated, he cried out, 'Jesus Christ, the bloody mixer's buggered!' As luck would have it, the fault, which had deactivated all his faders, had also made the microphone go live and his remarks went out all over Scotland.

Complaints started to come in and some elements of the press got hold of it and approached the church minister whose service had been so inappropriately announced. His response was a beauty: 'At times of stress, one must expect technical terms to be used.'

The other extra activity that came my way was a radio programme called *Beat the Band*. This was an old format where listeners would call in with a song title and win a prize if the band didn't know it. Our new elements were to make the listener sing the song with the band attempting to accompany them, and to use musicians who were not only knowledgeable and competent but also funny. Our approach was that anyone who phoned in to take part in such a programme had forfeited all rights to dignity and so they had the whotsit mercilessly ripped out of them.

Every member of the band was miked up and could contribute to the banter. Bernard Sumner was the pianist and leader, with Frank Pantrini on sax, Brian Payne on bass and Andy White on drums. Andy was known as the £7 Beatle after a newspaper article outed him as having been the session drummer on 'Love Me Do' and having been paid that amount for his work. 'Better rates than I'm getting here,' was his mournful reaction. He went off to America after one series, in the hope no doubt of improving those rates, and was replaced by Roy Sneddon.

I probably laughed more on that show than any other; I was always better at making other people corpse rather than losing it myself, but on this show I fell apart fairly frequently. Sumner was very quick, witty and often simply rude. Such was the level of suppressed hysteria that we could be set off for very little reason. One man who called in announced his song as, 'The Village Pump'. Now, in Glasgow, that last word had a sexual connotation at the time, and there was a certain amount of sniggering. When Sumner asked, in his sub-Kenneth Williams style, 'Anybody we know?', there was a long period of coughs, moans, whimpers, but no speech, and the poor bewildered caller was left to keep the show going with cries of, 'Are you there?' and, 'Will I sing it now?'

This programme also confirmed to me the ability of musicians to drink everything and anything at any hour of the day or night. Even I had to decline when offered a capful of Glayva at nine o'clock on a Sunday morning. *Beat the Band* developed a kind of cult following, and seemed to become something of a weekend hangover-cure institution. We took the show on the road, too, and played some of the small theatres around central Scotland, usually with an invited singing guest. We did one night at a full-sized theatre, the Ayr Gaiety, when I was specially delighted to meet our vocalist, Kathie Kay of *Billy Cotton Band Show* fame. Having said earlier I wasn't a hero-worshipper, I do admit to enjoying meeting people I've heard on the radio.

The show fizzled out when the suits saw the bills, mainly I think for Bernard's arrangements, and *Beat the Band*, while never actually axed, one year simply failed to come back from its annual break. Although it was twenty-five years ago, I still occasionally meet people who say, 'I used to listen to you on *Beat the Band*. It was terrible rubbish but good fun!' A typical Scottish compliment.

Back on the daily show, there was a steady procession of star guests. Billy Connolly came up as a prospect; he had gone through well-publicized marital difficulties and had begun his relationship with Pamela Stephenson, and the Scottish press had turned on him. As a result, we were told he would not answer any questions about his private life and would very probably walk out if the matter were raised. I happily accepted these conditions, as I knew there would be plenty of material for a good interview without delving into it, but I also felt there was a chance he might discuss it if I could get him in the right frame of mind.

He couldn't come in to the Glasgow studio so we had to do it 'down the line', with me in Scotland and him in a London cubbyhole. This could have formed a further obstacle, but in the event he warmed up quickly and was being as entertaining as you would expect. Soon he was relaxed and chatting away, when he dropped into his discourse the words, 'Pamela and the children'. This was the signal I had been waiting for, but if I crashed in with a crass question he might still walk, so I took the opportunity to give him a free kick against the Scottish papers by asking about his now fraught relationship with them. He took the chance enthusiastically and, after landing a verbal boot or two on journalists, softened and talked quite movingly about the difficulties of divorce and starting a new relationship, and the effects on all the parties, especially the children, of having the details played out in the pages of newspapers.

By the end of the interview, he had spent about half of it talking about the very subject that had been barred from discussion, and it had happened without having to ask a single direct question. Once again it proved that people, even famous people, like talking about the things that matter to them, and if you can create the right atmosphere of trust and intimacy, they can and will allow a little window into their inner thoughts.

Knowing that many of our guests were on the publicity treadmill with a book or film to promote, and may have been interviewed five times already that day, I attempted to seek out quirkier lines of enquiry. Mostly it worked quite well, since they enjoyed thinking of something other than stock answers to stock questions. The former *Sunday Times* editor and author Harold Evans said to the researcher after our interview that I had put questions he had never been asked before. Of course, that may have been a subtle insult, but my golden rule is, if in doubt, assume it's a compliment.

Not every star interview went to plan. A well-known TV

actor, publicizing a theatre tour, sat in his chair with a bored expression answering monosyllabically, if at all, and batting most things over to his director with a 'He can answer that.' I simply stopped asking Mr Famous anything and talked to the director, which irked him even more.

He seemed to fail to realize that the publicity interview is a two-way street; we got access to big names, they got bums on seats. He evidently felt he was well known enough to fill theatres without having to do this. His director knew better. Anyway, the Curse of Bruce, which rarely fails to strike anyone who has given me a hard time, worked very well as I have not seen this man on screen or stage for many years, whereas his then TV co-star is still a very big name. Cross the Bruce at your peril!

We had a number of regular contributors, including John Brown of the Scottish Film Council talking about movies, Gerald Warner with a witty essay, John Leese discussing food, and Emilio Coia on art. Emilio was a distinguished artist who both interviewed and sketched a famous Scot each month for the *Scottish Field* magazine. He was a small, dapper man with twinkling eyes and a natural charm. He used to phone up the female researchers and ask, 'Who is that?', and on being told would, from the other end of the line, continue, 'May I say you're looking lovely today.' They fell for it every time.

The journalist Sally O'Sullivan, who at that time worked for a Scottish Sunday newspaper, was also a regular visitor. Quite apart from her broadcast contributions, I enjoyed chatting with her about the latest gossip in the newspaper world. A new editor had been appointed at the *Glasgow Evening Times*, Charles Wilson, who had a reputation as a hard man of the press. I had asked a few people about him when someone casually remarked, 'Of course, you know he's married to Sally.' I didn't, and suddenly panicked that I might have unwittingly asked her whether her beloved husband was a complete bastard.

I decided to keep quiet and hope for the best, but the next week, when Sally came in, she said, 'I hear you're worried that you asked me whether Charlie is a ****. Well, you didn't. And he is!'

With the sheer numbers of people coming in and out of the studio each day, there was an inevitability about something going wrong and, sure enough, the day arrived when a man I had never seen before was ushered into the studio with no word of introduction. After the usual hellos and such like, I still had no clue as to who this man was or why he was here so I pressed the talkback button to ask for some notes, keeping it vague lest our guest should clock that he was completely unknown to me. There was no response from the other side of the glass since, it later transpired, the talkback had failed.

I tried a ruse I had been saving up for just such an occasion, and said, 'Just for level to set the microphones, can you tell me about yourself?', and he helpfully replied that he was the president of the Society of Ethical Stage Hypnotists. I relaxed a little, at least now knowing what I might be able to speak to him about, but there remained the problem of the name, which I had been expecting him to include in his little dissertation. I went for broke. 'How do you spell your name?' This could have ended in tears, if he had started saying, 'S – M – I – T – H,' which would have left me nowhere to go except weakly offering, 'No Y then?'

Luckily, though, he said, 'Yes, a lot of people use a K but it's Casson with a C, Peter Casson.' Bingo! I now had everything I needed and the interview could proceed. It turned out to be fascinating, even if I say so myself, as he had strong views on the way some hypnotists were using the members of the public who attended their shows. Or perhaps my judgement was coloured by overwhelming feelings of relief.

While I was enjoying the show, the flow of interviews seemed never-ending and I began to find I was losing curiosity about the guests; it was becoming a sausage-machine, and I was in danger of simply processing interviewees, in the manner of a bored New York immigration officer. As often happens, synchronicity takes a hand, and the prospect of regular, perhaps full-time, work at Radio 2 was beckoning.

Six

'Just Play Lots of Nice Music'

In early 1984, the new Controller of Radio 2, Bryant Marriott, called to offer me my own show on the network. The *Late Show* on a Saturday night would run from eleven till one with me simply playing music. I don't think I hesitated for more than a nanosecond. It would mean I would be working all week in Glasgow and travelling to and from London each weekend, but what the hell, I was young and it was the opportunity I had been waiting for.

Any new show on a radio station means the departure of an existing show, and in this case I was replacing Pete Murray on one of his two weekly programmes. His other one was also being dropped and he was leaving the station. I hated the feeling that I was at least partially responsible for this – the man was a broadcasting icon after all – and I was therefore a little uneasy when I met Pete at a social gathering not long after. I needn't have been, as he was kindness and generosity itself and has continued to be so every time we have met. His attitude taught me how to cope with career disappointments; if you must blame someone, blame the bosses who made the decision, but not the person who's got the job. The chances are they've been sacked a few times already; allow them the break.

The Saturday *Late Show* was produced by Geoff Mullin; he delivered a music plot, or running order, that was a little delight each week, hampered as he was by the usual lack of 'needletime'. The BBC's agreement with the music industry at that time was for only a limited number of commercial records to be played in any week: the needletime. It was never enough. Any other music needed to fill the schedules was to be by the corporation's own orchestras or session musicians, but 'live' in any event, with some library music or foreign recordings bought in for good measure.

A Radio 2 disc show needed about sixteen music items per hour, of which on our programme four had to be sessions. The traditional complaint by presenters was that the sessions stood out amongst the discs, either because the music was of a different style, too old-fashioned, or simply of a poorer standard. While there was some truth in those complaints from time to time, Geoff was careful to commission good sessions which blended into the show more easily and he placed them well in the plot, to make them less of a musical sore thumb.

My week now went something like this: Monday to Friday I would have breakfast with the family, then head off to the BBC for about half past ten, do the show through the afternoon and get home about seven o'clock on a good day. If there were any other things on, sometimes only just drinks with the team, I could be rather later. On Saturday I would pack up my overnight bag and head to Glasgow airport in the afternoon, catch the shuttle to Heathrow, plod over to Broadcasting House, do the *Late Show* and retire to a hotel room. On Sunday morning, it was up and off to Heathrow again, the 10.15 a.m. plane and home for Sunday lunch.

I wasn't spending enough time with my wife and children, and the cracks began to show. I was enjoying the company of one of the researchers on the show, but we were both married people and it never occurred to either of us that it could become dangerous, so the warning signs went unheeded. Trouble lay ahead.

1984 was a good year. A very good year. The Scottish show was successful, the Radio 2 *Late Show* had added audience and I was asked to sit in for Steve Jones on his lunchtime show. Paul Walters was producing this. Steve had only just got his daytime slot and it was proving very popular with the listeners. For one write-in competition, with a not terribly spectacular prize, Pauly told me they had received over ten thousand entries, a huge postbag by the standards of the day.

I would never have dreamt that Steve would be ousted from his show by the end of his first year. It was, however, still the time when BBC managers were much less answerable to the public than now. Schedules were there to be played with, and presenters were disposable. After all, the commercial market was much smaller and the corporation's attitude tended to assume that everyone wanted to work for them. Steve was an excellent broadcaster, whom I had known from his days at Radio Clyde, and deserved better treatment than he received.

Other changes were in the offing, one of them major. In the late summer Terry Wogan announced he would be leaving his breakfast show at the end of the year, to take up his three-nights-a-week television show. This news grabbed my attention. Terry was just about the best-known and most liked person in the country at that time; he could do no wrong. His show was hugely popular and his departure would leave a big gap. What interested me, though, was not the immediate succession, but the knock-on effect. If someone from the existing schedule was promoted to the breakfast slot, as I assumed would be the case, it might leave a space for me to slip in.

I felt Ray Moore was the man for the job, and that view was not simply based on bias due to his being a friend. He was already the regular stand-in for Terry, was known to the audience and had a strong personal following, as well as a distinctive, quirky sense of humour all of his own.

David Hamilton was the other name in the frame; he too would have done an excellent job. Either of those choices would have left a gap in the daytime schedule and I had, I felt, a good chance of filling the shoes of whoever landed the gig.

Sure enough, one evening just a few weeks after Terry's announcement, the phone rang and the familiar brisk tones of Bryant Marriott, the Controller of Radio 2, came ringing down the line. Bryant had been a jazz drummer and years of shouting above the sound of a Premier kit had left him with what you might call a carrying voice; not best suited for whispered conversation. He was using, for him, conspiratorial tones tonight though.

The exact details of the discussion are a blur now; his words, 'We wondered if you'd consider taking over the breakfast show,' knocked me sideways. It was completely, utterly unexpected, and all I can remember is tottering downstairs to tell Fiona with what must have been a baffled expression on my face.

Bryant had asked me to think about it and get back to him in a couple of days. I needed a lot longer. After the initial euphoria of such an offer, the cold reality of what might be involved started to bite. And the pitfalls seemed obvious. I was a completely unknown quantity in England; although there had been a couple of newspaper items of the 'People to Watch' variety after I started the Saturday night show, I was hardly even known to the wider Radio 2 audience, let alone the press and general public. And I was taking over from an icon. Comparisons would be made, probably to my detriment, and there might well be a hostile reaction. It was a classic poisoned chalice.

On the other hand, it would launch me on a national stage. With the confidence of youth, I knew I could handle the pressure and the exposure. Crucially, I knew that if it didn't work out, I would survive somehow, even if it meant going back to the shipping forecast again, which I would do quite happily. The fame, profile, notoriety, call it what you will, was of no real consequence to me; so with that firm feeling, I realized that I had come round to deciding to accept the offer.

Fiona was entirely supportive, even though it would mean the uprooting of our little family and a move south to a new life in London; she knew how much it meant to me.

This process took a few days, by the end of which Bryant phoned me again to ask if he could please have an answer as he would have to make other plans if I declined, so I said yes, and sat back to await the storm of activity that would follow the announcement.

During this period, there was intense speculation as to who the new presenter would be, and the bookies were taking large sums of money. To begin with, I was well down the betting, an outsider, and as I was one of only a handful of people who knew the real outcome, I ought to have hotfooted it down to William Hill and put not just my shirt on it but my entire wardrobe.

For some reason, I delayed doing it until the massed bets of the BBC management using their inside knowledge had pushed me into the favourite position, by which time I would have made about tuppence profit, so I never got to the bookie's window. The only time in my life when I would have in my gift the very definition of a dead cert bet, and I missed it.

For years afterwards, I would meet people who had been in the loop, and they'd say, 'I made a lot of money on you,' and I would smile thinly and say, 'Good for you,' through gritted teeth.

When the news broke, a press frenzy erupted and I was interviewed by everyone from *The Times* to the *People's Friend*. Almost everyone asked the same questions, and I immediately sympathized with all the interviewees who had passed through my studio as part of an 'all-stations' tour; their smiling presence must have been difficult to maintain after the twenty-fifth 'groundhog day' conversation.

The tabloids were generally happy with a phone call and a couple of good quotes; the broadsheets wanted to visit the house, meet the family and then go off and attempt some cod psychoanalysis of me. On balance, I preferred the tabloid approach. Their interest in me was clear; I was news and I would get a fair shake from them just now. If things didn't turn out well for me, they would very probably give me a kicking. It was straightforward.

The broadsheet people could be more devious; they might try to worm their way into your trust, either by pretending to be a bit socially gauche or shy, or by shameless flattery, and then go away and write highly judgemental pieces. If they got into your house, they would invariably ask to use the loo so they could have a snoop around. I caught one in our bedroom going through the drawers. I stopped doing home interviews after that.

The question I was most often asked was, 'Are you going into television?' I resented the implication that it would be some kind of promotion, although it's still a widespread belief today, and I had a terrible feeling that in many eyes I was not only expected to take over Terry Wogan's show, but his wider career and lifestyle too.

On the whole, though, my experience of being hot news was pretty painless, at least at that time. The intricacies and differing power bases of BBC management were to cause me more immediate problems.

My producer was to be Paul Walters. He was a tall, good-looking man, a fanatical golfer with, he had been told once, the look of Errol Flynn about him. Paul hadn't needed to be told that twice and even had a photo on his office wall of the legendary actor next to one of him wearing a Robin Hood hat. He was a lovely bloke. He had been producing Steve Jones's show and was still reeling from the news that the programme was being taken off to make way for David Jacobs at lunchtime. The bond between producers and their presenters is strong and management know that, so very often keep them in the dark. I asked him if he'd been given any inkling that the suits didn't like the show. The only criticism they had made, he said, was that they once said Steve should talk a little less. The great communications industry.

I became aware about this time that there had been a strong lobby in one branch of management for Ray Moore to be given the breakfast show, and while I didn't think that anyone would actively work against me, I knew that it wouldn't only be the general public I would have to win round. Ray himself, of course, was typically good-hearted about the matter and never let his natural disappointment affect our friendship.

Before I left Radio Scotland, I managed to corpse one of my colleagues, quite unintentionally, which is always the best way. The duty announcer came in to the show each afternoon to do a little package of trails for programmes later in the day, all scripted and very straightforward. Alister Smith was the man on call that day and he came in a few minutes early, while a recorded piece was going out. It so happened a photographer, Tom Kidd, was in the studio doing some publicity shots and we were all chatting away in a relaxed fashion. Smithy was a very good audience for stories and gags and had an explosive and infectious laugh. Somehow the subject of the Glasgow Empire came up and I told them a tale about a performer called G. H. Elliott. Almost everything about this story is unrepeatable in polite society, containing as it does not one, but two Very Offensive Words, so I will spare you the details, but when I got to the tagline, Smithy burst into violent laughter and couldn't be stopped. This set Tom and me off. Unfortunately, the cue was about to come for me to speak. I introduced Smithy in the briefest manner possible and left him to it.

Suppressing laughter is almost physically impossible. I didn't try, and Tom was actually on the floor, holding his stomach. Poor old Smithy attempted to keep a lid on it but his voice was constantly breaking into falsetto and there were several brief gusts of outright laughter, which he tried to pretend were coughs, peppering his trail for a deadly serious documentary on child poverty.

By the end of it, we were sore with laughter and wiping tears from our faces. Tom and I, that is; Smithy looked rather more concerned, realizing that he may just have done the equivalent of handing in his notice live on air. As usual, no one in management seemed to have heard it, and the only responses from listeners were to ask us to play it again, so his job was saved, but no thanks to me.

BBC Scotland gave me a good send-off, with a final show in which many previous guests came back to join in the occasion, and Emilio Coia presented me with the original of the sketch he had done of me for the *Scottish Field* magazine, which touched me greatly. At the party afterwards, I was presented with a fine set of golf clubs, which I tussled with for many years before realizing that the game and I were never going to be natural partners, but they still reside in my shed, as a memory of many happy years and some wonderful people.

On 5 January 1985, I left my temporary home in Chiswick in a BBC taxi at 6.45 a.m. and headed for Continuity H in Broadcasting House, London, to begin my tenure as Radio 2's breakfast host. I wasn't alone; a film crew from BBC breakfast television dogged my every step from leaving the flat to going on the air, so it was anything but an easy, relaxed first day. It was nice of them to take an interest, especially since I was going to be their main competition, but it's very difficult to behave naturally with a large camera and three people huddled round it everywhere you go. I was aware that many ears would be tuned my way, with a fair proportion of them likely to be critical, but I tried to do what I always did, that is, ignore the outside world and speak only to the listener.

My meetings with Radio 2 management had impressed upon me the need to play the long game; to ease myself into the slot and 'just play lots of nice music'. So, no format. I wasn't unhappy with this, as it gave me the freedom to go my own way, but a faint warning bell rang. The first day came and went; there was a flurry of publicity, followed by an outbreak of reaction, hardly any of which I read, as neither the good nor the bad was likely to be any kind of accurate guide.

Some people kindly drew my attention to quoted pleasant remarks about me; just as many seemed only too keen to quote in detail the nastier ones. On the whole, I would rather know when there's been a negative comment about me; after all, it might have some worth and I could learn from it. Well, that's the intellectual approach; in practice, I read it, mutter under my breath that the writer is a ****ing idiot and make a mental entry in my Big Hate Book. It does, though, always surprise me that some friends and colleagues can't wait to pass on the fact that you've been slagged off, without bothering to think whether you really want to know.

There was a strong positive postbag to the programme, and a small negative one, and I was told that in general that was the broader reaction. A loss of audience had been expected, and the wiser heads opined that it would take a year or even two to pick up again. Would I be given the time?

I was having good fun on air, and off-air having just as much. My announcing colleague from Scotland, Douglas Brock, had very generously offered me a room in his Chiswick flat and during the week I enjoyed a busy social life. Every record company, every plugger, every publisher seemed to want to take me to lunch, and I was only too happy to accept.

In those days, record company lunches were legendary. They seemed to have unlimited entertaining budgets and always booked the best restaurants and ordered the finest wines. The lunches would drag on until four or five o'clock, with port and brandy being brought round by weary-looking waiters in their shirtsleeves.

Naturally, as far as the BBC was concerned, there had to be some rules about the dangers of undue influence. It was acceptable for a presenter and producer to be taken to lunch by a record company, or plugger, or artist, so long as no attempt was made during the lunch to persuade, cajole, bribe, praise or even mention any record they might want us to play. Under those tight guidelines, we could eat and drink all day. As we did.

Paul was responsible for choosing the music, with the understanding that I could ask for, or veto, anything I wanted. He knew all the pluggers and record execs and what they were promoting but I very often didn't. I knew their names and sometimes which company they worked for, but in almost every case had no idea which record they were pushing, so I was incapable of being corrupted. They say there's no such thing as a free lunch but I think I came as near to it as is humanly possible.

We were playing a lot of new records at the time; indeed, the criticism most often levelled against the BBC was that Radios 1 and 2 were too close together. The problem lay, I felt, with Radio 1, in that it was trying to appeal to listeners beyond its natural age range. Ostensibly a teenage and twenties station, they had no qualms about going for the thirty- and forty-something market during the daytime schedule. The obvious way ahead was for the corporation to put Radio 1 back in its box and allow Radio 2 to serve its natural audience, but the suits were on the point of deciding on a course that would push Radio 2 into becoming an elderly persons' ghetto.

This would have its own effect on me later, but for now I was getting on with, as suggested by management, playing some nice music, old and new. About three months in, I felt the show needed some added elements. The listeners' letters were coming in but the programme needed more. I asked my executive producer, John Meloy, if we could have a selection of newspapers each day, not for me to read out slavishly, but to provide a little extra by way of subject matter and to allow us to be a little more current and informative. John was in agreement; he couldn't see a problem but said he would just run it by the production heads to be sure.

He came back the next day looking somewhat bewildered. 'They said no,' he muttered in a dazed manner. 'They said you couldn't have them because Gloria Hunniford sometimes reads out snippets on her show and they don't want a clash.'

I couldn't believe it. The breakfast show, the most high-profile programme in the schedule, was being denied a couple of quids' worth of newspapers each day because the after-noon show used a few lines from them. Gloria tended to read out showbiz gossip and oddities; that was not how I planned to use the resource. But they hadn't even bothered to check what kind of material I would need or how I would use it; all I got was a cold no.

When I met with one of the production heads not long after, I asked why I couldn't be given newspapers. 'Terry didn't need any features,' he said. I pointed out that for many years Terry had had Fight the Flab, his Racing Bulletin and such like.

'That was a long time ago when he was just starting,' came the reply.

'But I'm just starting!' I countered. The point seemed lost on him. There would be no papers and, by implication, no help.

At that point I knew that my time on breakfast would be limited. I was going to be hung out to dry. All I could do was try to ensure my survival.

I was getting requests to appear on lots of other things, some radio interviews, panel games and bits of TV. Mike Read was the Radio 1 breakfast host at this time and he was also presenting *Saturday Superstore,* the successor to *Swap Shop* on Saturday morning TV. I was asked to go on one week, and such was the rivalry between the networks, Bryant Marriott promised me a bottle of champagne if I could get a Radio 2 golf umbrella in shot during my appearance. When I readily took up the challenge, he added that it must be opened fully. I still happily took on the task.

I can't now quite remember my exact modus operandi, or what conversational ploy I pulled off to achieve it, but I both raised and fully opened the brolly, and Bryant, being an honest broker, duly handed over the bubbly.

I was contacted by Eric Morley that summer to ask if I would be a judge at Miss United Kingdom, in the days before the world turned against such shows. There was no fee as such but we would be paid expenses. The ladies on parade seemed curiously sexless, and the old criticism of the cattle market similarity had some weight, but I don't feel anyone was being exploited.

Those who charge such events as being inherently sexist may have a point, though; after the show, Eric handed over my expenses, a small wad of notes, by a method he had clearly been using for many years. While shaking my right hand, with his left he poked the notes into the breast pocket of my dinner jacket. With fellow judge, Anneka Rice, he followed the same procedure but, since she was unjacketed and wearing a low-cut dress, he smilingly poked the notes down into her cleavage. I was taken aback; judging by her expression so was Anneka, but Eric seemed blithely unaware of the possibility of offence being taken and moved on as if he were distributing the Maundy money.

Another approach that year came from TVS, the south-east regional ITV production company. Jeremy Beadle had devised a pop quiz which was going into production, and had suggested my name as its host. He would produce it and the executive producer was the highly experienced and professional John Kaye Cooper. We arranged to meet to chat over the possibilities.

My problem with meetings like this has always been my

overriding interest in radio. First and foremost, I see myself as a radio broadcaster. Anything else, even the great god television, is icing on the cake, and somehow I manage to come across as if I'm unenthusiastic or lacking in excitement in such projects. I had a very pleasant meeting with John, at which I obviously failed to shine, because word came back that he thought I might be a little too laid-back to work as the presenter, so they would go with someone else.

In later years, Jeremy was generous enough to say they had got it wrong and he ought to have made me a star on TV, but even though I'm biased, I'm inclined to think that John Kaye Cooper called it correctly. His instincts were accurate and I wouldn't have been right for that show at that time. And, besides, in my heart I didn't really want to be a TV star.

One TV offer which did come to a result was from *Countdown*. It was already thought of as a long-runner even after three years, nothing like the quarter-century and more achieved now. The producer, John Meade, was a gruff character who enjoyed doing business over a drink. Happily, so did I, and after a bit of sparring we agreed that I would make the first of what would turn out to be many trips to Leeds.

My first meeting with Richard Whiteley confirmed what everyone now knows, that the man you saw on the screen, with his slightly bemused air, was exactly the man you met away from the studio. He was an intelligent man with a keen interest in politics, and relished the contacts he made in that world, mainly, I think, for the gossip it gave him access to. He never lost a kind of wide-eyed enthusiasm for his work and he was always genuinely thrilled to meet well-known people, even though in many cases he was more famous than they were. I don't think he ever fully realized just how popular he was.

He was also one of the great lunchers of our time. Some years later, a meal was arranged for Richard, myself, Terry Wogan and Paul Walters, who by that stage was back producing Terry's show. We had a very good lunch, by the end of which there were four empty wine bottles on the table. So far, so restrained. Terry and Paul had to leave, but Whiteley was very keen to stay on and I was in no hurry, so another bottle was called for, and then one more.

By the time we rose from the table, we had consumed two bottles of wine each. I don't know about you, but to me that constitutes a pretty good day's intake and all I was ready for was to catch the train home and recover with a quiet evening. I casually asked Richard what he was going to be doing. 'Oh, I've a reunion dinner of the Old Gig-gleswickians,' he replied. 'It's always a terrifically boozy do. Looking forward to it!'

But that was Richard; never happier than when he was socializing with like-minded people. His untimely death robbed us of one of our great characters and one of the most honest and straightforward of men.

One further TV excursion took place that year: a show called *Names and Games* in which slightly famous people such as myself took part in not-terribly-strenuous activities. The only things I remember about this are lunching with Graham Chapman; Captain Sensible insisting that the charity our whole team played for had to be the one he wanted; and me falling off the back of a quad bike, in the process receiving a beautiful imprint of a tyre across the leg of my trousers. It was held at Butlins holiday camp in Bognor, and as the coach from our hotel came up to its gates, someone wailed, 'Bloody hell, it's Tenko!'

It rained all weekend, we were all eventually sent home with hardly anything shot, and the programme never made it to air. In the course of the few items we had been able to film, the director remarked that I should give him a call sometime as there might someday be some work we could do together. Like the fool that I am, I never made that call. Why? I don't know; diffidence perhaps, but probably just a wish not to be diverted from my main focus: the radio show.

It was at a press call during that weekend that the first question was put to me about my tenure on breakfast. I countered with a lame remark to the effect that I had a long-term contract, to the end of next week. When I saw the reporters dutifully noting the phrase down, I realized that it was being taken seriously and had to point out that I had, in fact, been joking. Much crossing-out and impatient sighing followed, and I made a mental note never to say anything to the press that I wouldn't wish to see quoted verbatim.

I had bought a little cottage in the Chilterns near Great Missenden and moved the family down from Glasgow, but it became apparent that I would very soon have to make a serious decision about my marriage.

Despite a number of attempts to put some distance between us, my feelings for Anne, the researcher in Scotland, had grown, and after much soul-searching and many sleepless nights, I decided that my future lay with her.

Let no one tell you that divorce is too easy nowadays.

There may be fewer legal obstacles to it, and less social stigma, but the emotional wreckage that it causes is deep, profound and long-lasting. The guilt I felt at being the cause of it all was a huge burden. The pain that Fiona, who was blameless in the whole matter, must have gone through is difficult to imagine.

As much as we could, we tried to protect the children from the fallout. Fiona and the boys would move back to Glasgow, and I would make full financial arrangements for their new life there, keeping up regular contact either by flying up for weekends or bringing the boys down to London.

The only small crumb of comfort came later at the divorce hearing, where the judge described the arrangements and our agreement about the children as 'admirable'. Fiona showed great dignity throughout and the credit is all hers.

An announcement to the press would have to be made, and I enlisted the help of a journalist friend, Arnie Wilson, to smooth the path. I foolishly gave the BBC a heads-up, since they needed to know of the possibility of awkward head-lines. I use the word 'foolishly' advisedly, as the first thing the corporation does with news like that is tell anyone internally who might have a stake. With dozens of people suddenly in the loop, it didn't take long before the story leaked, spoiling our nicely planned campaign.

The response of the press to a story depends on how they got it. If it was a press release that everyone is receiving, they're not so very interested and may just run a couple of paragraphs on page 15. If it arrives as a quiet tip-off that they are sure they have before anyone else, they'll splash it. Suddenly I was big news again.

It was to get worse, as a new broom had arrived at

Radio 2 to head up the Production department. Frances Line had been a producer in the department and had made good progress through the management strata, and now had come back at the top of the tree. Although we subsequently got on well, I found her a little difficult at first; but perhaps that was not entirely surprising, given that she had some hard decisions to make and one of them directly concerned me and my future. It was her view – more than that, her conviction – that I should come off breakfast and move to the mid-morning slot. On one fateful December Friday, she called me to her office and delivered the bad news. I would finish in April. There was a record company Christmas lunch going on in one of the Charlotte Street restaurants, so I went along and drowned my sorrows amongst the seasonal revellers.

In a way, it was a relief. I had been uneasy about the role from the outset and to have a resolution of any kind was good. But, and it was a huge but, it marked my tenure on the show as brief, fifteen months in total, and therefore a failure. I would have liked another year, or six months at least, to show what I could do. The audience figures were beginning to turn, and with the right backing and invest-ment it could be a great show.

On the other hand, would they invest? Or just continue to starve the programme of even a few newspapers? In a new slot I could start with a clean slate and make it my own. The mid-morning show I was being offered was a request show, a notoriously dull format which can easily descend into endless lists of names and addresses and everyone asking for the same few records they heard last week. Moreover, the show was only to last one hour; hardly a show at all. So I sat down and came up with a variation on the format with a couple of extra features, and determined to argue the case for at least another half-hour on the running time, to bring it into line with some other shows on the network. I made an appointment to see the Controller, and on the day was surprised to find not one but three people facing me across the table. It only struck me afterwards that they probably thought I was going to throw a wobbler and they had turned up in numbers to pin me down if I turned violent.

Whether I argued my case well, or whether they were simply relieved that I hadn't started swinging a meat cleaver above my head, they agreed to all my ideas, even to the extra half-hour. Maybe it wasn't much, but to me it was a face-saver and made the future look altogether brighter.

It was some small comfort, given the 'Ken Axed' publicity that would be bound to follow. Well, I could cope with a few negative headlines or 'told you so' gossips. A blow to the pride didn't trouble me deeply. What did was the inescapable feeling that my life was falling apart. I had lost both my marriage and my job in the space of a few weeks. I had gone from the very good year that was 1984 to what Her Majesty would call, in other circumstances, an 'annus horribilis'.

The BBC got the news of my departure from breakfast into the public domain fairly speedily and, of course, nobody wanted to interview me personally, being much more interested in who my successor might be. To my surprise, though, I received a lot of sympathy, in the press and from my colleagues; Jimmy Young, who up till that time had been perfectly friendly but a little distant, had come bursting into my studio shouting, 'Young man [he called everyone apart from Lord Reith 'young man'], I think they've treated you shittily!' From then on, he became a good friend and I saw much more of the mischievous and very, very funny side of him that didn't get enough exposure on air.

All this happened in the run-up to Christmas. Fiona and the boys moved north at the end of the school term and I closed up the house in Buckinghamshire, ready for sale. Anne was by this time resident in London but was going north to be with her mother over the festive season, so I was going to be alone in a small flat in West Ealing, probably drinking myself into a gentle stupor on Christmas Day.

Times like these are when the inherent goodness of human beings comes to the fore. As soon as Alma and Ray Moore got wind of the fact that I would be Home Alone, they immediately insisted I join them for the festivities. No sooner had they offered than Tom Boswell, the Radio 2 promotions man, and his wife, the radio journalist Irene Mallis, invited me over to their house.

I managed to take advantage of both offers, and had a really good Christmas, thanks to the kindness and thoughtfulness of genuinely good people. Ray and Alma had recently moved into a charming house on the common at Blackheath, and the memory of Ray slicing up onions for the stuffing with a Park Drive in his mouth, a glass of red teetering on the edge of the table and the Service of Nine Lessons and Carols on the radio is still clear in my mind.

Ray was the man I felt closest to in the broadcasting business. His view of radio accorded with mine. We had come into the business not for fame, or glory, or even money, but because we admired those we had heard who could communicate solely with the voice, who could create a whole character through inflection or tone and who you felt were talking just to you.

Ray was bemused by those who saw radio as a stepping stone on the path to television, or a way of keeping their name in front of the public, remarking of one colleague, 'Oh, he's not in radio; he's in *show business*!' Still today, I'm suspicious of stars of stage, screen and print who suddenly discover a lifelong love of radio when their careers need a little lift.

We regarded ourselves as jobbing broadcasters, with a special area of interest in music presentation, but who could turn our hands to anything. We had both been announcers and had come up in the tradition of taking any script and making sense of it, but relishing the freedom that a music show offered.

At this point in my life, I needed more work. As I had sold up in Glasgow, bought and immediately sold again the house in Buckinghamshire, funds were severely depleted. With all my outgoings for maintenance and travel, I worked out that after agent's fees and tax, I would actually be in deficit at the end of each month. I was a jobbing broadcaster, so voice-overs seemed the obvious answer. Like any market, though, it takes time to break in, and while being on radio seems a perfect shop window, most people in the advertising industry were too cool to listen to Radio 2 and only heard the voices on Capital or Radio 1, and therefore thought of them first.

Ray Moore, in a typical act of selflessness, offered me his contacts book, 'if you think it would help'. Help? Of course it would, but I simply couldn't accept the offer. Instead, I sat down with the *Yellow Pages* and the *International Film Yearbook* and listed every production house and recording studio I could find, and set about calling them and sending out tapes. Work began to trickle in.

One I was particularly pleased about was a commercial for a large publishing company. I didn't know what the specific product was until I got to the studio and found it was a well-known Sunday newspaper. In fact, it was the same newspaper which had, a few weeks after my marital break-up, published a 'Revealed!' story about Anne and me, quoting unnamed 'friends' and generally making our story rather more salacious, and indeed interesting, than was actually the case. I had been a little upset by the piece, not so much about what it said about me, but more about the doorstepping and intrusive phone calls that I knew my friends and family had had to endure.

The golden rule I discovered about these exposé-type stories is that your real friends don't talk to the press and the ones quoted are usually people you've hardly met and who know very little about you. The odd thing is that the papers never attempted to speak to me; they'd rather not, of course, as it might spoil the story they want to print. I'm not bitter, though; they have their job to do and we read the results – I was fair game.

Here I was being asked to promote the very paper which had done me over. Do I walk out in high dudgeon, or sit down and do it? Naturally, I chose the latter. It gave me a certain satisfaction to be paid back a little for the disruption they had caused. When the cheque arrived, I thought briefly about framing it as a memento, but one day later took it straight to the bank and stuck it in the account. I needed it too much.

The day after the Sunday story appeared, the dailies

followed it up and I even made front page of the *Sun*, a dubious honour. The following day, they splashed with some daft story trying to make mischief about Sarah Kennedy having lunch with a High Court judge. I immediately phoned her up and berated her for having the cheek to push me off the front pages.

The only thing you can do in a situation like that is to laugh it off; nevertheless, I did not enjoy my private life being focused on and I made the decision to keep a low profile in future. I had moved into Anne's tiny Ealing flat and all I wanted was to rebuild my life and keep my head down. This was not what the BBC wanted; their policy was that presenters should bring added value to the station by their outside activities and the attendant publicity. My view was that I was employed as a professional broadcaster and I would do the on-air job to the best of my ability. If they wanted someone to sing and dance across the media and have their picture in the papers all the time, they had plenty of other people who enjoyed that. I was content to be judged on my radio work.

The corporation grudgingly put up with my stance, and in any case, Derek Jameson was arriving to take over at breakfast, and there was no one more adept at placing stories in the press, even to the extent of dictating the copy down the phone to them. They would have plenty of publicity with him around.

Through Derek, I discovered that the papers will print almost anything if it's said to them loudly and confidently enough. Over the years the audience figures he told them rose exponentially, until he was claiming 10 million listeners a day. Statistically, this would mean that by the end of a week, there would only be approximately three people in the country who were not listening to him. No doubt he would convert them the following week. It was plainly nonsense, but it was dutifully printed and his massive audience became an accepted truth. I got on well with him, managing not to fall into the trap of blaming him for my ill fortune, but I can't pretend that his show was an easy listen for me.

One of the more irritating elements was that, less than a year after I had been refused even delivery of the daily papers, his programme was entirely built round the contents of that day's press. It didn't seem to inhibit Gloria's show at all.

Still, most people who work at the BBC get used to minor, usually unintentional insults, oversights and slights, and all one can do is mark them down as good stories to share in the pub and move on.

Seven

'A History of Inappropriate Levity'

I knuckled down to my new show in April 1986, and found that there was certainly no shortage of willing listeners to take part. I didn't want to fall into the trap of simply doing, 'Happy ninetieth birthday, Doris!' or, 'Hello, twins!' links, so I took the cards that came in and looked for something amusing or odd about the people or their message and 'poked gentle fun'. Oh, all right, 'took the piss'. It's what I did best.

Musically, though, it could be hard going. Because the official policy was to superserve the over-fifty-fives, priority seemed to be given to requests for songs from the 1930s. I have no problem with a wide-ranging music plot – in fact it's what makes and has always made Radio 2 stand out – but the balance had tipped too far and I had too many recordings of Carroll Gibbons and the Savoy Orpheans and comedy songs by Frank Crumit for my comfort.

Good can be found in any type of music, and I certainly learned a great deal about styles of the 1930s and 1940s, but I felt we were making a fundamental mistake. Old folk don't only like old music. People aged fifty-five or sixty don't think of themselves as old, and neither, these days, do seventy-year-olds, so feeding them a diet of music that dates solely from their youth simply serves to remind them of the ageing process. Everybody loves a little nostalgia, but nobody wants to live in the past.

Such new releases as we did play were of the very safe variety. Hardly any chart material made it on to our playlist. Even the Linda Ronstadt and James Ingram recording of the ballad 'Somewhere Out There' was banned because of its 'loud electric guitar solo', a frankly bizarre decision. As you can imagine, it was a tough time for a broadcaster in his thirties. It seemed to be even tougher for one in his forties, David Hamilton, who jumped ship to a commercial station in November 1986, saying he would 'rather play Madonna than Mantovani'. He had a point, and felt that he was likely to be sacked anyway, so decided to beat the drop.

I, too, had an approach from commercial radio at this time, their assumption being, not unreasonably, that I would prefer a more amenable music policy to work under. Naturally, it was nice to be asked; flattery works wonders. But getting out was not really on my agenda. Leaving Radio 2 would be, I felt, cutting off my nose to spite my face. I was on a national network, the show was popular and I was now getting good reviews, even from some writers who had previously dismissed my efforts. And I had a solid belief in the self-correcting nature of the BBC; that whatever odd avenues it sometimes gets led down, a balancing mechanism kicks in after a little while, common sense prevails and the status quo is restored.

I was sure that if I hung on, things would swing back. It took some time, though, and I had to plough through some pretty depressing music plots in that time. One day I met an old friend, one of BBC Scotland's most experienced Outside

Broadcast engineers, a man in his late fifties whose judgement I had always respected. 'You're sounding OK,' he said, 'but the music . . .', and he shook his head. Here was a man right in the target age group, and certainly no follower of trends, and if he couldn't stomach it, we were definitely getting it wrong.

Very often, engineers and studio managers are excellent barometers of a programme's worth. They know as they're making it if it's working or not. Even an intense dislike of a producer or presenter won't prevent them giving a grudging respect if it's due. And if they think something is rubbish, it usually is. They are at the forefront of broadcasting, and see it at its best, and worst. They also have to put up with long and unsocial hours and, in the case of Outside Broadcasts, the vagaries of the weather.

One OB engineer was working on a pro-am golf tournament at Turnberry, and was stationed well out on the course with a fairly primitive field telephone – of a type which would be easily recognizable to anyone who served in World War II – as his only means of communication with his colleagues a matter of half a mile away. This was in the days before mobile phones were available and without his large green boxed phone he was completely out of contact.

It so happened former President Gerald Ford was playing in this match, and the attendant Secret Service men were much in evidence. At one point, our engineer was attempting in vain to raise the control van, visible across the course, by furiously turning the ring handle and yelling down the phone, when, pausing, he watched a sharp-suited American agent take what appeared to be a pen out of his pocket and calmly say into it, 'Patch me through to the White House.'

On another occasion, an outbreak of flu had decimated the OB department, and several non-specialists had to be drafted in. The bug had hit the commentators too, and there was no one locally who could cover an important match between Scotland and an Eastern European country. One of the London football commentators was flown up to Glasgow at the last minute and got to Hampden just in time to start the broadcast.

He knew the Scottish players but had little idea of the opposition men, apart from the information in the match programme. The engineer sitting next to him was a music specialist with no knowledge of, and even less interest in, the glorious game, but all went fairly smoothly until the visitors made an unexpected substitution.

The commentator, who had only just got his tongue around the names of the foreign players, began searching through his notes for the subs' names, when the new man on the pitch suddenly upped and scored a goal.

He did his best to convey the excitement of this upset by shouting, 'The substitute has scored within seconds! Yes, he's only been on the pitch for the blink of an eye but already he's put the visitors ahead. The substitute, whose name . . .' and looked imploringly at the engineer for a prompt. The engineer leant over, lifted one ear of his colleague's headphones and whispered something.

With a relieved expression on his face, the commentator continued, '. . . whose name is Fuktifyno!'

Radio 2 was fond of the OB at the time, and one of the first I had had at breakfast was the *Railshow*, where each daytime programme came from a railway station somewhere in Britain. The thought behind this was, I imagine, to get out and meet the public as they made their way to and from work or in their home town. In practice, stations are not places where people spend much time. The average commuter probably arrives two minutes before the train is due and anyone with time on their hands may choose not to spend it at the end of Platform 3, unless they are of the anoraked variety.

We had a very nice photograph done for the *Radio Times*, with all of us decked out in hats and whistles next to an InterCity 125 at Paddington. Gloria Hunniford couldn't make it, so she was pasted in later, perched on the front of the engine like the figurehead of a four-master. When the allocation of stations came in, I had drawn a doozy: Reading. Others had holiday towns, seaside resorts and the like, and I had Reading. Because of the early start, someone had booked us all into a local hotel.

The BBC's practice then was to pay a set amount for overnight allowance, enough to cover a decent hotel room, and allow staff to choose how they spent it. Whoever had booked the hotel for us was obviously of the 'make a skin on your expenses' type, as it was cramped, down at heel and with nylon sheets on the beds. I hardly slept that night, and when I did I was woken up by the fire regulations falling off the door. Still, we'd saved £5 on the expenses!

The programme wasn't much better, as we'd been placed on an out-of-the-way bay platform where no passengers ever ventured, and in the unlikely event of anyone coming to the station specially to see the show, it emerged that they would have to buy a platform ticket before they could get in. All in all, not brilliant. Add to that constant interruptions from expresses thundering past, and drivers cottoning on to the fact that they could get on the radio if they sounded their horns while I was talking, and you can see it was something I wouldn't wish to repeat.

The BBC can, on occasion, be quite clever. Whenever it hears anyone saying, 'Never again!' it puts the idea on the back burner just long enough for memories to fade and the declaration to have been forgotten. So, two years later, the *Railshow* came up again and in a moment of weakness I said yes. This time, only David Jacobs and I would travel and we would go in the exhibition train to Morecambe, Llandudno, Skegness and other exotic parts. The same difficulties of access arose and we all remembered why we'd said we'd never do it again, but some fun was had and David was, as always, a delightful companion with a fund of anecdotes and a gift for telling rude jokes in an incongruously beautiful accent.

It was on one of these shows that I had my bum pinched. Odd though it may seem, I have not often been regarded as a sex object. Except in the sense that when I suggest sex, women object. However, on Llandudno station, in the middle of a group of people getting autographs from us and our guests, I felt my nether regions being tweaked. Naturally, I thought I was mistaken and carried on writing. When it happened, quite definitely, a second time, I wheeled round and saw a portly lady in her sixties, leaning heavily on a stick and trying to look innocent. I suppose I had hoped it would be some willowy twenty-five-year-old who'd assaulted me, and looked around in vain for one, but such was the nature of our audience that I had to accept that my allure seemed to work best amongst elderly arthritics.

Off the rails, as it were, there were several other outings;

Judith Chalmers and I presented a succession of summer OBs, from the Newton Abbot Steam Fair, Gloucester Cathedral and even one from the Paris Air Show where Judith, being the most visible of the partnership, got to sit in all the planes and interview the pilots and celebrities, and I got to sit in a makeshift studio and introduce the records with only one visitor, the editor of *Flight International*. Lovely chap, but no substitute for a ride in a Harrier.

No excuse was too feeble, and no link too tenuous to build an OB round. There was one to celebrate national Waterways Day, where Paul Walters and I broadcast from a narrowboat near Birmingham. We had recently been marvelling that the Two Ronnies had got away with a musical sketch based on Gilbert and Sullivan where one Ron had repeated, as in the original, the last three syllables of the line, 'A policeman's lot is not a happy one!' 'Happy one!' They had then done lines such as, 'What the Navy needs is more efficient ships.' 'Fish 'n' chips.' It culminated in one about *The Gondoliers*: 'As they ply their trade upon that far canal.' Slight hesitation and then, 'Fancy that.'

We had enjoyed that so much that Paul bet me I couldn't get the words 'far canal', pronounced in the offensive way, into the show. Naturally, I wasn't going to let mere taste do me out of a tenner so I did it, in an interview with a government minister no less, and happily collected the bet. In my early days I had set myself a small challenge of getting rude words into Radio 2 shows by devious means, such as mispronouncing the word *Barcarolle* and saying our orchestra had been intending to play 'bugger all', but had been persuaded to play anyway. I also managed to describe a picture I had been sent from a local paper of the footballer Luther Blissett leaning on the gate of the house he had just bought in Corfe Mullen. The house name emblazoned across the gate, I announced happily, was Far Corfe.

We had some good outings; we enjoyed getting out of the studio and I like to think that the programmes we did were interesting in some way, but repeated research showed that the majority of the audience likes Radio 2 to sound the way it always does, the same people in the same places every day, so OBs, costing more than the norm, as they were bound to do, became much rarer. Some I miss, like the Saturday afternoon spent on the terrace of a hotel in Torquay, sipping wine with David Suchet in full Poirot garb; others, such as the freezing morning at a waste recycling centre in Sheffield, a little less so.

Before the axe fell, a number of Themed Days somehow got through the planning process. Radio 2 in Paris took every daytime show, and a few others, across the Channel. I ended up in the newly opened Disneyland, which I thought was not too bad a draw until we heard that the entire site was 'dry'. The prospect of having no alcohol to recover from the hell of broadcasting alongside human-size Donald Ducks was too terrible to contemplate so we smuggled some necessary supplies in. As it happened, Walt's people did allow wine in certain parts of the complex, so we had more than enough to dull the pain.

RAF Day was one occasion when I drew one of the longer straws: Cyprus. Quite apart from the good weather, our host, Squadron Leader Dave Davenal, was so efficient that we had a guided tour of the island, halloumi on the beach and drinks in the mess within five hours of landing. The drink of choice for the staff there turned out to be brandy sours.

A huge pitcher appeared on our table, which, a bit like the everlasting bottle of Guinness, never seemed to be less than three-quarters full. In that warm climate, it slipped down like lemonade but had a rather more powerful effect. I was so impressed I immediately got the recipe and have kept and used it ever since.

We only just managed to operate the next morning; how these guys could fly military aircraft after a night on the sours, I will never know. It definitely was one of the better postings for that day; I got to broadcast from the turret of a tank. Gloria Hunniford's mission was to be winched out of a helicopter above the North Sea. For once, I seemed to have got the non-fuzzy side of the lollipop.

There was still a lot of live music on the network and I was being asked to present concerts with the BBC Concert Orchestra, to whom I would return many years later on *Friday Night is Music Night*, and the Radio Orchestra, as well as its subdivision, the Big Band. The old Scottish Radio Orchestra had been closed down in the early 1980s in a BBC-wide cull of orchestras that spawned the 'Keep Music Live' stickers which can probably still be found today on surviving Citroën 2CVs, alongside the obligatory 'Nuclear Power – No Thanks' stickers which were rumoured to be factory-fitted.

I was pleased to find some of the former members of that band had found their way into the ranks of the Radio Orchestra and that the London-based musicians were a match for the Glasgow ones in capacity for fun, although they had a slightly more responsible attitude towards keeping on the right side of sober when playing.

The Concert Orchestra was based at Golders Green Hippodrome and had some good pubs and restaurants close at hand. The Radio Orchestra played at Maida Vale Studios, which are located on a residential street, notoriously far from the necessities of life, so at breaks everyone ducked across to the nearby tennis club, whose committee seemed happy to overlook breaches of membership criteria when they counted the bar takings.

The popular misconception is that orchestral musicians are staid and sober, while rock stars are wild and drunken. The two are closer than you might think. Some rockers retire to bed at half past ten with a glass of mineral water; I've known plenty of tail-suited players who keep the bar open until five in the morning. One of the joys of orchestras is that, while each member is a talented and dedicated instrumentalist, together they can start to behave like the most unruly class of teenagers it's possible to imagine.

Shouting out rude words at quiet bits, giving cheek to the conductor and exchanging the most tasteless jokes; no wonder I like their company. Even during school visits, they know no restraint. Musicians tend to refer to players by the name of their instrument, such as, 'He's second trombone in the LSO.' One day, a group of youngsters were on an educational trip to see a BBC orchestra, and when the conductor, in an effort to engage the kids, asked brightly, 'Now, does anyone know the difference between the flute and the oboe?' one of the brass section shouted out, 'The flute's got bigger tits.'

Some years earlier, the well-known arranger and conductor Wally Stott had undergone gender reassignment. He had gone to Switzerland for the surgery and returned to work as a woman and under a new name, Angela Morley. This prompted Harry Secombe to remark, 'I've heard of leaving your heart in San Francisco but this is ridiculous!'

It was undoubtedly a brave thing to do and on her first day back, before the rehearsal began, the head of the orchestral committee felt he had to make a little speech. He was a hard-bitten player of the old school, but spoke movingly, concluding, 'I know how difficult it's been for you over the last few months but our respect for you as a musician hasn't changed and you'll get nothing but help and cooperation from us.' Then, as he made to sit down, he hesitated and added, 'By the way, I suppose a f***'s out of the question?'

It brought the place down, with, so it's said, Angela laughing as much as anyone. After all, she was a musician herself. In their world, potential offence is always outweighed by the volume of the laugh.

I made good friends with many players, and still to this day try in any concert to include lines in my introductions that might be appreciated by the band. Alan Bennett once said that he envied Peter Cook in their *Beyond the Fringe* days because he could 'make the band laugh'. It's true they are the toughest audience, which is probably why I feel I've got it right if they ever do.

Radio 2 had the luxury in the 1980s of access not only to an FM frequency, but two medium wave ones as well, and in the days before 5 Live it was the home of Radio Sport. For big events, the frequencies were split to allow music on FM and sport on MW, but most of the time attempts were made for the two to coexist within programmes, with Gloria being sent to the races in the afternoon and me having to include the draws for the FA Cup and the cricket tournaments in my show.

The rattling balls and the fumbling in bags were not great radio, but the drama of the unfolding draw was quite entertaining. I would usually hand over to a correspondent at the draw who would host proceedings and let the chairman or whoever shout out the numbers, and then identify the teams. Normally this worked like clockwork, but for one cricket event things started to go wrong. I handed over to Peter Baxter, who in his urbane fashion introduced the suits handling the balls and the draw began. After only a few names though, some hesitations crept into the number-calling and there was a distinct unease about the whole proceedings.

After a few more halting attempts, there was a pause and the chief ball-puller whispered to Peter that something had gone wrong. Well, that's not quite true; firstly, his whisper was more like a restrained shout and therefore clearly audible, and secondly what he actually said, live on Radio 2, was, 'We've buggered it up!' His economy of expression and accuracy were both admirable in their way.

I secretly envied Gloria her trips to the racecourses. I had a soft spot for the horses, while not really knowing too much about the sport, and I had a complete admiration for Peter Bromley, who was, for me, the king of racing commentators. His ability to describe a race was astounding, and I cannot recall him ever calling a finish wrong, even in the closest of races. And that's not to say he would sit on the fence: in photo finishes he would always offer his view as to which horse had passed the post first, and I never once heard him get it wrong.

I met him a few times at BBC events and on one occasion was able to introduce him to Jimmy Young, whom he had never met. They got on famously, but unfortunately both being a little deaf, and used to speaking in commanding tones, their lively conversation was heard right across the room by a fair number of the bosses they were moaning about.

The 1986 Commonwealth Games were to be held in Edinburgh and I was delighted to be asked to be the 'non-specialist' presenter working alongside Sport, the idea being that I, as a regular daytime voice, would be a bridge for the casual listener to the detail of the games, with the ability to ask the questions a non-sports fan would ask. Or, as it was usually put, the 'idiot' questions. I was supremely well placed to ask those.

I would be working as co-host with the wonderful Renton Laidlaw, one of nature's true gentlemen, and as it turned out I got to see a few events as well. At Meadowbank Stadium, it was planned that the impressionist Janet Brown would do her Mrs Thatcher and interrupt me as I was introducing the coverage. In fact, every time I opened my mouth to say something, she was to plough straight through me. I thought it worked well; too well, in fact, as a friend said to my brother, 'I heard Thatcher making a complete fool out of Ken on the radio,' and he wouldn't accept it was not the real thing he'd been listening to.

I was also sent out to the bowls venue. This was not a sport I would normally have been keen to watch but there was to be a visit by HM the Queen and I was to describe the royal progress. I was eager to have another bash at covering such an event after the less than glorious half-hour in Glasgow, and I would have alongside me the vastly experienced Bryon Butler, so nothing could go wrong. And it did go remarkably well, with one exception. We were in a little greenkeeper's hut or some such for our commentary, with a good view of the bowling green, but HM was to be on the far side and surrounded by crowds. We had the advantage of TV monitors though, so would be able to see everything.

The hut was a little small. This is not unusual; commentary positions are invariably cramped, cold and sometimes precariously placed. Sports commentators pull off magnificent work in the most adverse conditions. We were not badly off, but the confined nature of the box meant I was right up against the TV monitor as I did my reverent descriptions. It is a three-line whip on any royal commentary that what Her Majesty is wearing will be given full coverage and sometimes the BBC would, in their sexist way, add a woman to the team to provide that info. Those days were past and it was down to me.

I valiantly painted a picture of the Queen looking radiant (another compulsory element) in a yellow dress with red polka dots. Lovely. The only trouble was that HM was wearing a yellow dress with *white* polka dots. I had described the red tinge you see on everything when you're sitting too close to a TV screen. After that, I decided to give royal commentaries a miss.

Some years later, it was suggested to me that I might like to try another one, but I declined. Just as well, as when the idea went further up the management ladder, my name was vetoed on account of my history of 'inappropriate levity'.

Something must have gone well at the Commonwealth Games, though, as I was asked to take on the same role, that of interpreter to the Radio 2 audience, at the 1988 Olympics in Seoul. This was a much bigger operation, and I would be away from home for the best part of a month. After various uncomfortable injections and a long flight, I found myself installed in a newly completed high-rise hotel in the centre of the city.

My room was on the thirty-second floor; the high-speed lift journey up there felt like being in a space simulator. I swear my feet left the floor on the downward trips. From the room, there was a brilliant vista of the capital of South Korea; when you could see it, that is. Seoul had a horrendous pollution problem, with so many cars attempting to get into the city that they had a system where drivers could only use their vehicles every second day, odd-numbered licence plates one day, evens the next. Every morning, a thick, greeny-grey layer of smog sat over the city, well below my room's vantage point.

The hotel was not actually quite completed. Electricians were still wandering the corridors with coils of wire and there were carpenters carrying odd bits of wood around, but it was state of the art, with something I had never seen before in a hotel room: a heated bathroom mirror. No matter how long you ran the shower, the centre of the mirror stayed demisted.

Having got that right, the owners had failed in one central aspect: the air-conditioning. It seemed insufficient water had been put into the system or some such thing, but, whatever the reason, the result was that every single broadcaster in the BBC party came down with a sore throat and lost their voice to some degree. For a couple of days every report from the Olympics was delivered in croaking tones. The BBC doctor was travelling with us and he dosed us up with various potions, but I preferred self-medication, and the mini-bar's supply of fine old Scotch whisky got my vocal cords working again.

Once again, I was working alongside some of the doyens of sports broadcasting, including Peter Jones, one of the finest of his trade, whose wide experience of all types of event had stood him in good stead when he found himself having to broadcast throughout the unfolding Heysel stadium tragedy. His work on that night was exemplary, and without wishing to denigrate the ex-footballers who are now involved in commentary, I doubt if many could have risen to the challenge of describing the horrors of that night with such control, accuracy and sensitivity.

Former players have a lot to give to sports commentary in terms of insight and experience but, on radio at least, the *Test Match Special* formula works best: a seasoned broadcaster doing the main descriptive commentary, with a player giving the expert summary.

I watched Jonesy on a swimming commentary and was amazed at his ability to look at the action briefly, take a mental snapshot and then describe what was going on with his eyes on his notes, with only a few brief further checks right at the closing stages.

He was a famous charmer with the ladies, but could also schmooze the fellas effectively. At one Olympic venue, once the main business had finished, we were waiting for the *Daily Mail* sportswriter Patrick Collins to do a 'think-piece', or considered evaluation of the day's activity, before we headed back to the broadcast centre. Peter and I were standing a few yards away and chatting quietly while we could faintly hear Pat doing his three minutes' worth for *Sport on Two*. He finished up and after removing his headphones came over to us and said, 'Did that sound all right?'

Without missing a beat, Jonesy said, 'It was perfect, a

typical Pat Collins piece. You captured the mood of the day perfectly.' He had not heard one word of it; he'd been talking to me all the time, and yet his sincerity and convincing charm had Pat smiling happily and sauntering off with the praise of the top man ringing in his ears.

I didn't get out to many events; my role was to be the studio link man, so I was confined to a windowless room in the bowels of the broadcast centre for hours on end. After a couple of weeks of this I was beginning to get stir-crazy and it was only the company of Cliff Morgan, that great rugby player, fine broadcaster and proud Welshman that kept me sane. His endless fund of stories and cheery disposition were a life-saver.

His jolly little one-liners became more important as time went on and I can recall laughing for what felt like ages at his throwaway comment as he entered the office one day: 'And now a little song entitled, "Come on Down to the Airfield, Darling, You Can Kiss Me behind the Hangars".' Hysteria for hours. Without him, I would have gone crackers. Thank you, Cliff.

I was kept quite busy at the Olympics, to the extent that I saw very little of Seoul itself apart from the journey from the hotel to my airless cell in the broadcast centre. After work though, there was usually a general move to find a restaurant, and those of us who liked our food tried to find as many different eating experiences as possible. Not everyone was in the mood for experimentation. Garry Richardson seemed to subsist on pizza for most of the Games, and, on the occasion when he came out to a Japanese restaurant, baffled the chef by ordering steak and chips.

John Inverdale and I went one night to a tiny eating house

up a back street which was allegedly the best local restaurant in Seoul, where we would get authentic Korean food. It was good, although we had a strong suspicion we had been served the kind of meat legend has it the locals eat. It seemed our *bulgogi* may have been bulldoggy.

The advantages of having a doctor travelling with the team came to the fore on the return journey when he supplied us all with short-term sleeping pills, so that we would avoid jet-lag and arrive in London fresh and ready to resume normal duties. I dutifully popped mine, slept all the way back, twenty-two hours in all, and still suffered horrendous jet-lag for days afterwards, nodding off during the day and awake half the night.

The first gig I had on returning to home shores was a Scottish concert from the Radio Show at Earls Court in which I would be introducing Kenneth McKellar, a very funny man behind the formal singing. We were to be in full Highland dress for this show, yes, even on the radio, and for some reason I had foolishly decided I ought to be properly attired underneath the kilt, i.e. going commando.

I soon regretted this, as the stage was a high one and the audience were allowed to mill about right underneath it. I felt extremely vulnerable, especially when some local kids, presumably never having seen a kilted man in such close proximity, started trying to flick sweetie papers up my kilt. I was outraged, and came off stage fulminating about the behaviour of London kids, until I remembered that as a teenager I had gone unwillingly to see the Alexander Brothers, a traditional Scots act, at the Pavilion Theatre in Glasgow, and spent a large part of the evening trying to do exactly the same to them.

Prior to my brief flirtations with sport, I had been asked to take over a World Service show called *Album Time*. It was a half-hour programme which went out every week at three different times, and was just an excuse to play music that wasn't all hit tracks. Despite my stint only being originally for thirteen weeks, I carried on doing it for a full seven years, until the service decided to cut down on its musical output to concentrate on news. It was rather nice to receive letters from Freetown, Sierra Leone, rather than Bromsgrove, West Midlands, and I enjoyed my spell there, never really believing it was actually being listened to with any huge appreciation. However, a number of years in, I was at a BBC reception when I was told someone wished to meet me. The someone turned out to be Terry Waite. During his time as a hostage in Beirut, he had been allowed a radio and had tuned in to the BBC. He said, 'I never used to think that there was a need for music on the World Service, but I found listening to your show was really important in helping me get through the days.' To think that this man, who had spent months chained to a radiator with his life under constant threat, could have the kindness to say such a thing to me was utterly humbling.

In 1986, the Light Entertainment department came knocking and I was asked to join the long-running *Pop Score* programme. In its original form, Pete Murray was the presenter, with team captains Terry Wogan and Tony Blackburn, and it was the kind of quiz where correct answers were considered to be a luxury rather than strictly necessary. It was a forerunner of *Never Mind the Buzzcocks* on television, but less scatological, and of course, being radio, with no budget for comedy writers.

When Pete had left the BBC, he was replaced as chairman by Ray Moore, and Terry had left for TV, with his place taken by David Hamilton. Blackburn had recently gone off to commercial radio and was therefore persona non grata on a BBC network, so it was his seat I had to fill. Richard Willcox produced, wrote and did the warm-up for the show (you guessed it; no budget), and made the whole thing work. It was great fun to do and always began and ended with a drink or two in the Captain's Cabin, a pub squirreled away behind the Paris studio in Lower Regent Street, where almost all LE shows were recorded.

The Paris was a converted basement cinema which had been an LE outpost since the war and had a loyal regular audience who seemed to have been coming there since around the time of the Blitz. They turned up to everything from *Brain of Britain* to *The News Huddlines* and laughed loudly and applauded without prompting. Their highly individual characteristics were reflected in the standing joke: what has thirty-three legs and four teeth? Answer: the front row of the Paris.

After only one series, David Hamilton made his walk to commercial radio but I was delighted to find that Alan Freeman was to join in his place. Fluff was one of the kindest, sweetest guys you could hope to meet and made it clear he was up for as much insulting banter as could be thrown at him. With Ray and Fluff together, we had cornered the market in the nicest men in broadcasting. Not one episode was remotely like work.

Ray and Alma and Anne and I often got together for nights out. Ray was a non-driver so travelled everywhere by train or cab; Anne was a non-drinker so my lift home was assured, and therefore much 'Algerian bellywash', as Ray put it, was consumed. I recall him marvelling at the sheer size of his wine glass in one restaurant; 'This isn't just a glass,' he said in awe, 'this is a *schooner*!'

One night, at a Scottish-themed party we threw, he turned up wearing his old Scout kilt with, instead of a sporran, what he termed 'Alma's old Dorothy bag', in reality a small velvet purse, hanging from his waist. On another visit, he was delighted to find that I had contrived to build a shed upside down. This was a slight exaggeration in that it was a flat-roofed shed, and although the walls were the right way up with the window at the top (I'm not completely stupid, you know), I had managed to place the floor where the roof should be and vice versa. I must say that the instructions were very unclear and the components were very similar-looking. However, I've found this defence never seems to convince anyone and Ray was no exception. He had some-thing of a fetish about sheds anyway, having spent a large proportion of his childhood watching his father nailing down roofing felt and such things, so I became to him, and his listeners, the Man Who Built His Shed Upside Down, a similar case study to the Man Who Mistook His Wife for a Hat.

In his mid-forties, Ray was diagnosed with cancer, and in one of fate's crueller tricks, cancer of the mouth, which meant his speech was affected. To a man who loved broad-casting, and who rightly prided himself on his clarity of delivery, this was devastating. Physically, in other respects, he was pretty strong still and could have worked on for some time, but the one physical function he needed most was the one most affected.

He listened back to recordings of his show each day until

he decided his speech was no longer up to his own exacting standards and told the BBC he would have to give up. For reasons best known to themselves, they decided to replace him from the very next morning, denying him the chance to say goodbye to his loyal audience. No doubt they thought they were doing it for the best reasons but it was another cruel blow.

Ray survived for a further year and wrote a best-selling book about his experiences, but the illness had him in its grip, and he died in January 1989, just a few days after his forty-seventh birthday. I miss him still.

He had a good send-off, one of the things the BBC does organize very well, in All Souls' Church with the Syd Lawrence Band in attendance. At the drinks afterwards, I was talking to Jimmy Young, when a senior executive whom neither of us had seen for some months came up looking dreadful: thin, gaunt and grey. As he moved away, Jim turned to me and, in rather too loud a voice said, 'Tell Syd and the boys not to leave!'

During Ray's illness, I had been asked to take over his role as radio commentator for the Eurovision Song Contest and so began a twenty-year association with this annual farrago. I had watched Eurovision in the 1960s and had followed it through the 1970s and 1980s, so I was more than happy to take on the job. I liked the contest but fell short of being a fan, an attitude which I think matches the majority of the UK population.

The Eurovision Song Contest began in 1956. The United Kingdom did not take part. That was perhaps the last time we made a correct decision regarding this event, which has brought to us ever since a mixture of joy, sadness, anger and, chiefly, disappointment. Even our wins, much rarer now than in the 1960s, bring the worries of staging and, worse, paying for the next contest.

My own relationship with Eurovision has been ambivalent. Much as I enjoyed attending each contest and working on it, I have always banished it from my mind each May as soon as we land at Heathrow, and kept it there in limbo until the following January, when the rigmarole of finding another plucky loser begins.

One thing I have discovered over the years is that the true fans, who are lovely, kind-hearted people, always know every detail of every previous contest, and are happy to share their knowledge with you. Over-eager sometimes. When we did a Eurovision special edition of PopMaster once, we discovered that it was impossible to write questions they couldn't answer. They knew more than we did; the writers of the Danish entry in 1977, the backing vocalists on the Israeli song in 1982, even the names of the audience in Brighton in 1974 probably wouldn't have been beyond them.

This level of detail is not something my commentaries ever fell victim to, but the fans were mostly listening to Terry on TV, so I got away with it. My approach from the start was to describe the event in the hall, not the TV production, which gave me a great deal more freedom. A television commentator must follow the picture; on radio, I could go my own way, describe the frocks and the choreography if they warranted it but not if they didn't, ignore the tourist-puff 'postcards', and go off on tangents as the mood took me.

I can honestly say I never envied Terry his role as the TV commentator. Of course the vast majority of people watch it as a TV event, but the radio listening figure is higher than you might think; Eurovision on Radio 2 gives the network its biggest Saturday night listening figure of the year. And I like to think it's a discerning audience who, either by necessity or by choice, aren't in front of a telly.

And I found that, not for the only time in my life, I preferred being just out of the full glare of the spotlight. My first contest was in 1988 in Dublin. Terry was at the height of his fame on both sides of the Irish Sea and to travel there with him was like being on a royal visit. Everyone wanted to speak with him, be his mate, touch the hem of his garment. At the after-show bash, I offered to fetch a couple of drinks while he was waylaid by some people. I queued up, got the glasses, came back and found him still surrounded, but by different people.

I had long finished my drink and was beginning to look thirstily at his before he finally broke free and collected it. I said, 'I don't know how you cope with this.' He replied in a heartfelt tone, 'If I'd known it was going to be like this, I'd never have started.' It reinforced my belief that I really did not want to give up my relative anonymity.

I was happy to accept the benefits of his fame, though, which included the use of the Taoiseach's motorcycle outriders. We were all staying in the same hotel, and since a British delegation was held to be a slight security risk in the Ireland of that time, I was able to be whisked to the venue in the motorcade. Tearing up the roads past the queuing traffic and taking the wrong way round roundabouts with the blues and twos going is a lifestyle I might easily get used to. It was one of the attractions that made Dublin my favourite Eurovision destination of all. That, and the directness of the people. Everyone was in show business.

After one contest there, I was having a drink at the official reception with my manager, Jo Gurnett, when a tall fellow in casual clothes came up. 'Are you Jo Gurnett? I saw you earlier. I sing a bit and wondered if you'd like a tape of me, to see what you could do with it.' Jo asked him a few questions about his experience and he said, 'I only sing part-time. In fact, I only got in here because I'm one of the police outriders!'

We were being driven back in two cars to an address that for our driver was proving a little hard to find. The two-way radio to the lead driver Michael Devine crackled, with Mick giving directions. 'Where are you? OK. D'you see that sign that says "No Right Turn"? Well, turn right there!'

Dublin also gave us *Riverdance*, without doubt the most memorable interval act ever, and our commentators' tradition of drinking Bailey's on the night. It began simply enough, as there was a free Bailey's bar directly behind our commentary boxes one year, and at the interval, where I usually have a few minutes' free time while the music plays, I popped out and collected glasses for all. One led to another, and by the time we got to the end of the scoring a UK success was beginning to matter less and less to us. With the UK's loss of fortune in subsequent contests, an increasing supply of Bailey's has become more and more necessary.

Recently, with security checks increasing, a ban on bottles being brought into the event has become common. A simple solution has been found; our Head of Delegation, GB1, Kevin Bishop, decanted the Bailey's into an empty one-litre

191

water bottle. On the only occasion on which the contents were queried, he sweetly replied, 'Coffee,' and was nodded through.

His predecessor as Head of Delegation was Jim Moir, who eventually became Controller of Radio 2, to great acclaim. His years running the UK end of Eurovision were marked by general hilarity, as he chose to treat the whole thing as a 1950s prisoner of war film with himself cast as the senior British officer and the rest of us as gallant lads trying to outwit the devious foreigners. 'Look here, Bruce, we need a volunteer to go in there and teach Johnny Foreigner a thing or two. Think you're up to it?'

'Don't know, Sir, but I'll give it a bash and be happy to die in the attempt.'

Jim would be the first to admit that he's a big chap, and Terry is perhaps less svelte than he once was. One year, joined by producer Stewart Morris, himself a substantial figure, the three of them were crammed into a tiny commentary box no bigger than a small garden shed. I don't say the walls actually bulged but there was a rumour that Terry's words could hardly be heard above the creaks of straining wood. When the heat got up, Jim alleged that if the temperature in there increased any further, Stewie Morris would begin to melt and the hall would have to be evacuated.

I have so many great memories of Eurovision, good singers, fine songwriters, some decent songs, but rarely all three at the same time. Most of the happy memories are less of the contest itself and more of the pre- and after-show social gatherings. At my first Eurovisions, the audiences were made up of the great and the good of the host country. It was a black-tie event and the guest list might include the

Head of State, such was the kudos the contest was held to bestow in certain countries. In those days, the venues were conference centres or large theatres; now they tend to be basketball arenas with huge seating capacities, and the audiences have expanded and diversified to match.

The post-show parties used to be lavish and enjoyable; I recall some fantastic spreads in Ireland and Sweden, fresh seafood and fine wines. But as costs escalated, these diminished, and to mourn their passing is pointless. Time passes and things change.

I will, though, indulge in a little mourning for the loss of the live orchestra; the spectacle of fifty-plus musicians beavering away at each markedly different song was always entertaining, and the arrival on the podium of each country's conductor was a regular source of material for commentary. I always enjoyed the company of our own Ronnie Hazlehurst, especially as foreign hosts could never quite pronounce this very English name and mangled it beyond recognition.

Little Noel Kelehan from RTÉ (Radio Telefís Éireann) was probably the most frequent conductor seen at Eurovision in my time, and from the UK we called on the talents of Alyn Ainsworth, Ernie Dunstall and, in the very last appearance of a studio orchestra in 1998, Martin Koch, conducting our very own BBC Concert Orchestra. With so many entries being rock-based, the demise of the live band may have been inevitable, but I still feel its time may come again.

I described *Riverdance* as the most memorable interval act and, it's true, it changed the nature of that part of the contest forever. In fact, it changed the whole event, in that the competing countries no longer come out with a drum kit and a keyboard and just sing; we get a full-blown dance act and pyrotechnic display as well now. No vocalist can get a line out without four acrobats risking their lives and the obligatory great tongues of flame firing off around them accompanied by a dazzling light display; Eurovision's carbon footprint must be huge.

One other interval act sticks in my mind, in Switzerland in the 1989 contest. They had booked a crossbow specialist by the name of Guillaume Tell. An amazingly inventive name, I'm sure you'll agree. His shtick was to set up a circle of twenty crossbows, each with a balloon on the trigger. Each crossbow was aimed at the balloon on the next one, so that after he set off the first one, they would fire in turn in a kind of domino effect until the very last one, in front of which he stood with an apple on his head.

I didn't usually do a commentary on the interval, but something told me this needed a bit of description so I set about it. It had gone very smoothly in rehearsal, all the bows had fired perfectly and the last bolt had pinned the apple to the wall above his head.

On the live show, I described the interminable set-up, a good seven minutes of balloon-blowing and flourishing bolts above his head and then he was ready. Guillaume fired off the first bolt and placed the apple on top of his head as the crossbows thumped and the balloons burst. The whole thing took only about 10 seconds until the final bolt shot towards the apple – and missed! A good inch to the side. Better than too low, I suppose, but still, a terrible finish.

I shouted out, 'He's missed it! What a disappointment for him,' etc., etc. . . . until the video playback of the final moments appeared on the monitor and, miraculously, this time the bolt went straight into the apple. I was dumbfounded and began to backtrack, saying, 'Well, I could have sworn he missed,' as Guillaume came out brandishing an apple neatly skewered by a bolt. At this point my producer, David Vercoe, scribbled a note which read, 'The replay was the rehearsal VT – he DID miss!'

Hell hath no fury like a commentator misled and I proceeded to pour scorn on his performance and trickery. Foreigners, eh? You can't trust 'em. Give us Tommy Cooper any day; at least we got a laugh when his tricks didn't work. I still think that's where the rot set in for the contest.

I had been asked to do the *Eurovision Preview* programme for BBC1, working with the legendary TV producer Yvonne Littlewood. I had been booked simply to present and received a contract for that, but when I expressed a wish to write my own script, that contract was replaced with one on which my fee was tripled. Once again, the BBC's contracts department was working its peculiar magic; it certainly taught me where the money was in TV.

Yvonne was very understanding with me and only asked me to change one reference in the script, a small jibe where I described one buxom lady singer as looking like a barmaid. I think the worry was less about the singer's hurt feelings and more that the nation's barmaids might rise up in revolt at this comparison, and none of us wanted that.

Presenting this show gave me access to the sometimes primitive video recordings of each country's song. Very few other people had this information so I managed to put a bet on my choice for favourite before the bookies had settled their prices. Having missed out on my own dead-cert bet in 1984, I wasn't going to let this chance pass. Even though it was actually worth betting on the quality of the song back then, rather than its country of origin, which appears to be the only deciding factor now, I still got it wrong and lost my dosh.

In later years, I opened a phone account with a major bookie purely to place my annual bet on the Song Contest, until they got wise to who was calling and said they hadn't opened the book yet. Not that my choices ever won. Their money was safe from my expert forecasts. I had much more success in the BBC sweepstake, with wins in several years, but that was a random draw which I couldn't spoil with my great musical judgement.

In the twenty-first century, all you require in order to predict a Eurovision winner is an atlas. Neighbour votes for neighbour, and former Soviet republic votes for other former Soviet republic. It's all depressingly inevitable. In Switzerland in 1989, twenty-two countries took part; twenty years on, it's regularly over forty. It's too big and unwieldy, and the organizers seem to be behind the pace of change, allowing too rapid an expansion without anticipating the effects. In the commercial world, that's suicide; Eurovision is no different.

The growth of the competition has strangled the original concept. The idea that we're looking for the best new song in Europe is laughable. Songs no longer matter; spectacle is the only performance indicator, and geographical proximity or tribal loyalty outweigh even that. It really is time for Eurovision to go back to the drawing board and start again. Perhaps 2009's review of the voting procedure is the first step in that process.

*

By the later part of the 1980s the mid-morning slot had established nicely and I felt I had a strong rapport with the audience. Somehow, despite regular protestations of support and plenty of kind words, I felt I still hadn't quite convinced management of my worth. Partly, this was because all the network's publicity and promotion was based around Jameson, Jimmy Young and Gloria. They were the most publicly recognized faces, so there was a kind of logic to it, but I could never understand why majoring on them meant there had to be total silence about me, Adrian Love and John Dunn. At least I was in good company, but this policy has continued, and indeed narrowed to the present day, when Radio 2's promotional campaigns consistently only show the most recent, most visible recruits.

Good though they undoubtedly are, the fact remains that over 70 per cent of Radio 2's total audience share is provided by three shows: Sarah Kennedy, Terry Wogan and mine. And the biggest single show on a Saturday is not Jonathan Ross; it's presented by an eighty-year-old gentleman by the name of Brian Matthew under the title *Sounds of the 60s*. Why are these successes not trumpeted? Because they don't fit with the marketing ethos of attracting new young audiences by showing them faces they already know.

We have a moan but don't complain all the time. We don't really want a massive advertising campaign built around us; just a mention now and again would be nice.

The slight feeling I had developed in the late 1980s of having to check my back occasionally for knives, thanks to the BBC's continuing fascination with booking 'star' names, led me to accept an offer for pantomime. Oh, yes, I did. A charming man called Paul Elliott, who ran more than half the pantos in the country, offered me the chance to appear as Alderman Fitzwarren in *Dick Whittington* at the Richmond Theatre, a perfect venue as it was close to both work and home, and meant that I could carry on the morning show while treading the boards in the afternoons and evenings.

I speedily agreed, as Anne and I had been thinking about moving house and the extra money would cover the costs. We had an excellent cast: Robin Askwith, keeping his trousers on for once, fellow Scotsman Peter Blake, who had scored a success in *Dear John* on television and proved an eminently hissable King Rat, and topping the bill were Bernie Winters with Schnorbitz, and Su Pollard. This line-up was slightly irksome to Su, who, although very fond of Bernie, had come second to a performing dog on *New Faces* at the start of her career, and her views on cute canines had taken a downward turn ever since.

Luckily, Schnorbitz (who was a large St Bernard, for the benefit of younger readers) was almost completely torpid, confining himself to shuffling on and off stage at his cues and sitting stock still in comatose fashion between times, so was not likely to be a major threat in terms of scene-stealing.

It was an interesting experience for me, because although I had frequently appeared on stage as a host and compere, acting is a whole different matter. And acting in panto is different again, since you are appearing in a strange amalgam, both as a character and also as yourself.

I confess I struggled, first with the learning of lines, something I had never had to do, and secondly with the exaggerated movements so necessary for this kind of theatre. My fellow performers were encouraging but I know I was about as mobile as a Chippendale dresser for most of

'Ten Miles to London . . .' Su Pollard is Dick Whittington, while I give my all as Alderman Fitzwarren. Richmond Theatre, 1988.

Scott, me, Issy and Alasdair at my mother's eightieth birthday (1989).

A photoshoot promoting British menswear. Left to right: Derek Nimmo, Ernie Wise, Roy Castle, Terry Scott, Norman Vaughan, Bernard Bresslaw, me, Jimmy Cricket.

Queuing to get into the Cinecitta in Rome for Eurovision, 1991. Left to right: Jo Gurnett, Paul Walters, me, Terry Wogan.

My mother and my Aunt Isobel braving the elements on the north-east coast.

Interviewing David Suchet as Poirot at a Torquay outside broadcast.

Wilson, Keppel & Betty's World Tour. Me, Terry and Paul Walters at
the Wailing Wall, Jerusalem, for Eurovision, 1999.

Kerith with Kate in Ealing, 1999.

Kerith and a red-faced BBC spokesman in 1999.

Seeing in the Millennium broadcasting from Plockton Village Hall.

My three youngest children, Murray, Verity and (below) Charlie.

Hosting an open-air concert at Balmoral, 2005.

'Who's that with Ken?' you're probably wondering. Beyonce guested on our Tracks of My Years spot and was kind enough to agree to be photographed.

Every man should have his own bus.

the run, and I only really loosened up towards the end, by which time I had decided that I was out of my comfort zone and not doing it well enough for my satisfaction.

I hate the feeling of not quite hacking it. In a way I had felt similarly out of my specialist area at the Olympics, since my sports knowledge was only sketchy and I was heavily reliant on good production, but at least I was being used there specifically as a non-expert. In pantomime, I knew I was not doing it as well as my colleagues and I resolved not to put myself in such a situation again.

I did it as well as I could, and probably did get a little better by the time the run had finished, but being out of one's natural element is not a comfortable situation and I was relieved when we rang down the curtain for the last time. That said, I had a highly enjoyable time with truly sweet people for whom I have nothing but admiration.

We actually moved house in the middle of the run, two days before Christmas. It was the easiest house move I ever experienced, as I left home at half past seven in the morning and returned to a different house at eleven o'clock at night, with all the furniture neatly in place. Perhaps it wasn't terribly considerate to immediately pour myself a glass of wine and flop into an armchair, saying, 'Well, this all seems to have gone very easily.' I thought the hard stare was unnecessary, though.

A couple of weeks after the panto closed, Anne and I were married in a very quiet ceremony at Acton Town Hall, followed by a meal in a West End restaurant. And so I settled into what seemed to be a pretty good life: new house, new marriage and the radio show was doing well. What could possibly go wrong? I should have known better.

Eight

'If I'd Known I was so Popular, I'd Have Asked for More Money'

I should have suspected something when the BBC suddenly started mentioning me in public. In 1989 Frances Line became Controller of Radio 2 and gave a couple of press interviews in which she praised my abilities. She even sent me copies in case I had missed them. Naturally I assumed this meant that the status quo was giving satisfaction and would be maintained. Wrong. I was being softened up for a move.

Frances called me in to her office one Friday. These meetings are always on a Friday so you don't go back on air the next morning and slag everyone off. The belief is, after a weekend to consider, you'll have cooled off enough to stop yourself from committing professional hara-kiri.

The news she gave me was not good. She thought it was, though. I was being given the chance to launch a brand new programme that would expand the daytime style of broadcasting into a new area. This new area was late nights. My interpretation of the move was somewhat different. From my point of view, I was being taken off the mass audience of mornings and shunted into a dark-hours backwater.

I should look upon it as a promotion, Frances said enthusiastically, a mark of the trust they had in me. I saw it as tantamount to a dismissal. To be fair to Frances, she did believe in me and gave me some assurance about my future as well as a decent pay increase. The assurance was that I should do this for two years and then, if I wasn't happy, I would come back to daytime. I'm afraid I didn't put any weight on this at the time as I knew that the best of intentions are often overtaken by events, and the broadcasting landscape could look very different in the space of two years.

I could only see it as a slap in the face and, when the news eventually came out in public, I wasn't alone. 'Ken Axed Again' read the headline in the *Sun*. I was pretty morose, and for the first time in my career seriously considered an approach from a commercial radio station. Not for long, though. Radio 2 was my spiritual home; I knew the audience, they knew me, and the long view was the one I felt I could afford to take. My somewhat arrogant stance was that if management had temporarily lost their sense of direction, I would just wait until they'd got back on track again.

The plan was for me to replace Brian Matthew at night, where his *Round Midnight* show had been running for many years, and I would be replaced in the mornings by Judith Chalmers. Brian was, and remains, a fine broadcaster, and was very unhappy with the change. Mind you, his move was to *Sounds of the 60s*, which has been a consistent ratings winner ever since, and Brian is still there nearly twenty years later.

I knew Judy and liked her very much; we'd done several shows together. As usual, the broadcasters bore no serious grudges against each other, and we could all unite in blaming management for our disrupted lives.

No one has a freehold on a radio slot; there are no such things as squatters' rights in broadcast schedules, but I did feel a proprietorial interest over the 9.30 a.m. slot and would miss the audience who were so responsive at that time. A point of concern was that Judy could only do the show for six months as she had television commitments for the rest of the year. I felt that wasn't playing fair with 'my' audience; they ought to have some continuity. However, it wasn't my problem, and my priority was to get the new late-night show up and running. Phil Hughes would produce and he came up with a format of interviews and features, including a late-night newspaper review with the regional front pages faxed or phoned to us, which made for a strong and topical late-evening listen.

We launched in April 1990 to a good reception, but I struggled with the hours. I was a morning person; it was when my brain was ticking over best. I liked getting up, doing a radio show while fired up and then relaxing after. I couldn't seem to get used to getting up in the morning and waiting around all day to go to work just as everyone else was going home. Still, I buckled down to it and dug in for a long run.

The show ran from ten o'clock to midnight, and because some of our contributors would want to be tucked up under their candlewicks by that time, we pre-recorded some interviews. This meant I was expected in the studio by seven o'clock. Anne was working all day, so we would only see each other for about fifteen minutes before the BBC car came to whisk me in to Broadcasting House. The car, by the way, was a contractual stipulation as I was not prepared to drive myself home at midnight and thus stay alcohol-free for the entire week.

Then events took a strange turn; someone from publicity told me that they'd had quite a few letters of complaint about the fact that I'd been moved. Two weeks later, they came back and said that the number of complaints had reached 4,000. I was astonished – for a moment – then delighted.

The *Daily Mirror* columnist John Diamond wrote a piece in praise of me and received a further 5,000 letters of support. When I met him some time afterwards, he said they'd had many more sacks they hadn't bothered to open. He also admitted that he wasn't much of a listener really but his wife had suggested he do the piece, the lady in question being a certain Nigella Lawson.

As an aside, John and I were at a BBC dinner with a very senior executive seated between us. This person admitted at one point to being a fan of *I'm Sorry I Haven't a Clue* but was confused about something. Could we explain the rules of Mornington Crescent? Diamond and I went into a jokey explanation. 'Ah well, it's a complex issue of transportation and diagrammatic representation'; 'But, of course, let's not forget that when the joker comes into play, the whole basis of the action reverses,' and a great deal more jargon-laden rubbish until it slowly dawned upon us that our assumption that the executive was sharing the joke was wildly mistaken. The question had been deadly serious. We backtracked quickly and changed the subject. Chatting later, John was shocked that someone so high in the BBC hierarchy could fail to understand a key part of its output. I was not quite so surprised. A sense of humour and high office do not always go hand in hand. Listening to the output was also not always considered necessary.

The responses to my move to late nights surprised the BBC. They had not expected such a reaction. To be honest, neither had I. The old line, 'If I'd known I was so popular, I'd have asked for more money,' sprang to mind. One or two other papers took up the story to some degree or another, to the slight irritation of some at the corporation. At that year's Eurovision in Zagreb, I met up with the BBC's correspondent there, who said to me, 'I've been reading about you; you've become something of a cause célèbre.' To which, the senior man accompanying me said drily, 'Don't believe everything you read in the papers.'

Whether it had any effect, I don't know; sometimes, the BBC determines not to yield to campaigns just to show its independence of thinking. A more personal pressure for change came up; I really couldn't adjust to the hours. I decided that I would have to speak to Frances Line about it, without any great expectation of a fast solution being offered. I was wrong. She immediately offered to move me back into the daytime, but said at present she could only offer me the mid-afternoon slot or the early mornings. It was no contest; I asked to go back to the early show, where I'd begun my Radio 2 efforts. It was quickly arranged. My friend Chris Stuart, who had taken over the slot after Ray Moore's death, was tiring of the early starts and seemed happy to move to nights, and so a straight swap was effected, sold to the press as a conflict of body clocks.

So, after nine months of late-night broadcasting, I was back in the mornings. Not in my old slot but in a very nice place nonetheless. I was especially pleased when David Hatch, who had given me my first shows on the station, and who was now Director of Radio, popped into the studio on the first day and said he was personally delighted I was back on mornings. He wasn't half as delighted as I was.

I would have to face the tyranny of the alarm clock again, though. I've always needed a good eight hours each night and I was damned if I was going to go to bed at nine o'clock each evening, so I determined that I would not get up before five in the morning. This didn't leave a massive amount of time before being on air at six o'clock, but it was enough for a quick wash and brush-up, a Clarksonesque race into town and twenty minutes in the studio waking up before launching myself on the airwaves.

My voice was always still in my boots at six o'clock and the brain was still in bed, but by the time the show finished, seemingly in a trice, at half past seven, most cylinders were firing. Paul Walters was back producing me, and although he was an early riser and often in the office during transmission time, the policy of the day was for there to be 'No Producer Present'. In other words, the presenter was alone in the studio with just a technical operator and was trusted to get on with the job, make the right decisions and not swear or bring the BBC into disrepute. How very different from the current age.

Paul built the music running order weeks in advance, and he proved at that time to have an uncanny knack of picking songs that would prove either appropriate or awkward, depending on the news of the day. One morning there was a serious air crash, with the story developing while I was on air, with frequent interruptions for news updates. I accommodated all these, but found that we had just about every air- or plane-themed record ever made in that morning's running order. 'Leaving on a Jet Plane', 'High in the Sky', 'Up, Up and Away', were all in there, and I was tossing records aside like plates at a Greek wedding. I managed to avoid any unfortunate titles, until the very last newsflash, where the disc following was the Everly Brothers' 'On the Wings of a Nightingale'. Not appropriate, I thought, and as I had just about run out of other music I looked for a different track from their album. 'The Story of Me' sounded safe enough, so I cued it up, just listening to the first two notes of the song. The news, with its toll of dead and injured passengers trapped in the wreckage, ended and I played in the disc, with the first words from Don and Phil being, 'Rescue me . . .'.

1991 was the year of the Gulf War, and News Division were granted extra time for their bulletins, particularly the main seven o'clock one, which could stretch from its normal seven minutes to ten or more. Once again, music became a danger area but we managed to avoid any faux pas. On the day the war ended, news asked for a further extension, and as they finished at twelve minutes past the hour, rather than the expected seven, the first disc up had Sinatra singing, 'Give me five minutes more.'

A less obvious one, but which gave me material for a corny link, was on the morning of the national census, when every householder is expected to complete the form detailing all residents. That show began with John Denver and 'Annie's Song'. If you're struggling to find the connection, the first line he sings is, 'You fill up my senses.'

It was a happy year and I learned to cope with the early starts by nipping home after the show and topping up with a nap for an hour or two. Not every day, though, as I was busier than before. When I had been removed from daytime the year before, some others, like me, had seen it as an indication of a loss of commitment from Radio 2. The good people of Radio 4 offered me the chance to take over the Saturday morning holiday programme *Breakaway*. Bernard Falk had been presenting this, but the bosses had decided to move him to another show produced by the same department, *Going Places*. Tragically, Bernard died suddenly just a few weeks into the new order.

The reason Bernard was moved was because he was not often available to travel abroad for *Breakaway*, having his own production company to run in London. I was a bizarre choice to replace him, as I was, if anything, less available, having a daily commitment in London for Radio 2. It didn't seem to bother Radio 4, so it didn't bother me. And, by skilful manipulation of my holidays and, on one occasion, persuading the BBC that my daily show would sound very good coming from Orkney for a few days, I did manage to get out of London and do some features.

Everyone laughs when you say you've been to Jamaica to work, and I can't pretend it wasn't pleasant, but, and you can laugh again now if you wish, it *was* actually quite hard work. Well, not hard, but I was kept busy and didn't have much time to enjoy the island, as after completing our interviews I had to get back home to reassure Radio 2 that I still cared about them really.

In fact, I have much stronger memories of a trip to Alaska, probably because it's not a place I would ever seriously contemplate visiting off my own bat. Spectacular glaciers, icy waters and keen but entirely clear air; I felt quite at home. The wildlife was impressive: beluga whales so close to the shore you felt you could reach out and touch them and, at one point, a moose standing right in front of the car in the middle of town. The people were like the Scots, resigned to living in an unwelcoming climate but relaxed about it, and used to being an afterthought to their fellow countrymen to the south. They also had their fair share of eccentrics, including the woman who ran the B&B establishment we stayed in.

Jet lag had ensured my sleep patterns were all over the place, and on the first night of my stay I was awake at some unearthly hour and working on my laptop, my very first, which was about the weight of a small horse even without the battery attached, itself the size of a breezeblock. Tapping away gently at the keyboard, I heard another gentle tapping at my door. It was my landlady, dressed in what would have been described by the comic Rikki Fulton as a 'dianaphous neglyge'. In a Fenella Fielding-type voice she enquired huskily if there was anything she could do for me. Had this been a *Carry On* film and I more of a Leslie Phillips character, I would immediately have gone into 'ding-dong' mode. As it wasn't, added to the fact that in the looks department she was less Barbara Windsor, more Windsor Davies, I simply stammered in a quaking falsetto that I was fine thanks and just falling asleep. I stopped short of saying I was gay, and impotent to boot, but would have done if she hadn't given up and withdrawn. Besides, I was a married man. Even on tour. I was still slightly offended that she gave up so easily, though.

Back home, and after less than a year of doing the early turn, out of the blue Frances Line asked me if I would please go back to my 9.30 a.m. slot, adding words I never thought I would hear a BBC executive say: 'I was wrong.' It was a magnanimous thing to say and I was touched, even though she hadn't in all honesty got it wrong. She'd made a decision, tried it out and it hadn't quite worked, so she'd said as much and put things back again. I admired her for that. I've known an awful lot of people who wouldn't dream of owning up to an idea that hadn't worked, imagining that to do so is a sign of weakness. Real strength is being willing to try out new things, but being just as willing to admit it when the experiment hasn't come off. It had been worth a try, but I can't pretend I wasn't delighted that I was to be 'rehabilitated'.

Breakaway was a Saturday morning programme, broadcast live, so theoretically I could have continued with that, except for the fact that Friday was its main prep day and I would now be unavailable until the afternoon. This created all sorts of problems and so we had to part company. It had been fun and I had honed my formal scriptwriting skills, but returning to daytime Radio 2 well outweighed any disappointment. As for Radio 2, we had a new breakfast presenter, Brian Hayes, a surprise choice, but I thought a good one. Brian's fame was based round his LBC phone-in, where his famously direct, bordering on rude, responses to his callers had made him a must-listen. His reputation was that of a Rottweiler, but I had never heard him be abrupt with anyone who didn't deserve it and he was sensitive and patient, but never sentimental, with those who had something worth saying. In person, he was friendly and funny and I enjoyed his company and his broadcasts.

His predecessor, Derek Jameson, had shifted to nights, in a double act with his wife, Ellen. There are two schools of thought as to how this move came about and I leave you to decide which is more likely. One is that, having heard Ellen appear on a special with Derek, the BBC thought they made a quirky on-air team and were perfectly suited to a late-night chat show, and that such a ready-made hit would be an excellent way of introducing independent production to Radio 2. At the same time, following a policy of diversifying production bases, it would be the first major strand for the network to be produced from Scotland, and with Ellen having Scottish roots this made perfect sense.

The other interpretation was that Radio 2 wanted Derek off the network, so they offered him a package that would be so insulting he would resign. You move from breakfast to late nights; not only that, but it's four days rather than five. We'll still pay you, but you have to split the money with your wife, who will co-host. In addition (and, if this is true, they must have thought this was the clincher), you'll have to do the programme from Glasgow every night. Oh, and with an inexperienced production team. To their surprise, nay, shock, he said yes.

Which is nearer the truth? The decision is yours.

Derek and Ellen bought a flat in Glasgow and began their show, which developed into a cult hit as people were hooked by the Jamesons' nightly niggle-fest, with them transferring their sometimes decidedly snippy kitchen conversations directly on to the airwaves. Lots of people tuned in, without always being able to tell you why.

Brian Hayes fared less well as the powers did to him what they did to me and failed to allow him time to settle in the new slot and develop the audience. After a year, he was moved to a show which utilized his original skills as a phone-in host. Brian, being a gentleman, accepted the situation in a typically gracious manner. A radio professional.

Terry Wogan, the great Terry, the man born to present the Radio 2 breakfast show, returned, and the morning partnership we forged then has continued to the present day. I pop in to see him practically every day; we have a laugh, a moan, a rant about the latest excesses of management and politicians, and then get on with our work again. Every morning has been a joy.

In the early stages of my return to the mid-mornings, I had another case of the thankfully rare broadcasting condition of corpsing. It was during a two-way with Jimmy Young, and I cannot now remember what set me off, but I lost it completely and a record had to be played in. I mention it now only because while I may not remember the words that caused it, I do remember the real cause. I tend to be most susceptible to corpsing when I'm in a heightened emotional state, and the night before we had discovered that Anne was pregnant. Marriage number two, child number three. You'd best keep count; it gets complicated later.

Kate was born in the October of 1992, and so we had a nice new family. Anne and I, the two boys, a new baby daughter, and an inherited spaniel, whom I referred to as my step-dog. The boys came to London at least every month, flying down from Glasgow on a Friday night and back on Sunday. They were happy, bright lads and took to their new sister immediately. And as soon as she could talk, they started to wind her up and tease her. It's what brothers do. I had a new lease of life at work, we had settled into our house in Ealing and everything looked rosy. Sadly, the idyll was not to last.

But in the meantime, I was happy and fulfilled. It was around this time that I was caught on camera being disrespectful and using bad language to a national icon, none other than the sainted Pudsey bear of Children in Need fame. Before you rush to condemn me, there are mitigating circumstances which I will lay out in my defence. Radio 2 had, at that time, engaged its first marketing team to work alongside and in cooperation with the publicity office. The two marketeers and the pair of publicity officers boasted one of the finest line-ups of surnames I have ever come across: Rock, Blott, Holdom and Nutt. You could not make it up.

In charge of marketing was Roger Holdom, who managed to persuade BBC television to publicize the Radio 2 music marathon, the twenty-four-hour request show in aid of Children in Need. They gave us three slots on BBC1 through the evening to tell viewers about the opportunity they had to phone in and pledge money to hear their favourite pieces of music. The wheeze was that I would appear on screen in an interesting location with Pudsey in attendance and between us we would soon have the coffers rattling. Edinburgh was settled on for the location and so off we trooped for the evening.

Younger readers should look away now, as I have to reveal to you that when you see Pudsey bear on screen, occasionally it is not the real Pudsey. It's a man in a suit. I'm sorry, but there it is. You had to know.

Roger was to be Pudsey for the evening. He was an excellent marketing man, all buzzing ideas and enthusiasm, but as a costume performer he lacked something. Coordination, mainly. We were to record our pieces in Princes Street, in front of the National Gallery with the floodlit castle in the background. A lovely idea, marred only by a constant down-pour of rain which necessitated my carrying a huge golf umbrella, totally obliterating the view behind me. Edinburgh is a cold city at the best of times, and this being November, it was doing its job even better than usual.

We had three pieces to record, and each time, Roger, as Pudsey, either missed his cue or stopped in the wrong place or faced in the wrong direction. To be fair to him, life can't be easy inside a bear suit, largely insulated from outside sights and sounds. At least he was warm and dry, though.

I am a patient man, and managed to do retake after retake without complaint, but then on the *rare* occasions when Roger got his bit right, I would fluff my lines, making what should have been a short task stretch over a whole evening. By the time we had got to the final piece, to be played out at close-down, the cold and damp had seeped into my bones, and the iron had entered into my soul.

When Roger walked boldly into shot and crashed straight into me, I could take no more and broke into my spiel to add, 'And Pudsey's f***ed it up *again!*' The crew were delighted, having a nice cut for their Christmas outtakes compilation, but I felt I had committed a mortal sin by swearing at Pudsey. I consoled myself that it was not the real Pudsey, as he would have hit his marks perfectly, and I was really only swearing at a marketing man, which is, as we know, perfectly justifiable and acceptable. But it is still a matter of shame to me that I uttered those words to even a substandard Pudsey and I have done all I can for Children in Need ever since as my penance.

*

The end of my second marriage in mid-1995 came as a shock. Quite literally, as I had not seen it coming. Only a few weeks earlier I had given an interview to an old friend, Willie Hunter of the *Glasgow Herald*, and had talked of my contentment, both professional and domestic. I really should learn not to tempt fate.

I sensed something was not right with Anne, but the ostrich tendency is strong in me and the head stayed firmly buried in the sand. Eventually, one night, when she looked thoroughly miserable, she admitted that she was not at all sure she wished to remain married to me. You can have an inkling, even a strong feeling that something is wrong but still, when the confirmation comes, be knocked sideways by it. I had not for a second imagined that the relationship I had left my first wife and children for could end as suddenly and as finally as this. I was completely at sea.

Later, friends expressed surprise that I had been on the radio every day sounding chirpy through all the upheaval, but the reality was that only the radio show and the escape it offered kept me afloat. That, and my determination that I would remain a hands-on parent to my daughter. I had always regretted that, even though I saw my sons regularly, I simply couldn't be there for them as much as I wanted, with a 350-mile gap between us. I would not let that happen again. Once the dust had settled, we agreed Kate would live five days with me and five days with her mother. This meant I wouldn't be a weekend-only dad and could play a complete part in her upbringing, school runs, doctor's visits, the lot; she had her own bedroom in each house and quickly adapted to the new regime – a lot quicker than I did.

My life for the next several years was an odd mix; I was

a single parent with care, leading a busy and abstemious life for half the time, with a two-year-old to feed, bathe, clothe and entertain, but I organized myself and, after the initial panic of finding oneself totally responsible for a small child with no one else in the house to share the duties, I discovered I was, even if I say it myself, quite good at it.

When Kate went off to her mother's, my lifestyle changed and I was living the life, as one of my friends imaginatively put it, of a playboy. A slight exaggeration, but I did the usual midlife things: joined a gym to look fitter, sold the sensible family car and bought a convertible, went to parties and drank too much.

It took a while, getting on for a couple of years, when our divorce was finalized, but eventually I toned down the parties and drank a little less, although not before spending an entire afternoon and early evening getting plastered at an industry event and then attempting to make my way home by tube. God knows how, but I had managed to negotiate the tube network from an unfamiliar station and change to the correct train for home when I began to feel a little unwell. I decided fresh air would help so got off the train at Barons Court station. I made for the exit gate but couldn't locate my ticket anywhere about my person so decided just to sit on the bench on the westbound platform for a few minutes to get my breath back.

I woke two hours later. I had been fast asleep, drooling no doubt, in full view of every packed Piccadilly Line train through the entire rush hour. I was very grateful at that moment for the anonymity that radio provides. I stumbled on to the next train and reeled home, my ticket having made a miraculous reappearance in my pocket, and went straight to bed.

The following morning, when I got up for work, I found my clothes, in order from socks to coat, in a long trail from the bedside to the front door. It was that day I decided that I really couldn't carry on like this; I had to get over it, stop wallowing, cut down the drinking and begin living a new life.

One thing I was definitely sure of: I would not be getting married again. I was in my mid-forties, divorced twice, with three children, and to even contemplate throwing myself back into the maelstrom again was madness. Wrong again, although I couldn't know it at the time. Mystic Meg had nothing to fear from me.

In the meantime, I was dating again, always around my parenting responsibilities, and very happy at work. Jim Moir had replaced Frances Line as Controller of Radio 2 and immediately signed me up to a long contract, followed by an extension of the show time to its present length, 9.30 a.m. to midday. And I had been joined by a new producer. Well, not exactly new; Colin Martin was one of the longest-serving producers in the department and had been running the *John Dunn Show* for several years. We fell to talking one day and he remarked that he'd been looking for a new challenge recently and had ideas for my show. In my enthusiasm for shaking up every facet of my life I had wanted to move the programme on too, and we discovered that we had a shared wish to brighten and modernize the music policy.

We both wanted to work together but we couldn't just go to the bosses and suggest it; that would be a sure-fire way of having the idea rejected. We had to make them think they'd thought of it first. So I mentioned to my executive producer that I felt the show needed a fresh approach but I couldn't think of any producer who would be right for it. A few days later, Colin was chatting with the same exec and idly remarked that he was an admirer of mine but felt that the show had unrealized potential. He said later he could almost see the light bulb coming on above the man's head. Next day, I had an approach from a very smug-looking executive who said, 'How would you feel about working with Colin Martin?'

'D'you know, I'd never thought of him,' I said slowly. 'But – it could just work. Yes, the more I think about it, it's a brilliant idea!' Exit one beaming exec, leaving two very contented working colleagues. Once you know how the BBC works, you can get it working for you.

Colin had faultless musical taste and set about altering the sound of the show without alienating its existing listeners. That sounds such an obvious approach that you would think it hardly worth noting, but you'd be amazed how many times changes in radio are pushed through without careful enough thought about how the current audience will react. Ours liked it and the figures reflected that. In addition, Colin suggested a quiz might bring some added value to the show, so between us, with the invaluable addition to the think tank of pop maestro Phil Swern, we came up with the format and the title for PopMaster.

Our intention was always that it should be a tough quiz, but that our accuracy must be absolute. Ed Stewart was running a quiz in the afternoon at the time which seemed regularly to have people challenging its answers and I was determined that ours should be above criticism, hence the importance of having Phil, Dr Pop, on board. From the age of about ten, he had bought every single in the Top Ten every week, forming a vast collection which he kept in an ever-growing part of the family home in Wembley. Even when he eventually sold off his collection of vinyl, he started again replacing everything with CDs. No one is a better, more knowledgeable compiler of pop quizzes.

Everyone, with the possible exceptions of Brian Sewell and the Archbishop of Canterbury, believes they know about popular music and we banked on the likelihood of those people wishing to show off that knowledge, so the standard of questions was set pretty high. Soon enough, it became apparent that the level of expertise out there was consider-able, so the bar was gradually raised higher and higher until we reached the status, I like to think, of the *Mastermind* of pop.

Not that everyone who applied was quite so expert. We had several zero scores, and one or two people who were so overcome by finally getting on to the quiz that they dried up after one correct answer. Almost everyone will say, and it's true, that 'it's more difficult when you're actually on the radio'. The questions are misheard, or adrenaline spits an answer out before it's been properly considered, but either way some daft things are said. One exchange I recall ran like this:

'The brothers Derek and Alan Longmuir were members of which seventies boy band?'

'The Osmonds?'

'No, they tended to be called Osmond, as a rule.'

I kept a relatively straight face for that one but failed miserably when one contestant was accompanied throughout her answers by her pet cockatiel. I'm not entirely sure why but I find the sounds parrots and other 'talking' birds make inherently hilarious. Perhaps I was influenced by a parrot joke at an early age. Parrots look funny for a start and simply squawking is enough to get me going. If they can manage a word or two, I'll laugh like a drain, and if they can swear; well, I'm completely poleaxed with no hope of recovery

The cockatiel in question had no words at all, rude or otherwise, as far as I could make out, but what he did have was timing. Perfect comic timing. Just after I had finished a question, he'd interject with a querulous, 'Aaark?' and I would start to snort. The poor lady gave her answer and the bird would add an approving, 'Awwk.' This continued for the ten questions, by which stage I was barely able to say any more words than the cockatiel, and our contestant thought she had caught me on a medication-free day.

The prizes were hardly life-changing; an inflatable chair and a shower radio, evolving into a CD wallet and a digital radio, but most contestants simply wanted to be on the quiz to show how much they knew, and, in some cases, how little. And then there was the 'Can I say hello to a few people?' problem. Sometimes we are treated to a litany of relatives, friends, workmates and pets before getting anywhere near the ubiquitous 'and anyone else who knows me'. Maybe I should have stamped on it from the start, but it's too late now, and anyway, it affords some harmless pleasure to those involved.

Over the years, my excellent producers, Ken Phillips and the current and longest-serving, Gary Bones, have tweaked the format and difficulty, but a real problem arose in 2007, when the BBC was hit by the phone-in controversy. It had started on commercial television, and what is still often forgotten is that their transgressions in this area were much worse than the corporation's. Our response, I'm afraid, allowed the impression that the BBC was as guilty as the others to take hold. A blanket ban on any competition with a phone-in element was hastily introduced, meaning that perfectly innocent quizzes, such as the Goal of the Month and, of course, PopMaster, were bundled in with the dubious ones.

This blanket ban was, I felt, a huge overreaction; in an effort to show that the corporation was taking it seriously, it only gave the impression that the top management had so little idea about what was going out on their services that their only option was to take everything off. Worse, it took ages to get things back on again.

I felt personally affronted; it seemed to me that my own honesty had been called into question. I deeply resented the implication that my quiz was in any way under suspicion and fired off an intemperate email to my immediate bosses. I received sympathetic replies, but the Director of Radio, Jenny Abramsky, said, ruefully, that it could take as long as six weeks to clear everything up and get PopMaster back on air. Six weeks! That seemed a lifetime. If I had known it would actually take ten long months for the BBC to finally discover that there was, and had been, nothing at all wrong with our procedures, I may possibly have been in prison by now doing a twenty-five-stretch.

In a long tradition of BBC own goals, this seemed a classic. We were indulging in a corporation-wide *mea culpa* and tarring all of our mostly innocent output with the same guilty brush, all the while diverting attention from the proven wrongdoing of our competitors.

Immediately after the initial suspension, I fought fiercely to get some form of PopMaster back on; a major element of its popularity was the listener taking part in the car or at home, shouting out the answers before the on-air competitors could. Why should they be deprived of their enjoyment? We quickly introduced Celebrity PopMaster and a willing array of famous people came out of the woodwork to take part. Some really knew their stuff; from *Emmerdale*, Tony Audenshaw and, particularly, Charlie Hardwick dazzled with their knowledge. Richard Drummie from Go West became the eventual celebrity champion, and Rob Brydon not only knew all the answers but delivered them in my voice.

Others knew a little less; in fact, most of the celebrities knew very little, but their floundering attempts made for, I hope, an entertaining listen.

A bizarre side effect of the ban on phone calls showed itself. When we tried to get the extremely knowledgeable BBC News presenter Jonathan Charles on, we were told that while he could do it on a line from Television Centre he couldn't do it over the phone from home as that would make him a member of the public! Similarly, we were told that BBC staff could not take part but freelancers working for the corporation could. This meant that, from the Radio 2 newsreading stable, Charles Nove could appear but Fran Godfrey couldn't. Quite why two people doing what to the listening audience was exactly the same job should be treated completely differently I could never fathom. We were suffering from arbitrary rules, over-zealously applied, with a notable absence of common sense.

Celebrity PopMaster continued for far longer than we had anticipated, and the lack of a clear date for the restart of the normal competition, plus a few false dawns along the way, occasionally left us up a famous creek without a celebrity paddle. But someone always rallied round and we kept it going, with a full return early in January 2008 for a remark-ably unchanged public quiz which seems as addictive as ever.

At work, I had long since decided that I would only accept jobs that I was comfortable with, wanted to do and would enjoy. I had sat through enough corporate dinners waiting to make a speech to know that the discomfort was rarely worth the pay cheque. I had been a panellist on sufficient strange TV game shows to know that there were only a very few places on the medium that I would want to show my face. But, give me a nice voice-over or the chance to stand up on stage with a live orchestra, and I would be the proverbial schoolboy hopping up and down with my hand in the air.

The live concerts had been sporadically coming my way for a few years, but now the chance to make them a more regular part of my diet came, when I was offered some programmes in the *Friday Night is Music Night* series. I had last done one in 1982; obviously I had impressed so much it took the BBC a mere fifteen years to come rushing back to rebook me.

I love doing them; as I found out in the 1970s, I enjoyed being with musicians, especially those who could arrive, sight-read a complicated piece of music, play it perfectly and think nothing of it more than simply doing what they were paid for. Precisely the qualities I admired in broadcasters, although I've found in both professions that sometimes, if it looks too easy, people believe it really is.

Any live music show is going to have the odd problem, and stories of near-disaster are not too difficult to find. There was the night at a stunning English cathedral where the afternoon rehearsal had finished early to allow Choral Evensong to take place before the live transmission at half past seven. A long lay-off is always dangerous for musicians as the nearest pub is usually held to be the place to while away the hours.

In the evening, an instrumentalist, who was only required for a couple of numbers, came back rather well refreshed some time after the show had started. He tiptoed to his instrument in front of the audience, which included the Bishop, the Mayor and sundry other dignitaries. His arrival would have been less noticeable, it must be admitted, had he not been carrying a glass of red wine in one hand and a cigarette in the other.

Compounding the difficulty, he then tripped over a raised flagstone, health and safety officials being less prevalent in the seventeenth century, and fell headlong on the floor, sustaining a small cut to the head. Being a professional, though, he spilled not a drop of the wine. He merely dusted himself off and continued to his seat, where he nipped his cigarette, placed it and the wine glass on the lid of a handy piano, and beamed at the open-mouthed audience while wiping away a small trickle of blood from his cheek. Who said there's nothing to see at a radio show?

It wasn't only the performers who had been known to misbehave; even producers could occasionally go off the rails. One incumbent of the post 'popped out for a few minutes' during the rehearsal break at half past three one day. When he failed to return for the second part of the afternoon his PA and the studio managers just carried on. When he had still not returned by transmission time, there was nothing to do but plough on regardless. He eventually showed up fifteen minutes into the live programme, entering by the rear door of the stage area and processing through the orchestra while they played. He had two heavy-looking carrier bags with him that clinked loudly and insisted on greeting each player he passed with a 'Hello!' or 'How are you?' He made it to the control cubicle and promptly fell fast asleep for the remainder of the evening. Strangely, the programme review board later that week praised it as having been a particularly well-produced edition.

If tales like these don't reflect particularly well on the main character involved, they do show the tremendous professionalism of everyone else involved in such shows, where every person from the conductor to the studio porter knows exactly what they have to do and gets on with it without histrionics. *Friday Night is Music Night* is totally rehearsed and performed in the space of eight hours. The conductor and singers arrive at half past one and have a piano rehearsal, then the full orchestra, most of whom won't have seen the music until that minute, arrive at half past two, rehearse until six, go off for a bite to eat, and the live programme goes out from half past seven until quarter past nine.

On television, they'd want about a week to do all that, but on radio, it all happens in one working day. And they do it all again next Friday, too. You really are getting your licence fee's worth there.

Some of the guest singers have provided moments of fun. One man fell asleep in his dressing room after the rehearsal and awoke to hear the opening bars of his first live duet wafting through the speakers. He made it on to the studio floor in his street clothes just in time for the first chorus. After that, it became the custom for the producer to fetch the singers in time for their cues. One famous soprano was being accompanied to the stage when she suddenly clasped the producer's hands in hers. As she swept out to face her

Ken Bruce

adoring public, he discovered that she had used the gesture to deposit her chewing gum in his palm.

And then there was the little Spanish tenor who went with the crew to the pub after a show in Llandudno, discovered it was karaoke evening, stepped up, sang 'Nessun dorma', and won the first prize of free beer for the table for the rest of the night.

It's a fine old institution, *Friday Night*. It's been running for over fifty-five years and to some ears might sound a touch old-fashioned. I prefer the word traditional; it brings the sound of a live orchestra to the public, and indeed to some present-day performers unused to such luxury, and as well as the popular stuff it plays some music that might not get an airing anywhere else. It seems to me to be exactly the sort of thing the BBC ought to be doing.

My responsible parent/carefree bachelor split personality lifestyle kept me pretty happy during the late 1990s. My daughter was at nursery during the day, so I could drop her off on the way to work, and do any voice-overs that came my way in the early afternoon before picking her up on my way home. Any offers of evening work were either refused or deferred until a non-parenting part of the month. Social events were treated the same way.

I'd got used to living on my own. Until Anne and I separated I'd always been either living with my parents, married or sharing a flat with someone, but now, for half the year at any rate, I was alone in the house with no one else to consider. To my surprise, once I got used to it I found I quite liked the space. There were downsides; an occasional empty weekend with nothing to do and no one to see. But, largely, the situation I found myself in was good. I had had a couple of relationships but wasn't looking for anything too serious; my lifestyle militated against regular dates anyway. And I was still quite sure that I was finished with marriage.

That all changed at Eurovision 1998. The United Kingdom had won the previous year with Katrina and the Waves singing 'Love Shine a Light', and we would have the honour, if that is the correct term, of hosting the next one. Birmingham was chosen as the venue and the presenters would be Terry, of course, joined by Ulrika Jonsson. We all met up for a thoroughly enjoyable lunch in London beforehand and I looked forward to a fun competition.

The contest was notable for a number of things: it was the last time the show was hosted in the UK; it was the final one in which a live orchestra was used, our own BBC Concert Orchestra doing the honours; and it was where I met the woman who would become my third, and final, wife.

Kerith was working as a researcher on the *Jimmy Young Show*, having come to Radio 2 only a few months earlier from another branch of the BBC. Volunteers to work on the radio part of the operation had been called for, and since her parents lived near Birmingham, she had put her name forward. We met on the Thursday, when a promotional trip to Warwick Castle had been arranged; we independently managed to get lost on the way round and found our way out together. The following day, while stuck in the studio, we discovered that we had many mutual friends and acquaintances and liked a lot of the same music.

I was unattached at the time and, I discovered, so was she. She had the great advantage of being beautiful, warm-hearted and funny. By the Saturday of the contest, I was more than a little interested but was unsure how she, being sixteen years my junior, would react to some old lecher making advances. The contest was a terrific production, the good old BBC showing our so-called friends in Europe how such a show ought to be run. Kerith's work completed, she was able to sit in the auditorium and watch it, while Paul Walters and I crouched in our little hut backstage. For some reason, I had to announce the UK voting results in vision that year, in addition to my radio commentary, so had to don a dinner jacket and black tie for that section, retaining my jeans and comfortable trainers out of sight below the desk. Television is all artifice, you know. I slipped away from our post-show get-together to find Kerith at the wrap party, where we had a couple of drinks and a dance, after which we parted with me saying I'd call her during the week.

Feeling pleased with my night's work I returned to the hotel bar to find Terry and his wife Helen had been joined by Ulrika and her then boyfriend Stan Collymore, along with, surprisingly, Richard Whiteley, his partner Kathy and some friends. I fell into a night of pretty heavy drinking and found myself, long after the others had left, propping up the bar with the Irish broadcasting contingent. During the course of this evening, I may say, I was propositioned in the most direct terms not once but twice by attractive women, and even by one man. It was probably my most popular night ever, or would have been had I taken up any of the offers, but my interest had been sparked by Kerith and I wasn't in the market for a quick one. Besides, my ever-protective manager, Jo, had stayed up to keep an eye on me and every time I looked as if I was in danger, she stepped in and shifted me over to the other end of the bar. Finally, at half past five in the morning, she took a firm grip of my elbow, said, 'Right dear, you've had enough, time to go off to bed,' and propelled me to the lifts. Not for the first time, she had saved me from myself.

During the following week, I suggested to Kerith that we meet for a bite to eat, and to my surprise she agreed.

It turned out we were both wary of new relationships; I still held my aversion to any idea of marriage but did feel that I was starting with a clean slate. Looking back over my two marriages, I realized that my divorce from Fiona had left me with some pronounced feelings of guilt, which I had kept well suppressed. I had been very happy during my second marriage, but that happiness had been bought at the price of someone else's pain, and that was lodged deep in my mind. When I was divorced from Anne I felt, in a way, the books had been balanced. I had been asked to pay off my debt.

It meant that this new relationship with Kerith could start in an uncluttered, clean and guilt-free way. We were both completely free agents, no one else had any claim over us and we owed nobody any explanations. After my untidy love life of recent years, it was wonderful to be able to allow matters to develop at their own pace with no outside influences. We had come into the relationship without any encumbrances, but that is not to say we didn't have baggage. We both, in our different ways, had past experiences to draw on and had pretty firm ideas about what we would and wouldn't want in the future. Despite the odd few disagreements, we found ourselves growing closer until, when Kerith was experiencing some difficulties with her flat, it seemed only natural for her to move her things in to my house, and soon enough after that we were discussing marriage.

The fact that I had been so adamant that marrying again was not a possibility only confirmed to me that to be even contemplating such a move meant I had found the right partner. We were, quite definitely, in love. And so, two and a half years after meeting, we married in September 2000. Since this was to be my final marriage, the wedding to end all weddings was called for. We asked our mutual friend Canon Roger Royle, whom Kerith had met in her earlier BBC career and with whom I had presented the first live *Pause for Thought* on Radio 2, to conduct the service and invited as many of our families and friends as we could manage, the final guest list topping the 200 mark.

The service was in the beautiful setting of St Bartholomew's in Smithfield and at Roger's suggestion the nearby Old Brewery became the venue for the reception, for which I booked the Pasadena Roof Orchestra to provide the entertainment. This completed the circle of life nicely; having been born in a pub, or at least a nursing home that became one, I was now, nearly fifty years later, being married in a brewery. At least it proved that, despite all evidence to the contrary, I *could* organize a piss-up in one.

We sang, we danced, we had a run on an open-top bus and after it was all over we went off on honeymoon to Mauritius. We had discussed fully the prospect of a family, which, despite my staring fifty in the face, we very much wanted; without too much delay, Kerith 'fell' pregnant, to use the quaint old Scottish phrase which makes it always sound like an unfortunate accident, and in January 2002 our first child, Murray, was born. Every child is special, but Murray turned out to be more special than most.

Nine

'Smelly Dogs, Singing Osmonds and Other Guests . . .'

There weren't any warning signs to begin with, although Murray's had been a difficult birth which ended in a ventouse delivery, where at the final stage the child has a suction cap placed on its head and is pulled out by the doctor. This left the little fella with a rather odd shaped head with a slight protuberance at the back, which we were assured was to be expected with this delivery and would diminish quickly.

It didn't recede much at all, and to this day he still has a slightly prominent area at the back of the skull, much less noticeable now and covered by hair anyway. But he progressed normally and hit all his targets for the first year or so, only showing a tendency to suffer stomach upsets and frequent colds.

With hindsight, he was a slightly withdrawn child and a little less sociable than perhaps he might have been, but not overly so. For those early months he was a bright, happy, normal baby. He began crawling, 'bumming' along for quite a while before getting the full hang of it, and walked at about thirteen months. He started speaking, too; well, only a couple of words, really, like 'bus', and then two words together, 'A plane.'

Kerith planned to go back to work when he reached eighteen months, and we took him along to a nursery where he ran in enthusiastically and played with the toys, so, relieved that we'd found a place where he'd be happy, we arranged for him to start there. It didn't quite go to plan. On his first day at the nursery, he cried and cried. It got no better for several days but he did settle at the nursery after a while, and was much happier, especially when being welcomed by one of his favourite staff.

However, he showed less and less inclination to play with his peers; alongside them, yes, but interacting with them, no. And his speech seemed to disappear. The few words he had been using weren't forthcoming anymore. At home, he was still a loving and smiley boy so we assumed that this was simply a temporary setback, possibly a reaction to the difficult start at nursery.

When he had still not spoken after his second birthday and a meeting with the nursery staff revealed that his interaction with the other children was not improving, we took him to our GP, who immediately referred him to a specialist.

The first 'specialist' we saw seemed to have some hard and fast rules about what was normal and what wasn't. When she asked if he played with dolls and brushed their hair, we answered with a slight laugh, 'No,' and she declared, 'That's not normal.' I pointed out that I had two older boys, neither of whom had shown any inclination to dress dolls or attempt hair styling, but she was unmoved. She offered us no positives, only negatives.

We decided we needed someone who adopted a less rigid

definition of what constituted unusual behaviour and saw a senior specialist. He assured us that there would be no rush to diagnose, which was a comfort, but even then, in our hearts, we knew that something was not right and we were aware that our son's behaviour was tending towards the autistic. Our specialist advised against looking up symptoms on the Internet as there could be all sorts of explanations for his lack of speech and social skills. Of course we did a great deal of research, always looking for cases where children had suddenly started speaking after three or four years, with normal progress thereafter.

There were lots of such kids, but there were also many for whom such a loss was symptomatic of something more serious. Our doctor studiously avoided using the A-word in his meetings with us. It took until his full diagnosis, just prior to Murray's third birthday, before he even mentioned 'autism'. By this time we were already ourselves of that opinion so it didn't come as a surprise. But I can't pretend it wasn't a blow. It was not easy to accept that I had an autistic son.

Some people say that after such a diagnosis you have to grieve for your lost child. I don't like the terminology. Yes, you can regret the lost opportunities, the potential difficulties and the changes it will mean to family life. I remember one of my early reactions was sadness that I wouldn't be able to tell him bad jokes and hear him laugh at them. But my child is not lost. He is simply different. And we share a lot of laughter together in other ways.

Most people know something of autism, but many know only the most visible of autistic traits. Why should we know more? Like most conditions, we only take a detailed interest when it strikes close to home. To a lot of people, an autistic boy (and it is mostly boys – 80 to 90 per cent) is someone with an amazing talent: drawing exact replicas of once-seen buildings; calculating the day of the week from any birth date; playing complex piano pieces from memory. Certainly, some autistic people can do these things and more besides, but there are many who, while intelligent, have no particularly astonishing ability. And the range of symptoms and behaviours on the autistic spectrum is huge.

One thing that binds them all is a difficulty with communication or social skills. Autistic people have trouble empathizing with their peers and family or seeing matters from another person's viewpoint. According to some, it's an exaggerated maleness, which, while harsh on the benighted men of society, may not be that far off the mark.

As to its causes, well, no one really knows. There seems little doubt that it has, in part at least, a genetic cause, and affected families can often find examples of people with such traits scattered through the family tree, but of course, until recently, the medical profession was not very good at diagnosing the condition. And there's a strong belief in an environmental cause, but no one seems to be able to agree on exactly what that might be. A number of parents believed, and still believe, that the MMR vaccine had an effect, although there is no scientific evidence to back this. Some say their child changed overnight after receiving the jab. I've no doubt it did and it must be almost impossible for such parents not to link the two. But my child's behaviour seemed to change the day he started nursery, and no one would claim that preschool education was a factor. Some traumatic events just seem to trigger a more obvious appearance of symptoms which in any case don't truly begin to show until the age of about eighteen months, coincidentally just when these jabs are being given.

We were told that autism is a life-long condition, that there was no cure or treatment as such, but that it was difficult to predict how any child might develop. In some cases, the diagnosis becomes irrelevant as the child grows into an adult who has adapted to the world and can enjoy fulfilling relationships and jobs. Others may need care all their lives. The autistic spectrum is so wide that there never seem to be two sufferers exactly alike.

When Murray was diagnosed, Kerith was pregnant with our daughter Verity. We were advised about the possibly hereditary nature of autism, which caused us some concerns in the early months, but she has proved to be unaffected and our youngest, Charlie, born in 2008, thankfully shows no signs of the condition either, although we still keep a watching brief on him just in case. It has been and will be difficult for them growing up in the shadow of an autistic older brother, having to make allowances for his ways, and trying to understand that they cannot get away with bad behaviour that he seems, from their point of view, to be allowed to. We moved out of London and Kerith gave up work to look after the children and give Murray in particular a more structured life.

Let me tell you a little about Murray. He is now seven years of age, lively, active, sometimes too much so, tall for his years and good-looking. He does not speak. The few words he had as a toddler disappeared and now he communicates his wants and needs by taking you by the hand and leading you to whatever or wherever it is he wishes. He can also use a picture exchange system known as PECS in which he will use pre-printed pictures of everyday items together with an 'I want' card to make up a sentence strip. As to his comprehension, he seems to understand what we and his teachers are saying to him but doesn't always show this understanding or act on it. Mind you, this kind of selective deafness must be familiar to many other parents.

There are many small dilemmas like this faced on a daily basis. How much of his behaviour is autistic and how much is normal? Is he ignoring me because he doesn't understand or because he simply doesn't want to do what I ask? Is he angry and frustrated because he can't express himself or is he just having a grump like any other child?

He attends a specialist unit attached to a mainstream school where the staff are well tuned to the ways of autistic children, and can be integrated into normal classes when both he and the classes are suitable. He responds well to the structure of the school day and the one-to-one attention he receives there. I cannot praise the work of the teachers and assistants too highly.

At home, where life is less structured, he can be a bit of a handful. His behaviour has hyperactive tendencies; he seems constantly on the move, running from one end of the house to the other, and is a born climber. He can cross the living room without touching the floor by standing on the back of the sofa, the radiator covers, the mantelpiece and the window-ledge. In the garden he will climb fences and gates and can frequently be found standing on top of the shed.

The house doors must be kept locked as he has escaped in the past. Even some internal doors are kept bolted as he has a strong affinity with water and would flood the bathroom and kitchen by running the taps. To combat this, we give him controlled water play at the kitchen sink where he can have five or ten minutes to get the urge out of his system. Any longer and he becomes over-stimulated and can't easily be diverted. The rest of the time, the taps are kept tied up. We truly need eyes in the back of our heads, but anticipating what he'll be doing and where he'll be can make life simpler. And checking quickly when things have become suspiciously quiet is always wise.

In common with a number of other autistic children, he has sensory issues. He feels some things less intensely than the rest of us. For instance, his pain barrier is higher and his appreciation of pain is delayed. In other words, he can be causing himself some damage before he knows it. It hasn't happened to him but we are always aware that, in water play, he could scald himself with hot water before his pain receptors would make him withdraw his hand.

In one case at school, through no fault of the staff, he got his finger caught in a closing door, but he didn't yell until it had been well and truly trapped. No serious damage was done but curiously, when the pain did fully hit him, he cried out his first and, to date, only fully formed sentence: 'I want my mummy.' That is why I say he does not speak, rather than he cannot speak.

His other sensory difficulties are to do with oral stimulation. He has shown improvement here but when he was younger he would try to eat inappropriate things, either for the taste or the texture on his lips and tongue. Earth, small stones and particularly leaves seemed almost irresistible to him and it's amazing he didn't have more stomach upsets than he did.

When he does become ill for whatever reason, he can't tell us what's wrong, where it hurts or how he feels. We have simply to respond to the symptoms we see. Luckily, he is a very strong and healthy boy so it doesn't arise often. When it does, he seems just to want to take to his bed and lie there until he feels better, which can happen almost instantaneously; one minute he's flat out, pale and quiet, next, he's running down the stairs and raiding the fridge.

While it's always a relief to see this remarkable recovery, I have to admit we have sometimes quite appreciated the peace and quiet that descended on the house while he was confined to bed.

He has also become an accomplished escape artist. To him, garden fences and gates are like Everest and K2 are to mountaineers; they exist to be scaled and conquered. His interest in all things do to with water attracts him to neighbours' ponds and the full-size trampoline next door is almost irresistible. We have very understanding neighbours. His disappearing tricks have even involved him coming downstairs from his bedroom one evening, opening the front door and, in bare feet and pyjamas, running off towards the local playground in the pitch dark.

That was one of the more frightening moments we've had with him; although I noticed his absence within minutes, he was rounded up very quickly by some sharp-eyed local residents, who are wonderful about keeping an eye out for him. We still shiver at what might have happened to him though, and our external doors are now kept firmly locked.

Every parent of an autistic child will have had similar experiences; some better, some worse, but never exactly the same. But for all the worries, the constant state of alert, the mopping up of mess, and the moments of sheer exasperation, we wouldn't change much. Autistic children are capable of great affection and our little boy is a great hugger, smiler and laugher.

He is a tactile boy and will often sit on a visitor's lap with no warning, or fling his arms around their necks. With female visitors, there is every likelihood he will snuggle into their chests. This can be charming from a six- or seven-year-old, but will be rather less so when he reaches sixteen or seventeen, so this is one of those areas where the well-used mantra, 'That is not appropriate,' will come into play.

The question of how you help to change the behaviour of an autistic child is interesting. While they will understand what you are asking them to do, or not do, they will not know why. To them, the world is a straightforward place. They do what we would all do if we were not held in check by concern for others' feelings or best interests. Taking turns is a lesson that is hard for them to learn. If told they must, they will usually comply, but won't easily be able to see why the other person should want his turn as much as they do. The norms of civilized behaviour have to be learned as rules, rather than the innate understanding that a normal child will develop.

The children who are verbal can be direct to the point of rudeness. If they tell someone they look very old, or have a big nose, it's because they do. They're simply telling it like it is, and the concept of offence doesn't come into their reckoning. If someone asks them, 'How old are you?' they will very probably have the same question shot back at them: 'How old are *you*?'

These are delights ahead for us, if Murray ever does speak.

He might well just begin talking away one day, or his spoken vocabulary may only ever stretch to a few words, or it may never happen at all. We have no way of knowing at present. He is not silent by any means, and has his own repertoire of little noises and near-words, which means he is usually trackable by sound. He can certainly communicate, though, by leading you to the kitchen sink if he wants water play, or placing your hand on the fridge door if he's hungry, but we spend a lot of time interpreting his wishes and offering the wrong thing, which he can find frustrating.

Frustration can lead, in some children, to challenging behaviour in the form of fits of anger, yelling and, in some cases, hitting out. Parents are taught calming strategies for such times, though often it's just a case of managing the situation until the child has quietened down. On a bad day, Murray can seem very angry and be difficult to calm. He can be awake for much of the night and be crying or shouting. Thankfully, these times are rare. More often, he is happy and exuberant, or even over-stimulated and a bit of a handful. As I write this, last night he caused a minor flood in the kitchen by removing the tumble drier tank and spilling it, followed by the emptying of two bottles of shower gel on to the hall floor while Kerith was putting our daughter to bed and I was giving the baby his bottle. It's not a typical night, but it's not untypical either.

For all the problems and challenges, there are plenty of moments of great happiness. Each little milestone that he passes is a cue for the kind of celebration more associated with a set of A-starred exam results. A well-timed visit to the bathroom is a cause for major congratulation and a few extra moments of eye contact or an unexpected hug are golden moments. The first time he responded to and delivered back a high-five was glorious.

Do I regret his autism? Yes, of course. Modern life is difficult enough without the lack of understanding of its basic tenets that autism causes. I worry about his ability to cope once we're not around, and if he needs a high level of care, who will provide it? As autistic children are often very intelligent, they can soon begin to realize that they are different, and that can lead to great upset. I hope he will turn out to be one of the many autistic adults who learn to cope with society and lead near-normal lives.

Would I want him cured? Some parents have gone on record as wanting their children to remain autistic and, in a way, I can understand why. They are open, honest and vulnerable and they bring out the best in us. I firmly believe the world would be a better place if everyone had direct experience of an autistic child in the family. But if the question is, would I want him to participate fully in society and have as complete an understanding of the world around him as the rest of us do, the answer is a definite yes. But if he could retain some of that lovely innocence, that would be a bonus.

The feature on my programme which gives this book its title, The Tracks of My Years, began as a Christmas idea in 1999 to get some stars of the music world talking about their favourite records, those which either influenced their own music-making or brought back a special memory of childhood or career. From the start, we noticed a terrific eagerness to take part. Musicians like nothing better than talking about music and in private conversation can never be stopped from telling you about their favourite old records or new artists they've just found. All we were doing was asking them to share these thoughts with a wider audience.

Almost everyone who compiles a list says they could have included a couple of dozen more tracks quite easily. We tend to ask for fifteen tracks, which are then whittled down by the producer to ten, after which we check with the star involved if they're happy with the final choice. Sometimes, one will be changed but largely they remain as they are.

This is not always the case. Al Stewart, the 'Year of the Cat' man, seemed a bit miffed that his list had been tampered with or, in his view, torn to shreds, but once he got talking about the tracks we had left him with, the old enthusiasm kicked in and he softened. Some others, either through misunderstanding the concept or seeming self-absorption, have chosen their own records. Neil Sedaka was one such; almost everything he picked was his own recording, or, when another singer did make an appearance, it was with one of Neil's compositions. He made for a good interview, though; a fascinating man with a huge back catalogue of hit songs. I had been taken to one of his shows a few years back. Naturally, I knew his music and liked it, but I wasn't desperately keen to see him; however, his performance and the sheer number of familiar songs he'd written won me over.

Some stars' choices have been surprising. Paul Weller, the Modfather, the star of the Jam and the Style Council, whose list would, you might have thought, be full of edgy, hard music, actually came up with Percy Faith's Orchestra and 'A Summer Place', a classic piece of 1960s lounge sound.

It was less the music, more the memories it conjured in that case. Robert Plant, who, again, might have been expected to favour heavy uncompromising rock, wanted a large number of mainstream 1960s pop recordings.

It's also gratifying to see older, established artists choosing some of the latest talent. Duffy, Elbow and Amy Winehouse get frequent mentions, and even singers with the lengthy background of Andy Williams and Glen Campbell obviously listen to a lot of new music. Glen, incidentally, brought his guitar into the studio with him – I believe it's practically glued to his shoulder anyway – and accompanied each of his choices with several bars of musical illustration. Sometimes, a fascinating insight gets thrown up by such interjections. In Glen's case he revealed that he was the session guitarist on Frank Sinatra's recording of 'Strangers in the Night', and that Sinatra had simply come in, taken off his hat, stood at the microphone and sung it straight off. They had it first time really, but got him to do it again just for safety. He never did more than three takes anyway, thinking, quite rightly, that his performance wasn't going to get any better for repetition.

Sinatra featured in a number of stars' reminiscences; Petula Clark recalled the time when she and her husband Claude had gone to a party at his house, where after a certain point in the evening, Frank took out a gun, a 'piece', and laid it on the table. His was followed by several others', laid down by a collection of some of the bent-nosed and cauliflower-eared heavies present, upon which Claude and Petula decided that an early night might be advisable.

Tom Jones chose Robert Palmer's recording of 'Addicted to Love', not just because of the song, but for the laugh he'd had watching Robert on an American chat show. Palmer was famously northern and never lost or even adapted his Batley accent. When the show's host remarked on the video for 'Addicted To Love' and the powerful effect the raunchy women in it had had on him, Robert replied, 'Aye, but you should have seen them before make-up. They were a right busload.' There is obviously no direct translation of this quaint old English phrase in the American version of the language as the host was utterly baffled and after a short embarrassed silence moved on to another subject.

Glen Campbell may have played his guitar when he chose his tracks, but Donny Osmond sang. One or two others have, too, but Donny was the first to do it and it quite unnerved me. In musicals it happens all the time; two people are having a perfectly amiable conversation and then one bursts into song for no apparent reason. On celluloid that's acceptable; in a radio interview it's unexpected, to say the least. When we got to each of his choices, he would say, 'That's such a great song!' and then start singing it. Not just a couple of notes either; he gave us three or four lines at least. Having someone sing a substantial proportion of a song directly at you, holding your gaze throughout, is not something that happens in real life, at least not to me, so I had trouble deciding how to react. In the event, I adopted a kind of silly half-smile and gazed back at him, hoping he couldn't read what I was thinking on my face: 'Has he finished yet? What do I say? God, he's off again.' He was a lovely bloke and it made for a good interview, but suddenly thinking, 'Is this man crackers?' swiftly followed by, 'Is he dangerous?' is not a situation I wish to find myself in too often.

These are celebratory interviews and we do not set out

to court controversy. One day, though, it came looking for us. My guest was the theatrical impresario and former actor and singer Bill Kenwright. He chose, as so many do, an Elvis song, saying it was to remind him of the time Elvis came to London. Even my slow reactions picked up on this fairly promptly; surely Elvis's only time on British soil had been the famous brief stop-off at Prestwick Airport in 1960 on his way home from his GI service in Germany?

No, said Bill, Elvis spent a day in London in 1958, and proceeded to tell the tale. It had been told him by his friend Tommy Steele. Before his transformation into an all-round family entertainer, Tommy was our first rock 'n' roll star, denounced in the pulpits as a moral curse and corrupter of youth. Mind you, so was Cliff.

Tommy Steele was our answer to Elvis and, so the story went, the American star had called his British counterpart and during the course of their conversation Tommy suggested he should come over to London and be shown the sights. So, strictly incognito, Elvis made the journey, met up with Tommy and, no doubt with mufflers and flat caps to confuse the fans, they had a day doing all the tourist traps of our great capital.

At the end of it, Elvis slipped back out of the country and Tommy vowed to keep his trip out of the public arena. One night, many years later, he had told Bill of this memorable day and, more years later, here was Bill revealing it on national radio, saying as he did so, 'I'll probably get into trouble for this.' How right he was.

As we recorded it, I said to Gary Bones, my producer, 'We've got a good one here, better tell the Press Office to get ready for a busy day.' Sure enough, as soon as it went out on air, the phones rang, and the next day the papers were full of it.

'Elvis's Secret Trip to London!' yelled the headlines. Bill's phone seemed to have been ringing off the hook and some journalists had got through to Tommy Steele himself, who declined to confirm or deny the story, other than to say he regretted that a special private moment for two young men had been revealed to the wider public. What he said to Bill in private I've no idea, but I hope they're talking now.

Did it happen? Did the two rock icons of the time spend a fun day together going round the sights of London? Or was it a late-night story told by one actor to another as the wine slipped down and embellished accordingly? Only Tommy Steele knows for sure; and he ain't saying.

Almost everyone who has contributed to The Tracks of My Years has been charming, eager to share their enthusiasms and talkative. Elvis Costello not only gave a fascinating interview, but also stayed behind, sitting on the metal cabinet at the back of the studio, chatting about the singing career with the Joe Loss Band of his father, Ross McManus, and the young Declan's visits to watch him at the Hammersmith Palais. Jools Holland brought in not only his choices for the list but a box of other records to play us in case we hadn't heard them. It's that wish to share the joy that they've found in music that I find so appealing.

Some, though, a very few, seem not to have taken any trouble over their selections, or, on odd occasions, to have left the choice to someone in their record company. They have very little to say about any of the records, and talk only about their own latest release. Worse still are the ones who turn up wearing sunglasses and keep them on during the interview, only removing them if we take a photograph at the end. It's a pet hate of mine and I regard hiding behind shades indoors as just plain rudeness.

For lack of engagement in the process, though, I have to go a long way to beat one guest whose identity I will not reveal, save to say that she was a well-known female singer.

This person arrived in the studio accompanied by a teenage girl and toting a small dog. I'm tempted to call it a little shih-tzu, but I have no idea of the real breed; it was, at any rate, one of those small brown lapdogs that are so difficult to warm to. Much like its owner. Making pre-interview conversation, and in an effort to establish a common bond, I lied about the attractiveness of her canine companion and remarked that I too had a dog. In all other cases, this sort of line leads to an interested response and an animated conversation about the joys and otherwise of dog owner-ship. People who genuinely like dogs never let a chance like that go by. Not this time. A silent nod of the 'So what?' variety and a blank look were all I got. My sympathy for the dog rose. Its keeper did not seem much of an animal lover. I expect he'd been chosen for his wardrobe suitability.

While we set up the recording, our guest spoke to her teenage companion, for whose presence no explanation had been given. I supposed that she was a niece or family friend or some such. It was only well after they had left that I discovered she was a total stranger who had been standing outside the BBC awaiting the star's arrival and on telling her how much of a fan she was had been promptly invited inside by her and waved through security as part of her entourage. This, I may say, a matter of months after the terrorist bombs in London. And here she was in a broad-cast studio. Frightening.

Back at the interview, things got worse. The lapdog had obviously been on too much Pedigree Chum as he started farting and soon the studio had taken on a distinct aroma of dog flatulence. And then, our star's pièce de résistance. Her mobile rang. Now this sort of thing happens from time to time. Forgetting to switch off a mobile is common; even mine has gone off before now. All you can do is stop and go back over the last little bit. It's not a problem and everyone to whom it has happened has offered profuse apologies all round and got on with the job in hand. Not her. When her mobile went off, she answered it. That's right, she took the call.

Not only that, but where you or I might have laughed and explained we couldn't talk right now because we were recording a radio interview, she actually had a conversation lasting a minute or so. I stared at her for a bit, then slowly looked through the glass, where I could see her PR person burying her head in her hands. When she hung up, I left a pause to allow her to say sorry or at least acknowledge the interruption, but not a word was forthcoming. I felt my anger rising but simply said, 'Perhaps we can pick up where we left off,' and asked icily polite questions thereafter.

She never did apologize but her publicist came up to me afterwards and said, 'I'm sorry,' to which I could only say I was sorrier for them.

Compare and contrast this behaviour with that of Victoria Beckham, who was sweet, natural and chatty, and when she spotted my computer screensaver picture with a photo of my then baby son and the dog curled up together fast asleep, came over all 'aww' and talked away about children, both hers and mine.

I suppose that may be the major thing I've discovered about the famous: I can't bear those who behave in a starry fashion, all attitude and 'speak to my people'. I've met so many of the biggest names who turn out to be friendly, down-to-earth and self-effacing. Sometimes the trouble is caused by the entourage, who try to insist on ground rules, like certain aspects not being asked about or not permitting the taking of photographs.

We always ask in advance about pictures for the website, and ask again before we take them, just to be sure. I have one prized recent photograph, which I stuck on the studio wall for a time, of me and Beyoncé. I just found it hilariously unlikely that the two of us should be snapped together, and encouraged everyone viewing it to say, 'Who's that with Ken?' She was very helpful and immediately agreed to our photo, but one of her entourage stepped in as the camera was being readied with the words, 'Not too close.'

At first I thought they meant I should keep a decorous distance between us and keep my grubby little hands to myself but realized they actually meant the nature of the shot. I felt I had to say, 'Trust me, standing next to me, she's going to look good.'

As these interviews are mainly the artist talking about their musical passions, I don't have to do as much research on them as for a major in-depth piece, so I do a quick bone-up on their life and career before they come in and keep all that in mind for the chat. I've always had a good short-term memory and can retain a fair bit of detail, but it doesn't stay there long and can have vanished two minutes after they've left the studio.

Sometimes, if I'm too relaxed, it can go quicker. Once, interviewing Sheryl Crow, I started calling her Sharon for some reason, I think because I had just been talking on air about someone with that name. When the concentration lapses, so does the memory. I'd called her by that name three times before she very gently corrected me. I blushed to the roots of what remains of my hair. She was very sweet about it, with a 'Hell, I don't remember my own name sometimes,' but it's the kind of stupid mistake I hate to make. Anyway, she must have forgiven me because she came back on the show a couple of years later.

It took me back to an incident right at the beginning of my career, when as a staff announcer I was presenting one of my very first *Night Beat* programmes in Scotland. As usual, anyone with a new book out and doing the rounds of the radio studios was welcome fodder for us. This night it was an American gentleman named Dan Dale Alexander who had written about the then revolutionary idea that arthritis could be eased by the taking of cod liver oil. As I say, any topic sufficed if it filled the slot.

In my introduction I called him Dan Dale Anderson; why, I have no idea, but he certainly didn't like it. When I wished him good evening he launched into a short rant, beginning, 'Why does everybody get my name wrong?' I grovelled a bit and the interview went OK after that, but I wondered about his fiery reaction. It turned out that in the long round of radio chats, being asked the same questions over and over, the only changing element had been the variations on his name that everyone seemed to have tried out, culminating in the last one where he'd become Dan Dare. No wonder he was getting a bit shirty by the time I had my go at altering his moniker.

A man's got to have a hobby. I believe the first person to say this was a husband discovered wearing PVC and accompanied by a sheep. My own shameful secret is only slightly less embarrassing: I own a bus. To be fair to myself, I'm not alone in this bizarre pursuit; there are five of us, so in truth I own about fourteen seats and a little over one wheel of a 1960s Routemaster.

Charles Nove mentioned in passing one day that he and colleague Steve Madden had heard some old London buses were coming on the market and looking for good homes. For reasons I cannot immediately explain, I said, 'Count me in,' rather in the same way men in pubs are apt to shell out for dodgy merchandise after one beer too many. I had no drink on board at the time but had always fancied driving a large red bus, and on being assured we could pick one up for only about £3,000, I added my name to the consortium.

With one other name added, that of the National Lottery's 'Voice of the Balls' Alan Dedicoat, we brassed up and collected her one January day in 2005. Since then, a younger, wiser head in the form of David Sheppard has joined our group and it won't surprise the owner of any old vehicle to learn that it has cost us a small fortune to refurbish and maintain her. In an effort to recoup some of the outlay, we have been hiring her out for weddings and parties and have recently added a second Routemaster to our collection, such has been demand. I occasionally drive for these events, but as soon as any passenger realizes who is up front, I'm assailed by cries of, 'Moonlighting?' and, 'Don't they pay you enough at the BBC?' To which the only correct answers are, 'Yes,' and, 'No.'

Kerith is patient enough to allow me out to play with the Boys' Toys now and again, and she can be sure I'm not getting up to mischief as it's keeping me out of the pubs and I certainly won't be meeting any loose women.

Marriage to Kerith has allowed me to have the settled family life that escaped me in my earlier attempts. It's been a long time coming, but I finally seem to have got myself to the state of mind where my wife and family are the most important things in my life. My career is the servant of my family and not the other way around.

Kerith and I are entirely happy together and I find I cannot wait to get out of London and home to her and the kids, Murray, Verity and, last but not least, Charlie. (And I do mean last. Six children is, I feel, probably sufficient.) We have put down our roots in rural Oxfordshire. For years, I had been promising myself a move back to Scotland, my reason being, I think, a wish to lead a more peaceful, down-to-earth life than media-centred London could offer.

But in our village in Oxfordshire, I've found the perfect compromise: the open countryside and grounded lifestyle, while still being within commuting distance of London, where the broadcasting work is. With three young children, retirement is not going to be an option for some time, besides which, I still enjoy hugely the whole experience.

I've had a daily show on Radio 2 for twenty-five years. Put as simply as that, it seems a settled existence, like a Dickensian clerk turning up day after day to fill in his ledger, expecting to walk away with a gold watch at the end of it. Well, it hasn't been like that; for the first ten years or so, I never had a contract longer than eighteen months' duration, and it's only in recent times that I've had the comfort of knowing I had two or three years' guaranteed work ahead of me. I've never had the vista of unbroken service stretching before me, which for a broadcaster is a good thing.

A certain insecurity of tenure keeps the reflexes sharp, but also stops that feeling of institutionalization that can stifle enthusiasm. When I was offered my longest ever contract, at three years, initial pleasure gave way to a slight feeling of being trapped, a sensation of being chained to a radiator for too long a period. It's the freelance mentality; I am not a number, I am a free man! That romantic notion soon gives way again to sensible practicality and the realization that being paid to do a job I love in a place I feel happy, and in the company of people who make me laugh on a daily basis, is not exactly a hardship.

Every morning, Terry gets me started at half past nine with some random remark, utterly unpredictable in its topic, for which you have to be on sharpish form as any slug-gishness of the brain is going to be obvious; and if you weren't awake before, you will be afterwards.

Later, Jeremy Vine will lope in with the details of his programme, which we manage to discuss in a rambling, tangential manner for some minutes, and in between times, I'll have been joined periodically by Lynn Bowles for the travel. Lynn is a gem. She takes all kinds of abuse from me, and gives plenty back. I like to think that many connect with us as we reflect the state of their own marital relationships:

a sort of armed truce, with regular skirmishes, no clear winner ever, but a kind of mutual dependence on each other.

Lynn would describe herself as a presenter's labourer; there to help out, hand me conversational tools and then back away to leave me to get on with it. She does a lot more than that. I always know that whatever conversational oddity I throw at her, she will have something to say, and not just that, but something worthwhile. It's a rare gift, and her presence in my studio flies in the face of my golden rule about co-hosts.

The trend towards double-heading and the increased use in mainstream radio shows of presenters from television seem retrograde steps. Of course, there are plenty of television people who are good on radio, and may have even started there, but too often a famous face is parachuted into a prime radio slot with no experience of or particular aptitude for the medium. Stand-up comedians are also seen as a ripe recruiting area, and here, too, there are many who have a real gift for the intimate communication that radio needs, but there are far too many who simply come on and do a version of their act. Loud, larger-than-life performances work in clubs and theatres, but not on radio.

The worst effect of this is that radio people, presenters who have come up in the medium and love it for its difference to the other forms, don't get a sniff at the biggest jobs now. Managements have lost their gifts as talent-spotters, and are too content to rely on a proven public profile to garner an audience. A famous face or name can bring in a certain number of new listeners to a programme, but if it isn't any good, they won't stay.

Programmers, too, have become obsessed with content,

with statisticians logging the speech-to-music ratio of particular shows simply by counting the seconds, without taking
account of what is actually said. Quality content is worth
striving for, but you can't measure it. Find a presenter with
presence and the quality will follow.

These observations are not complaints about my own
career; I've been lucky enough to find and keep a job I love
for over thirty years. I worry about youngsters keen to work
in radio now. The part I found hardest at the outset was
getting my foot through the door, getting on to the first rung
of the ladder. I think it's easier to do that today; there are
so many more radio stations all over the country that you
can practically walk up to the front door and find yourself
working there the next day. Provided you don't want paying.

But getting any further seems much more difficult, and
it appears that those who want to be famous at all costs are
leapfrogging those who want to become good at what they
do and stay loyal to their medium of choice. And the training
opportunities are not there; the kind of job I found in 1977,
where you could do five different types of broadcasting in
a week and learn how to cope with them all, does not exist.
Add to that the formulaic systems of some parts of commercial radio, and the news content bias of BBC Local Radio,
and there's nowhere for a young broadcaster to learn how
to take a list of unrelated music and make a programme out
of it with no more back-up than his or her own wits. I hope
the industry finds a way soon of investing in and encouraging young all-round radio professionals.

As for myself, I seem to have ended up, quite unexpect-
edly, doing the same job on the same station for twenty-five
years. It hasn't seemed anything like that length of time to

me, and I hope it hasn't seemed a life sentence for listeners. What the future holds, who knows? The day we stop being open to new challenges is the day we should hang up our boots. All I know is I never finish a programme without feeling a lot better than I did at the beginning, and to pay for that kind of therapy would cost a fortune. As I've said, I don't intend retiring any time soon, or any time at all really, and I'm rather afraid in the year 2044 you may read about a ninety-three-year-old broadcaster having to be dragged, kicking and screaming, from a radio studio on the island of Muckle Flugga with the cry, 'I'm good for another year!' echoing round the room.

As a broadcaster from another generation used to put it: 'If you have been, thanks for listening.'